KATRINA M. PHILLIPS

Staging Indigeneity

Salvage Tourism and the Performance of
Native American History

The University of North Carolina Press *Chapel Hill*

This book was published with the assistance of the Authors Fund of the University of North Carolina Press.

Set in Arno Pro by Westchester Publishing Services
Manufactured in the United States of America

The University of North Carolina Press has been a member of the
Green Press Initiative since 2003.

Library of Congress Cataloging-in-Publication Data
Names: Phillips, Katrina M., author.
Title: Staging indigeneity : salvage tourism and the performance of Native American
   history / Katrina M. Phillips.
Description: Chapel Hill : University of North Carolina Press, 2021. |
   Includes bibliographical references and index.
Identifiers: LCCN 2020038250 | ISBN 9781469662305 (cloth ; alk. paper) |
   ISBN 9781469662312 (paperback ; alk. paper) | ISBN 9781469662329 (ebook)
Subjects: LCSH: Indians of North America—Public opinion. | Indians of North
   America—History. | Heritage tourism—United States. | Indian tourism—
   United States. | Pageants—United States. | Theater and nationalism—
   United States. | United States—Historiography.
Classification: LCC E98.P99 P47 2021 | DDC 970.004/97—dc23
LC record available at https://lccn.loc.gov/2020038250

Cover photo by author.

Staging Indigeneity

For my parents, Jerry and Karen Wilber

Contents

Illustrations, Maps, and Table

Acknowledgments

I am, like my father, often stubborn and independent. However, I have been reminded time and time again throughout this humbling and gratifying journey that, in the words of the indomitable Velma Kelly in *Chicago*, I just can't do it alone. Any errors in the final product, though, are mine and mine alone. I earned my PhD in History from the University of Minnesota (U of M) in 2015. My adviser, Jeani O'Brien, has read every single word I have ever written—and many of them many times. I am eternally grateful for how she has motivated me, encouraged me, and guided me since I started grad school. After my first son was born in 2013, she never flinched when I brought him to our workshops on campus or the end-of-semester parties at her house. She never doubted that I would finish my degree, and her faith in me helped me get to the finish line. I can never repay her for the time she has dedicated to me even after I earned my degree. Thank you, Jeani. Other faculty members at the U of M were also crucial to my success. Kat Hayes's feedback was instrumental in shaping this final product. David Chang pushed me to challenge myself and expand my horizons, which has made me a better scholar. Kevin Murphy, Brenda Child, and Barbara Welke's insights and comments urged me to look beyond my initial research.

The American Indian and Indigenous Studies Workshop has been my academic home since my first year of graduate school. Many, many thanks to all those who read my jumbled, nearly incoherent thoughts and helped shape them into what they have become. These colleagues include Amber Annis, Jess Arnett, Marie Balsley Taylor, Adrian Chavana, Akikwe Cornell, Michael Dockry, Caroline Dönmez, Jesús Estrada-Pérez, Macey Flood, John Little, Samantha Majhor Alton, Hana Maruyama, Sarah Pawlicki, Juliana Hu Pegues, Bernadette Perez, Elan Pochedley, Kai Pyle, Megan Red Shirt–Shaw, Agléška Rencountre, Jacob Rorem, Sasha Suarez, Naomi Sussman, Jimmy Sweet, Joe Whitson, Kelsey Young, and many more—and I'm sorry to anybody I may have missed. Grad school colleagues in the Department of History at the U of M (including Laura Luepke, Ellen Manovich, Melissa Hampton, and Joanne Jahnke-Wegner) also shaped earlier versions of this project, and I thank you all. Joanne has been a dear friend and a confidant since our first year of grad school, and she has proven time and time again that even somewhat disparate bodies of work can create more meaningful scholarship. Kasey Keeler and Rose Miron have become two of my dearest friends and colleagues, and not just because of our affinity for Wisconsin sports teams. My dear friend Dr. Ruth Knezevich Morshedi shared with me the trials and triumphs of graduate school. Kyle Geissler, William Lucas, and Drew and Teresa Herman showed up at talks I gave around the Twin Cities, even when I protested that they must have had something better to do those nights. I thank our friends who always asked about my research and writing (and who genuinely wanted to hear about it), and who have been constant sources of encouragement along the way.

Sarah Rickert and Liz Huninghake babysat for us as I wrote in grad school. I also want to thank the teachers at our sons' Montessori school and our district preschool program for loving and caring for our boys and for playing a crucial role in their education. Balancing motherhood and academia has not been the easiest thing I've ever done, and I want to recognize the role that those who have cared for our sons over the years have played in the development of this book. Elizabeth Pihlaja, Heidi Ganser Lang, Kimberly Wydeen Johnson, Sarah Rickert, Shannon Balow Gates, Martha Rohde, and Erinn Liebhard have been wonderful friends since our undergrad years at the U of M (Go Gophers), and I am so grateful for your friendship. Years ago, on my very first research trip, Brian and Moira Sharkey refused to let me take a cab to their house, even though multiple delays landed me in Boston in the middle of the night. Their hospitality was, and still is, much appreciated. A few years later, Chris and Brooke Amys (and Taylor and Luke) welcomed me to North Carolina with open arms and homemade pizza.

This work has also been shaped by numerous conference panels and presentations over the years, and thank you to my fellow panelists and the audiences who have helped move this forward. It's been an honor to present alongside Clyde Ellis, Linda Scarangella McNenly, Linda Waggoner, Adriana Greci Green, and Amy Lonetree, among many others, and I'm thankful to have found academic homes and friends in these conferences.

When I joined the faculty at Macalester College, my list of friends and people I have to thank grew even more. I first came to Macalester as a fellow for the Consortium for Faculty Diversity, a program administered through Gettysburg College. I held a predoctoral and a postdoctoral fellowship before joining the faculty full time. Ernie Capello, Linda Sturtz, Yue-Him Tam, Karin Vélez, and Chris Wells have been kind and gracious mentors in the History Department, and they've helped me become a better scholar and a better professor. I also need to give credit to Louisa Bradtmiller, whose advice and institutional knowledge have been incredibly helpful. I want to make sure I acknowledge Alexis Lodgson, Ellen Holt-Werle, Ginny Moran, and Brooke Schmolke for their help with my research and sharing their time with me in and out of my classrooms, whether it's tracking down hard-to-find sources, sending me links to things in our campus archives, or helping me with technical issues around fellowship applications. Those who work behind the scenes rarely get credit where credit is due, and I would be remiss to leave them out of these acknowledgments. I also presented this research at the Humanities Colloquium and Conversations about our Scholarly Lives. Rebecca Wingo became an amazing confidant and writing partner. Amy Elkins, Leah Witus, and Crystal Moten became friends as well as colleagues, sharing the highs and lows and the ups and downs of being junior faculty juggling work, career, and life all at the same time. I'm grateful to Jess Pearson for her advice, words of encouragement, and *Friends* quotes, and for being my accountability buddy. Jess read the entire revised manuscript and offered kind and detailed suggestions—while we were on sabbatical.

Thank you to Katie Aulwes Latham and Michelle Epp in the Grants office at Macalester College for their help in not only finding but applying for grants and fellowships. A Wallace Scholarly Activities Grant from Macalester College, which allowed me to hire Kasia Majewski as a summer research assistant, also supported this project. She's heard me say it countless times, but there's no way I would have finished the first draft of this book without Kasia. She spent the summer before her senior year transcribing interviews, tracking down sources, reading chapter drafts, and combing through the finding aid for the Institute of Outdoor Theatre in order to chart close to 200 historical pageants and outdoor dramas going back more than a century. And she did all of this while working on her honors thesis. Athena Hallberg spent her summer break searching for sources to help refine the book's arguments based on the feedback from the readers, and her research skills helped get the revised manuscript in on time. This project was also funded by a Career Enhancement Fellowship for Junior Faculty from the Woodrow Wilson National Fellowship Foundation, which helped cover half of my sabbatical.

Dale Sauter's expertise with the Institute of Outdoor Drama/Institute of Outdoor Theatre archives at East Carolina University's (ECU) Joyner Library was crucial in the completion of this manuscript. I thank him for sharing his time with me, and I thank the countless employees at the Joyner Library who pulled box after box of archival materials for me during my trips to ECU. Thanks to the Ross County Historical Society and Bill Gover at the Bayfield Heritage Association. Thanks to Connie Karlen and the Inter-Library Loan staff at Macalester, and to all the student workers in the library who tracked my revision progress based on the books they pulled. The Hennepin County Library—and the ability of its librarians to send books to my local branch— also proved incredibly helpful. Mark Simpson-Vos at the University of North Carolina Press has guided me through the publication process and patiently answered every single question I've had along the way. Thank you, Mark, for helping shape this project and bring it to fruition. Thanks to Jessica Newman, Dominique Moore, and Catherine Robin Hodorowitz for their help as well. The two anonymous readers pushed me to think about these productions in ways I'd never considered, and I am truly grateful for their time and their thoughtful suggestions.

To my grandmothers, Margaret Pascale (Ogichidaakwe) and Irma Wilber, who were without a doubt the two strongest—and funniest—women I have ever known: I miss you more and more each day and, while I like to think I've made you proud, I bet you would think my little boys hung the sun and the moon and the stars. My in-laws, Gary and Kathie Phillips, have helped us in innumerable ways. To Jeff and Jill Menzel; Tad, Sara, Ella, Lucas, and Ryan Campana; and Abby, Billy, Grady, and Eden Wiberg—thank you for not taking it personally when I spent countless holidays reading and writing. My parents, Jerry and Karen Wilber, have been my most enthusiastic and ardent supporters, from ballet and piano recitals to my first NAISA presentation in Sacramento to today. I had written a long, rambling paragraph, but when it comes down to it, there is nothing I can say except thank you, thank you, thank you for all that you've done for me. I hope this book and your grandsons are adequate repayment.

And last—but certainly, certainly not least—there is Jake. He gamely tried to help me with the math portion of the GRE, proposed to me the year I applied to graduate school, and married me a month into the first semester of my PhD program. Jake has cheered me on ever since, all while earning his MBA and building his own business. Our sons, Leo Jacob and Max Francis, were born in 2013 and 2016: the first when I was writing my dissertation, and the second two months before I started as an assistant professor. To my boys: I love you—a lot, even.

Staging Indigeneity

Discovering and Defining Salvage Tourism

This book is my father's fault. I recognize that this requires explanation. I am an enrolled citizen of the Red Cliff Band of Lake Superior Ojibwe, and our reservation is in northern Wisconsin on the south shore of Lake Superior. It borders the tourist town of Bayfield near the Apostle Islands National Lakeshore, whose twenty-one islands and twelve miles of mainland shore have been dubbed the "Jewels of Lake Superior" by the National Park Service. While tourism played a minor role in Bayfield's economy in the nineteenth century, by the 1920s it became one of the last natural resources to exploit once the local quarrying, commercial fishing, and logging industries were nearly exhausted. The Bayfield Apple Fest is one of those tourism endeavors, an annual event in the fall that celebrates the region's fruit industry and gives lodging and restaurant owners a much-needed economic boost before the icy hand of winter makes tourists think twice about trekking north.

The festival started in 1962. Jim Erickson, who opened Erickson Orchard in Bayfield in 1954, was on his way to deliver apples in North Dakota. He got a flat tire driving through Duluth—the largest city for many miles around. He'd left the spare tire at home, and by the time his brother came to help him he'd sold twenty-seven bushels of apples out of the back of the truck. Even more astonishing for Erickson was the number of people who had no idea where Bayfield was or that Bayfield was home to numerous apple orchards. Several months later, he attended a meeting with local luminaries who wanted to encourage people to come to Bayfield in the fall as a means of extending the tourism season. He told his story about the flat tire and the twenty-seven bushels, suggesting that an annual festival could "bring the people to the apples" instead of the other way around.[1] And so the Apple Fest was born, bringing with it an annual influx of tourists from across the state and across the Midwest. It has become a pilgrimage for many, including those of us whose ancestors have called the region home for centuries. Nearly every year during my childhood, my mother and I would drive to the reservation on the first Friday of October and go to the Apple Fest with my grandma on Saturday. I delighted in the caramel apples and apple bratwurst and apple everything, while my mother and grandmother browsed the vendor booths that covered several Bayfield city blocks.

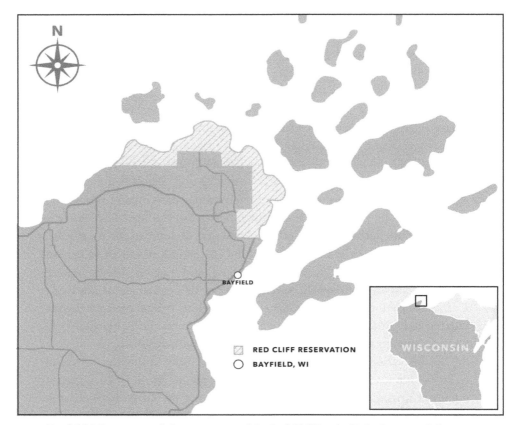

Bayfield, Wisconsin, and the reservation of the Red Cliff Band of Lake Superior Ojibwe. Map by Josiah Donat.

My grandma died in 2002, the winter of my senior year of high school. Our trips to the reservation became more and more infrequent after I moved away for college. Nearly a decade later, I was a graduate student in history at the University of Minnesota when my dad called me. The Apple Fest was that weekend, he said, and I should come home and go with my mom. It was the last thing I wanted to do on a weekend during the semester. I had books to read and papers to write, but those who know my father already know how this story ends. I went home, and that Saturday—just like we had throughout my childhood—we drove toward the reservation. I had forgotten about the traffic jams and the massive influx of tourists that overrun Bayfield, a place that Dennis McCann has called "emphatically a tourist town."[2] My mother, anticipating the traffic detours a few miles north, turned off Wisconsin Highway 13 onto Hatchery Road, which turned into County Highway J. She paused at the junction of Valley Road and County J, her mind mapping the easiest way to Erickson Orchard. These were roads she had traveled countless times since her childhood, roads whose names she had long forgotten because she did not need to remember them—she knew exactly where we were going.

We drove straight to Erickson Orchard to buy our apples. I had long wondered why we always went to Erickson's on our annual Apple Fest excursions, and why Jim Erickson would greet my mother and grandmother with enthusiastic hugs. When I finally asked my mom several years ago, she hesitated and said she would write it down for me. Her response was illuminating, and I realized how deeply entrenched my family had been in the local economy:

> When we would come to Wisconsin for vacation and it was strawberry picking time, we would pick strawberries for Jim. He would drive out to the reservation in his big truck and stop at people's houses. When we were young, we mostly were the runners for Mom and Aunt Emily. . . . The adults would pick and we would walk the carriers to the weight station. We had a ticket and they would punch it, we'd bring it back and carry the next one from the field. I wish I knew how much they paid. It was extra money for us but income for others. Mom said if we wanted to go to the movies or roller-skating, then we had to earn money to do that.

This was work for the women and kids, she told me, who would also pick raspberries and apples for him. After my grandparents moved back to Wisconsin, my grandma still worked for Jim if he needed extra help. "Jim always treated us very well," my mother said. "It didn't make a difference that we were from the reservation. I know that is why we worked for him. We were day laborers."[3]

This story of my family's participation in the regional economy is not unusual. Scholar Chantal Norrgard has traced how Ojibwe people in Wisconsin have long participated in the regional economy through their seasonal rounds and traditional livelihoods as well as the industries headed by non-Natives. Norrgard also demonstrates the significant role the Ojibwe played in the tourist industry, working as guides, performers, and domestic servants and by producing and selling commodities, even in light of tourists whose insistence on a "wilderness" vacation came with the expectation that Native workers only participated in specific forms of labor.[4] Similarly, William J. Bauer Jr.

Erickson Orchard and Country Store, which opened in Bayfield, Wisconsin, in 1954. It is one of nearly twenty orchards and berry farms in Bayfield County. Photograph by author.

has highlighted how Round Valley Reservation Indians in California used different forms of wage labor, like hop picking, alongside seasonal agricultural labor to ensure the survival of their families.[5]

But I knew none of this on that fall day as we wove our way through Erickson's store. As you might expect a historian to do, I found my way to a small bookshelf in the corner. I picked up a small book with an imprint of a Native man wearing a headdress and the title *Indian Pageant Cook Book*. It was a publication created by the Bayfield Civic League as a fund raiser for an Indian pageant that had first been staged on our reservation in 1924.[6] The Apostle Islands Indian Pageant, I later learned, was promoted as a tourist endeavor that would "give the people of America a historical record of the first Americans: thus preserving for all time something of the beauty, customs, glories, rites and romance of the Indians of Wisconsin."[7]

I began, as we historians do, with some basic questions. What, first of all, was an Indian pageant? And perhaps more importantly, who decided to stage one on the south shore of Lake Superior in the early 1920s, and why? Why was it produced for only a few years? Was this an isolated event or indicative of a larger trend? As I fell deeper down the rabbit hole of research, I realized that the Apostle Islands Indian Pageant, while unique in many ways, was also part of a broader shift in tourism and public conceptions of Indians and Indian history. I found other Indian pageants throughout history and across the country, all of which were designed to draw tourists to a particular location in order to witness dramatic reenactments "in the exact spots" where the exciting action had originally occurred.[8] From New York to California, as early as the 1900s and continuing today, enterprising towns have used narratives of American Indian history as the basis for dramatic, tourist-centered performances.

As early as 1909, New York and Vermont collaborated on the Champlain Tercentenary Celebration of the Discovery of Lake Champlain, which included numerous performances of Indian pageantry.[9] The Minneapolis Chapter of the Society of American Indians presented "The Indian of Yesterday," a pageant of "Indian forest life," in 1920 in conjunction with a lecture by Dr. Carlos Montezuma titled "The Indian of Today."[10] Two weeks later, residents of Lyon County in southwest Minnesota gathered in Marshall to celebrate the county's fiftieth anniversary with a pageant that depicted "the chief events of the state, county, and town."[11] Medicine Lodge, Kansas, presented the first Medicine Lodge Indian Peace Treaty Pageant in 1927. The pageant commemorates the treaty signed by members of five nations—the Apache, Arapaho, Cheyenne, Comanche, and Kiowa—in 1867 that set the southern border of the state and cleared the way for white settlement throughout the region.[12] The American Indian Exposition in Anadarko, Oklahoma, took advantage of the popularity of the All-Indian Fairs at Craterville Park, which began in 1924. By 1938, the fair had become the Exposition and included a historical pageant deemed an "innovation in entertainment."[13] Similar productions occurred at the Forest Theater in Ticonderoga, New York, and in the Casa Grande Ruins National Monument in Arizona from 1926 to 1930. Benjamin Black Elk participated in pageants in the Black Hills of South Dakota in the 1930s and 1940s, and Frank Hopkins, a founder of the Fort Ridgely State Park and Historical Association, staged pageants in Minnesota into the 1950s. Famed anthropologist Ella Deloria was commissioned to write a pageant for the North Carolina Indians of Robeson County in 1940.[14] Nearly four decades after the Champlain Tercentenary, the *Song of Hiawatha* pageant, which used Henry Wadsworth Longfellow's poem as creative inspiration, premiered in Pipestone, Minnesota, in 1948.[15]

This is by no means an exhaustive list. Instead, it demonstrates the geographic and chronological reach of these productions and their popularity around the country. As I continued to research the Apostle Islands Indian

Pageant, I discovered dozens of pageants and performances that were staged in Wisconsin throughout the nineteenth century. Newspapers promoted numerous Indian powwows, dances, and historical pageants in 1921 alone, from Green Bay and Wisconsin Rapids to Keshena and the Wisconsin Dells, that hoped to lure tourists to their respective performances.[16] The Apostle Islands Indian Pageant opened in 1924, and plans were already underway for "a bigger and better show next year," less than two weeks after the pageant's first season ended. The program for the second pageant reminded visitors, "We'll meet you in 1926 at the top o'Wisconsin" for the third annual pageant, an event that garnered little, if any, publicity.[17] The Apostle Islands Indian Pageant was a short-lived endeavor, but it helped lay the foundation for later tourist enterprises in northern Wisconsin.

As I kept finding more and more of these productions, I found several that, to my surprise, had not suffered the same fate as the Apostle Islands Indian Pageant. This book centers on three productions that, as of 2020, are still performed on an annual basis. The Happy Canyon Indian Pageant and Wild West Show has been produced in Pendleton, Oregon, in conjunction with the Pendleton Round-Up since 1916. *Unto These Hills* has told the story of the Eastern Band of Cherokee Indians in the years leading up to removal in the shadows of the Great Smoky Mountains in Cherokee, North Carolina, since 1950. The final production, *Tecumseh!*, has been produced by the Scioto Society in Chillicothe, Ohio, since 1973. There are others, such as the "Ramona" Outdoor Play (formerly known as the "Ramona" Pageant), based on Helen Hunt Jackson's 1884 novel of the same name and staged in California since 1923.[18] But "Ramona" is a work of fiction, one that Jackson hoped "would do for the Indian a thousandth part [of] what *Uncle Tom's Cabin* did for the Negro."[19] As Michele Moylan demonstrates, Jackson's dreams weren't that far from reality: *Ramona* has never gone out of print, and it has been printed hundreds of times in dozens of editions.[20] Despite various dramatic embellishments, Happy Canyon, *Unto These Hills*, and *Tecumseh!* are all grounded in history. *Trumpet in the Land* opened in New Philadelphia, Ohio, in 1970, and uses the 1782 massacre of ninety-six Christian Lenape Indians at Gnadenhutten by a Pennsylvania militia—an event also known as the Moravian Massacre—as its central story line. While *Trumpet in the Land* appears in chapter 5 alongside *Tecumseh!* and a third Ohio drama, *Blue Jacket*, it does not play a starring role in this book. The three productions at the core of this book all rely on the pairing of nobility and historical tragedy. The Moravian Massacre is more than tragic, and yet there is a distinct difference between *Trumpet in the Land* and the other three: the absence of nobility. All four are driven by audience sympathy toward the Indian characters, but Happy Canyon, *Unto These Hills*, and *Tecumseh!* recast their historical characters and narratives within the context of American nation-building and nobility. Gnadenhutten does not fit that mold, nor does it maintain the same status in the American collective memory as Tecumseh or the Trail of Tears.

Like the Apostle Islands Indian Pageant, countless other pageants and dramas centered on Native people, histories, and stories have opened and closed, whether after a few years or a few decades. *Blue Jacket* opened in Xenia, Ohio, in 1982 and closed in 2008, the same year the *Song of Hiawatha* pageant in Pipestone, Minnesota, called it quits. Tourism is a fickle industry, one whose life depends on the whims and desires of those with the time, money, and desire to travel. Hal Rothman has called tourism a "devil's bargain," noting, "Despite its reputation as a panacea for the economic ills of places that have lost their way in the postindustrial world or for those that never found it, tourism typically fails to meet the expectations of communities and regions that embrace it as an economic strategy. Regions, communities, and locales welcome tourism as an economic boon, only to find that it irrevocably changes them in unanticipated and uncontrollable ways."[21] This book examines these three productions through the convergence of tourism and history, the centuries-long contestations over citizenship and identity, and the continued use of Indians and Indianness as a means of escape, entertainment, and economic development.

Creating Salvage Tourism

In this book, I argue that these three productions epitomize what I call "salvage tourism" through the way they use American Indian history to help rescue regional economies. Salvage tourism combines the theoretical framework of salvage ethnography with the practices and yearnings of heritage tourism, meaning the experience of traveling to places and taking part in activities that aim to represent the stories and the people of the past. Salvage tourism is explicitly tied up in trying to salvage American Indian cultures before Indians, in the minds of non-Natives, die off, change, or degenerate from their ideals of a pristine Indian past. Salvage tourism builds on ideas of a nostalgic past through the nation-building practices of tourism and the creation of a distinctly American identity—one that can only really be achieved with Indians. The merging of these literal and figurative productions, in turn, allowed (and still allows) tourists to find sanctuary, safety, and security in the performance of a remembered past. By performing the act of tourism and by witnessing these performances of the past, tourists partake in what we might consider a historical communion. These collective acts reiterate and reify a national identity that is grounded in Indigenous history. Tourism, nostalgia, and authenticity converge in the creation of salvage tourism, which is about more than the salvation of the evaporating environment or culturally based productions. It becomes necessary in order to salvage the tourists themselves.

Tourism was a flourishing industry in the eastern United States by the 1820s, emerging at a pivotal moment in American society as Americans were working to define their national identity in opposition to Europe. Richard Gassan characterizes these early endeavors as "pilgrimages to wild-seeming scenic spots that were, in fact, well-tamed," a phenomenon that would influence the industry throughout the nineteenth century and beyond, and tourism would soon play what John Sears calls "a powerful role" in America's invention of itself as a culture.[22] Tourism was intimately tied to constructions of what these newly minted Americans considered the wilderness, a seemingly vast and slightly terrifying expanse that, according to Roderick Nash, was created in a context of fear and opposition.[23] Tourists followed the pioneers and the frontier westward, desperately seeking to reaffirm their connection to America's past while validating their belief in America's future.[24] As pioneers sought to claim and conquer the wilderness, tourists traveling to or through what was once deemed untamable would be the final stamp of subjugation. Once civilization overpowered the wilderness, tourists could, in their eyes, rest assured that the previous inhabitants had been similarly subdued.

Toward the end of the nineteenth century, many Euro-Americans began to frantically search for something familiar, something comfortable and reassuring. The Industrial Revolution had forced them into a confrontation with modernity. It had transformed not only the physical but the socioeconomic and cultural landscape, and international crises had brought millions of immigrants to American shores. The rapid growth of cities led to a greater stratification between the urban and the rural, and technological innovations and transportation breakthroughs seemed to have irrevocably altered the American way of life. Trying to find solace in the past, they sought a simpler, more pastoral time—a time that never existed as they imagined it. Rather, they were longing for an imagined past that served to create and define a shared experience and a shared identity. The pull of nostalgia, which fuels a collective rejection of the present and the future in favor of the past, rippled through the country.

The affection that many Americans had lavished on the burgeoning urban environment gave way to hostility and discontent toward cities and civiliza-

Audiences are privy to a scene from the Apostle Islands Indian Pageant, which was staged on the Red Cliff Ojibwe reservation in northern Wisconsin in the 1920s. Photograph by Gil Larsen, courtesy of the Bayfield Heritage Association (1980.2.160).

tion, leaving many Americans to instead turn to what they considered the thrilling *un*civilization. The rise of automobile ownership and the expansion of the highway system and railroads, coupled with the growth of American leisure culture, allowed tourists to flee "bureaucratized lives in steamy hot cities for the northern edges of civilization, where they hoped to brush up against something refreshing and authentic."[25] Many turned to nature, traveling by train or automobile to more remote areas of the nation, including some of the first national parks. The changing nature of vacation, coupled with the rise in transportation technology, afforded more Americans the opportunity to become tourists, spending anywhere from several days to several weeks away from the place they called home. Despite the rapid advancement of technical and industrial enterprises, many Americans seemed to be always looking back, always reaching for the singular element that would clearly create, reiterate, and claim the idealized America of the past. America, long defined by its "newness" in relation to other established nations, has continuously wrestled with a collective anxiety around defining and creating an American identity.

For those with the time, resources, and ability to travel, tourism became a confluence of the past and the present, a production illustrating a distinct moment in time that had to be seen before the inexorable flood of modernity washed it away.[26]

As tourists turned to nature, they also turned to American Indians as a way to solve their identity crisis. Alan Trachtenberg argues that the Anglo-American fascination with American Indians from the 1880s through the 1930s was a reaction to the waves of immigrants who "posed a threat to nationality," while American Indians were evidence of "national distinctiveness and proof of nationality."[27] The national identity crisis European immigrants had prompted transformed the idea of the American Indian from "savage" foe to "first American" and ancestor of the nation, a nation that had vigorously and violently fought to eradicate them from their homelands and strip them of their children and their cultures, their languages, and, essentially, their existence.[28] Indian pageants were tangible methods of acknowledging the roots of America by acknowledging Native history, albeit a history that was produced by, packaged for, and consumed by non-Natives. American identity has long been tied up in its proximity to Indians and Indianness, and these ideas of national identity are connected to the public commemoration of pageantry. This commemoration does not focus on Indians in their present state—as contemporaneous to Americans—but in the notions of these perceived ideas. These fears and questions around commemoration and national identity coalesced in the civic pageants that popped up around the country. David Glassberg's study of American civic pageantry has shown that many of these productions were largely community-based celebrations established to commemorate particular events, such as a town's centennial.[29] At its peak, according to Glassberg, thousands of Americans in hundreds of towns across the country joined in civic celebrations by acting out dramatic episodes from their town's history.[30] However, the majority of these pageants' plotlines did not focus on local American Indians. Many included scenes of idyllic Indian life before the coming of the white man, only to have the Indians exit early in the production in order to demonstrate how "inevitable progress, not white conquest, brought about the end of Indian civilization."[31]

Similarly, John Troutman argues that the appeal of Indianness arose from its "apparent cultural authenticity in an unseemly, inauthentic, vapid modern world—a world in which popular fantasies of Indianness serve as an antidote to the fabrication and immediacy of modernity."[32] My work argues that this sense of authenticity, this required component of salvage tourism, centers on touristic demands for what is real (or what tourists consider to be real). These productions do not simply reproduce history. They attempt to salvage it by zeroing in on the "sheer spectacle" of Indigenous history, highlighting their productions' "artistic excellence" and promoting their shows as "one of the most mesmerizing dramas in the nation."[33] Philip Deloria argues that the romanticization of Indianness played an important part in "the movement of antimodern primitivism and helped lay the foundation for a modern American identity."[34]

The late nineteenth century also saw the rise of anthropology and salvage ethnography. Congress established the Bureau of American Ethnography (BAE) in 1879 as a research unit of the Smithsonian Institution that focused solely on American Indians.[35] Convinced that American Indian languages, rituals, songs, and dances—not to mention the Indians themselves—would soon disappear, ethnographers like Frances Densmore rushed to salvage what they assumed was left of pristine Indian cultures before they vanished. In 1907, Densmore wrote to the BAE regarding "the interesting material among the Chippewa that would soon be lost forever."[36] Densmore was among those convinced that Natives and their languages, rituals, songs, and dances would become "relics of the past, relics of a race that would either disappear or sacrifice the practices in order to assimilate into an assumed detribalized American social fabric."[37] This desire to save, to preserve, and to keep Indigenous cultures for posterity shaped the creation of salvage ethnography, which emerged in the same historical moment as anthropological displays of humanity in world's fairs and the growing popularity of Wild West shows.[38]

Ethnography was not the only means by which Americans strove to preserve a particular vision of the past. Tourism productions also offered an opportunity to experience a distinct moment in time before modernity made it impossible to revisit a particular place. Jane Desmond contends that emergent "cultural tourism" offered wealthy vacationers a dose of what she calls "anthropological contact with selected primitives," meaning just enough contact to "reinvigorate through contact with the 'authentic' and 'natural' those suffering from ennui because of the deadening pressures of modern, urban life."[39] It is in this loss, this ostensibly inescapable elimination of indigeneity, that salvage tourism emerges. Like salvage ethnography, salvage tourism is not about saving the "vanishing Indian." Instead, it centers on saving Euro-American idealized ideas about Indians. By saving snapshots of what they consider to be expressions of Indianness in its purest form, salvage tourism underpins the notion that Indian cultures and Indian people are static and unchanging; when they inevitably change, they are no longer considered Indian. Salvage ethnography and salvage tourism hope to reenact these moments, to recapture that purity. These peculiar notions—the idea that one can freeze and capture a moment—draws nostalgically on a moment, conveying this history in a way that seeks to secure the unadulterated and uncontaminated past. By deliberately positing themselves as the purveyors of regional Native and non-Native histories, pageant and drama organizers and producers sought and continue to create, curate, publicize, and popularize a version of history that would appeal to tourists. This appeal relies on non-Natives' desire to find themselves in history, to salvage their ideas of the past by re-creating the Indigenous past and calling it authentic.

Salvage ethnography attempted to preserve Indigenous culture, and salvage tourism is an attempt to save the economy, bolster generalized ideas of Indian history, and define American tourists' sense of self. The nation had built its culture and its identity around the continual settlement of the continent, and Indian-centered tourist endeavors linked Indians and Indian history to what were, for white Americans, formerly Indian lands. By the late nineteenth century, the growing sentimentalism for the apparently dominated and disappearing wilderness turned Native peoples and places into commodities. Non-Natives' sense of inherent superiority linked them to the national myth of the American frontier, allowing everyday Americans to travel and see the wilderness through the eyes of a genteel vacationer, not a violent conqueror.[40] The sense of salvage and its focus on loss and extinction stresses the "pathology of cultural loss in the absence of any real experience with the normally operating small community."[41] Additionally, as Marita Sturken contends, the deep investment in what she calls "the concept of innocence in American culture" connects with how this culture processes and engages with loss.[42]

Salvage tourism is a process and a practice created by and performed for non-Natives. It is characterized by the power of nostalgic urgency, the need to participate in a performance of remembering and memorializing. Salvage tourism revolves around the intent to salvage the past, to save it from disappearing into obscurity. Salvaging is different from preserving, although both actions seek to save and encapsulate something (or someone). It requires transformation and reinterpretation; in this sense, it is the commodification of a distinct historical narrative around Euro-American ideas of the loss of Indigenous history and culture. Salvaging a house, for instance, is not the same as preserving or restoring it. It involves taking architectural pieces—the fireplace, a chandelier, a window—and reusing them in an entirely new and different context.[43] These pieces, once plucked from their original spaces and places, become a commodity, something with value, something that can be charged with meaning—and charged a pretty penny to obtain. As the salvager, as the owner, one can manipulate and modify it. To commodify something is to turn it into something that can be bought or sold, something deemed useful or valuable. Tourism, meanwhile, turns people, places, events, and experiences into commodities.

The creation and, more importantly, the continued production of these dramas epitomize salvage tourism through the use of American Indian history in order to salvage regional economies through tourism by creating a sense of tradition in a particular place. The tension between creation and preservation is critical: one is tied to knowledge production and the other is advertised as a product for consumption. As local economies faltered, American Indians, Indian history, and images of Indians became the most promising and potentially profitable regional tourist endeavors. Organizers and promoters clearly recognized—and continue to recognize—the economic potential of these productions.

Salvage tourism does not directly apply to the Indians whose histories inspired the dramas. Instead, their histories become commodities, a neat package sold to non-Native tourists who dream of the imagined Indians of the past. The commodification of Indianness, meaning the mechanisms through which Indians, their history, and the landscape were (and often still are) turned into products that must be immediately utilized before modernity inevitably obliterates them, created a market for salvage tourism, especially following the popularity of Wild West shows in the late nineteenth and early twentieth centuries. The prominence (and profits) promoters collected demonstrated that there was, in fact, a market for tourism industries that centered on American Indians. Opportunistic town boosters explicitly exploited non-Native fascinations with Indians and Indian history to encourage tourism to these specific regions. The key gesture in this commodification is the means through which organizers and producers took something that seemed to be vanishing or out of reach and made it eminently available through purchase. It is not for use, per se, but for memorialization.

American Indian historical pageants and outdoor dramas produce and package a theatrical version of a Euro-American idealization of Indigenous history for tourists. Happy Canyon, *Unto These Hills*, and *Tecumseh!* were each created in a moment where traditional economic systems were no longer profitable. Spurred by regional economic anxiety, local boosters, residents, and businesses reached not for Indians but for Indianness. In these moments—in the 1910s, 1940s, and 1970s—when participation in the conventional economic system was not working for anyone, we see a reflexive reaching for Indianness, searching for the imaginary over reality. That these moments recur and produce a similar impulse for salvage tourism is worthy of note. The seemingly inevitable, regrettable, and long-past erasure of Indianness led to its reification in these performative spaces.

Marguerite Shaffer argues that the tourist landscape of the late nineteenth and early twentieth centuries became a space to participate in a ritual of citizenship in order to validate the tourists' identities as Americans.[44] Shaffer contends that from the late nineteenth century through the middle of the twentieth, tourist industries created and marketed tourism landscapes as "quintessentially American places, consciously highlighting certain meanings and myths while ignoring others, deliberately arranging historical events and anecdotes, intentionally framing certain scenes and views into a coherent national whole."[45] Tourism advocates built a catalog of American tourist attractions that manifested what Shaffer calls a distinct national identity, encouraging "white, native-born middle- and upper-class Americans to reaffirm their American-ness by following the footsteps of American history and seeing the nation firsthand." Promoters who taught tourists what to see and how to see it "invented and mapped an idealized American history and tradition across the American landscape, defining an organic nationalism that linked national identity to a shared territory and history."[46] Additionally, Sturken's term "tourists of history" and the cathartic "'experience' of history" allow tourists to define themselves as both part of and distant from what they see.[47]

These pageants and dramas that showcase and help explain salvage tourism have been ubiquitous in the United States since the early twentieth century. The geographic range of these productions shows the broad reach of connecting tourism and indigeneity, while their temporal range—from the early twentieth into the twenty-first century—highlights their continued resonance with and relation to local economies and, in some instances, civic reliance on these productions as a means of economic survival. The range of these productions, from location and era to subject matter, underscores the reliance on Indigenous historical narratives for the creation and maintenance of these local tourist economies.

Each of these three productions premiered in a particular age when questions of citizenship were hotly contested. The Pendleton Round-Up and the Happy Canyon Indian Pageant and Wild West Show opened amid national debates over Asian immigration. *Unto These Hills* began during heightened Cold War tensions and the push to terminate American Indian nations as the final nail in the coffin of assimilation. *Tecumseh!* debuted in the wake of the civil rights movement, on the heels of national demonstrations by groups like the American Indian Movement, and on the brink of the nation's bicentennial. In each of these moments, as anxieties over identity, citizenship, and belonging intensified, Pendleton, Cherokee, and Chillicothe turned to two things that could serve as a temporary escape: Indians and tourism.

The Differences between Historical Pageants and Outdoor Dramas

In 1950, a North Carolina newspaper gleefully noted that the business of producing "outdoor pageant-dramas" that dealt with American history was booming. "Besides the theater aspect," the paper continued, "communities found such attractions good for business."[48] This particular craze had started a mere fourteen years earlier. Written by Paul Green for Roanoke Island's 350th anniversary, *The Lost Colony* was an instant success when it opened in 1937. By 1939, *Time* magazine crowed that the island, after remaining "obscure, poverty-stricken, almost unpopulated" for generations, now had a "boom-town look—new stores, cottages, hotels," thanks to the drama's success. President Franklin Delano Roosevelt was among the drama's 70,000 visitors in 1937.[49]

According to Laurence Avery, the people of Eastern North Carolina were frustrated by the "neglect of that important event by historians and in the popular mind."[50] Local residents and businessmen, including the Roanoke Island Historical Association, decided that a historical, dramatic presentation would be the ticket for not only fame and prestige but, in what will be a recurring theme throughout this book, the potential for economic prosperity. They had long held a local celebration on August 18 in honor of the birthday of Virginia Dare, the first English child born in America, and by the 1930s they were preparing to celebrate the 350th anniversary of the colony. Dedicated community members, along with assistance from the Works Progress Administration and the Federal Theatre Project, brought their history to life.[51] They tapped Pulitzer Prize–winning playwright Paul Green to bring the history of Roanoke Island to the stage, and plans for the production were soon underway. Green was likely inspired by Frederick Koch, who was a playwright, professor at the University of North Carolina (UNC), and the founder of the Carolina Playmakers at UNC. Koch had written a pageant called *Raleigh: The Shepherd of the Ocean: A Pageant Drama* in 1920 to commemorate the tercentenary of Sir Walter's execution, and Green's script for *The Lost Colony* had many parallels to Koch's previous endeavor.[52]

Two of the biggest issues facing the organizers of *The Lost Colony* were where audience members would come from and how they would get to the drama. As Avery wryly notes, "It wasn't because the area was densely populated that the Wright brothers went to nearby Kitty Hawk some years earlier to test their flying machines."[53] Tourists would have to come from hundreds of miles away, and there was not a particularly easy way to get to the island. It would take a variety of transportation methods, ranging from several ferries and a "floating road" of asphalt "suspended on steel cables hitched to pilings over several miles of swamp that would swallow anything falling into it" to packed sand or dirt roads. Creating *The Lost Colony* was a mammoth undertaking, requiring the assistance of the Civilian Conservation Corps, the Rockefeller Foundation, the University of North Carolina at Chapel Hill, the Federal Theatre Project, the United States Postal Service, and the United States Treasury.[54] Nevertheless, the people persevered, and *The Lost Colony* premiered on July 4, 1937, for an audience of 2,500.[55] The drama was a hit. Frederick Koch proclaimed that Green had reclaimed "the ancient and honorable art" of pageantry, which he considered to be the most democratic of all the arts because all may have a part, he wrote: "poets, players, designers, singers, and dancers." He could not think of a better way toward a "spiritual expression of our American life" than through this dramatic form.[56]

In 1952, Samuel Selden, who directed the Carolina Playmakers at the University of North Carolina at Chapel Hill and had a hand in a number of outdoor dramas, explained the popularity of the art form that drew nearly 350,000 people to five outdoor dramas the previous summer. Besides the fundamental urge to "escape the confines of our cramped way of living in a modern world," the desire for freedom that led people to drive to the seashore, the mountains, or the country to find an outdoor drama, he cited the "insatiable interest each of us has in the history of our country." Writing in a collective voice, he noted the pride in "our political and social ancestry." In an era of cynicism and discouragement, he outlined a need to be assured of the "brave spirit which gave our nation its early strength."[57]

Outdoor dramas—also known as symphonic dramas—are said to have their roots in medieval times or even ancient Greece. In many of these productions, the audience is at least presumed to be somewhat familiar with the historical events behind the drama.[58] These dramas are distinct from the historical pageants that dominated the American landscape in the late nineteenth and early twentieth centuries. Historical pageants primarily centered on fostering or boosting civic pride, and were defined as a dramatic presentation where "a running theme (or a series of incidents) takes the place of a plot, and in which large numbers of people participate."[59] Pageants were not and are not plays. They are what Laurence Avery calls "chronicles, with events following one another as historical chronology, not dramatic necessity, dictated."[60] Pageant characters were not what we expect to find in a play or a musical. Rather, they were representatives of prominent figures who, if they spoke at all, would step forward and give speeches like "I am George Washington. I led the Continental Army in our glorious War of Independence from the British crown, then accepted the verdict of my fellow countrymen and became the first President of these United States of America."[61]

Paul Green insisted that *The Lost Colony* was not a pageant.[62] Instead, he called his newest creation a "symphonic drama," not simply because of the use of music, but because all of the elements of the theater—music, song, dance, and pantomime, among others—worked together within the production. "It's not a perfect-fitting term," Green once admitted, "but the best I can find, better than music or musical drama. In the original sense it means 'sounding-together.'"[63] In his author's note for *The Common Glory*, a drama he wrote in 1948, he reiterated that he used the term "symphonic drama" to mean "that type of drama in which all elements of theatre art are used to sound together—one for all and all for one, a true democracy."[64] Green's definition of symphonic drama changed over the years. By 1957, he called it "the blending of all the arts and elements of stagecraft—music, dancing, folk song, choreographic movement, sound effects, pageantry, masks when needed, mental speech or what not—all working like the cooperative sections of a symphony orchestra in moving forward the characterization and story line of the piece."[65]

David Glassberg has convincingly demonstrated that traditional historical pageants declined in the years before World War II. These pageants were usually staged to celebrate a distinct event in a town's history, and they were often a onetime production. They would be performed a few times, mostly for local and perhaps regional residents, with local leaders and community members in the majority of the roles. However, these pageants did not necessarily disappear. Rather, they were replaced by Green's concept of a symphonic drama to serve as a long-term economic stimulus. Kermit Hunter, the author of *Unto These Hills* and a number of other outdoor dramas, believed that the motivating factor in outdoor dramas was "a small, energetic community determined to revitalize itself through a grand tourist attraction in the form of a permanent outdoor production."[66] *The Lost Colony* had transformed Roanoke Island's economy, and communities across the country—mostly small, rural communities—saw outdoor drama as a path to fame and economic prosperity.

As historical pageantry fell out of favor in the interwar years, a number of factors influenced the growth of what would become a powerful player in popular culture. Frederick Koch, a pageant-master, dramatist, and professor whom David Glassberg calls "the major figure in American folk drama in the 1920s," joined the faculty at the University of North Carolina in 1918. Koch wrote and produced a number of historical pageants, but he focused most of his energy on the Carolina Playmakers, a group of UNC students who wrote and produced original, one-act plays inspired by North Carolina.[67] People like Koch, who led the movement of artistic shifts away from pageantry and toward other forms of dramatic interpretation, had significant impacts on their students, some of whom would become major players in their own right.

Paul Green was one of Koch's students who cut his teeth on pageants before developing his own style.[68] The Carolina Playmakers staged a number of Green's plays, including *In Abraham's Bosom*, which won the 1927 Pulitzer Prize for drama.[69] His script for *The Lost Colony* would be one of nearly a dozen outdoor dramas Green would craft in his lifetime.[70] While playwrights and dramatists like Green helped build the canon of outdoor dramas, the 1963 establishment of the Institute of Outdoor Drama (IOD) at the University of North Carolina codified the rise of the genre.[71] Mark Sumner was hired as director the following year, a position he held for the next twenty-five years. Sumner would help launch more than thirty outdoor dramas in twenty-six states, and he also offered advice and assistance to countless other communities that hoped to start new shows or that hoped to improve or sustain their current shows.[72] He was called "the de facto leader of the American outdoor historical drama movement," and the organization named a lifetime achievement award after him following his retirement from the IOD.[73]

Sumner and his successors at the IOD have fielded hundreds of phone calls, letters, and emails from communities across the country and over the years. In a 1967 report, Sumner noted that the "expanding interest in things historical, the awarness [*sic*] of the tourist dollar, and a feeling of cultural worth have led an increasing number of communities to investigate the value and method of outdoor drama development."[74] The report outlined successful components of some outdoor dramas, but it also offered suggestions for improvement. Sumner and his colleagues saw the report as a tool not only for "the beginning community planning group" but also for "the individual theatre artist concerned with working in outdoor drama for the first time."[75]

The sheer number of requests for information, contracts for feasibility studies, and fully realized productions underscore the significance of these dramas. Outdoor dramas flourished in the decades following World War II, and there are likely a number of reasons why. The United States had just emerged from an era that saw two world wars and a great depression, and Cold War anxieties tempered the postwar elation. The nation was holding onto a sense of deterioration that lingered from the Great Depression and the war years and, as they had for decades, Americans turned to tourism as a means of building national identity. The surge of dramas in the 1950s and 1960s was the tangible convergence of economic recovery and stability in foreign policy. The development of a national highway system allowed Americans to travel farther and faster—and they did. The IOD, now known as the Institute of Outdoor Theatre, holds the records of more than 180 dramas that premiered from 1907 to 2010. There are, undoubtedly, more outdoor dramas staged by local communities in this period that were not in contact with the IOD, as well as those that, for whatever reason, never reached the stage. Even without those additional records, the geographic and chronological range of these productions underscores the fact that these dramas were an integral part of the American tourism industry.

Outdoor dramas require a number of things. They require a collection of dedicated organizers and volunteers willing to devote months, if not years, of their lives to see the drama from dream to reality. They require a plot of land big enough to hold an amphitheater and parking lots, and the drama's location needs historical significance. Lastly, and perhaps most importantly, outdoor dramas require a story. The success or failure of an outdoor drama may hinge on the story's ability to tap into the audience's emotion, to make the members of the audience feel as though they are, quite literally, reliving history. Harry Davis, another influential behind-the-scenes player in outdoor dramas, argued in 1957 that, while Broadway plays could focus on any conceivable theme, outdoor dramas were invariably connected with "actual events and personalities of the past." He continued, noting, "Another important feature of the historical play is its direct, indigenous relation to the locale in which it is staged. In nearly all instances the dramatized story, rooted in historical fact, is presented on or near the site where the real story took place. This imparts a valuable spiritual quality into the performance, since it becomes a sort of pilgrimage to holy ground."[76] With that in mind, small towns and bigger cities across the nation tried to capitalize on their histories throughout the twentieth century, working to turn the people and events of the past into tourist capital.

The ideas and ideals of democracy manifested themselves through the dramas, the reviews, and the writings of theater folks. Green himself dreamed of a "real people's theatre," one besides the movies. He wanted a theater where plays were written, acted, and produced by and for the people, "for their enjoyment and enrichment and not for any special monetary profit." He believed in what he called the decentralization of the theater, arguing that American dramas had been bottled up in "the narrow neck and cul-de-sac of

Broadway."[77] Harry Davis proudly noted in 1957 that family tourist groups made up an overwhelming proportion of the audiences at the dramas. This "theatre of the people," he wrote, was born in ancient Greece, was nurtured in Caesar's Rome, and came of age in Elizabethan England. Its revival—400 years later and a continent away—lived on in America, "whose history is young."[78] William Trotman concurred, noting that, out of the thousands of people who traveled to see *The Lost Colony* every summer, the composition of a typical audience "is not half so sophisticated as one on Broadway, for it is much more representative of a cross-section of the American public."[79]

The idea of democracy ran through the heart of countless symphonic outdoor dramas. A fund-raising brochure from the Ohio Outdoor Historical Drama Association, Inc. (OOHDA), the organization behind the *Trumpet in the Land* drama, proclaimed, "Paul Green has said, 'These theatres should be the theatres of the people, and these plays should show the greatness of America.'"[80] This idea of democracy—both in the makeup of the audience and the nature of the dramas themselves—is key to understanding a contentious element of outdoor drama: historical accuracy. Some scholars have summarily dismissed outdoor dramas based solely on the authors' focus on the "spirit of history." Historian John Finger, for instance, has argued that *Unto These Hills* is more mythology than history.[81] But historical accuracy is not a hallmark of outdoor historical drama. Despite the historical component of symphonic dramas, their writers often focus on the drama instead of the history. In 1959, Edwin S. Lindsey argued that writers of outdoor drama, like Green and Hunter, aimed to dramatize "the *spirit* of history" (emphasis in original). They were not concerned with the accuracy of historical details, Lindsey continued, because "they are writing drama, not history."[82]

As both a historian and an unabashed fan of the theater, I find this contradiction and contestation fascinating. Those who turn their noses up at Broadway musicals, for instance, often insist that they don't like musicals because nobody ever breaks out into song and dance in real life. Theatergoers, on the other hand, willingly suspend reality. We don't really believe that Glinda (*Wicked*) can fly or that cats can sing in harmony (*Cats*), and we don't really believe that the founding fathers could rap (*Hamilton*). Outdoor dramas walk a delicate balance between realism and fantasy, even as they publicize and profit from their historical connections. That's how Pendleton claims the American West, Cherokee claims the Trail of Tears, and Chillicothe claims Tecumseh. Even as the Happy Canyon arena is backlit by the lights in Wal-Mart's parking lot, its audiences take ownership of the fact that the Oregon Trail passed through town. Even as the cast in Cherokee reenacts removal, the members of the audience feel as though they sit on hallowed ground. Even though Indians were forcibly removed from Ohio, audiences in Chillicothe are inundated with the knowledge that they're sitting on Shawnee homelands.

But there's a dark side to playing fast and loose with history for the sake of drama. By fashioning themselves as the purveyors of history, playwrights like Hunter and Green had the power to twist the narrative for other purposes. The heroes of the dramas become the heroes of history, the heroes of America. Some might scoff at the seriousness of this study. It's just a show, they might say. But for the millions of people around the country who have sat in star-lit amphitheaters, this may be their deepest engagement with the stories they see on stage. They may leave Pendleton without considering how the Confederated Tribes of the Umatilla Indian Reservation (CTUIR) spend their other fifty-one weeks of the year. They may leave Cherokee believing that Tsali laid down his life for his people, even as scholars debate the truth behind this story. They may leave Chillicothe believing that Tecumseh, not Tenskwatawa, was the Shawnee prophet. The history of America is enmeshed with the history of American Indians, but the democratic ideals espoused by writers of outdoor dramas overshadow the truth behind the scripts. Green, Hunter, and their contemporaries were not scripting the histories of Indians— they were scripting their idyllic histories of America. Gregory D. Smithers, writing about the implications of historical inaccuracies in Hunter's *Unto These Hills*, contends that Green's pioneering way of writing historically in-spired epics allowed him to "teach Cold War audiences about the importance of learning from the mistakes of the past so that the democratic trajectory of the American Republic was not derailed."[83]

Regardless of the plot line, America was the star of each drama. From the North Carolina coast to southern California, outdoor dramas cultivated, pro-jected, and reified a nostalgic image of a storied past that gave Americans a collective history and creation story. Like their historical pageant forerun-ners, many dramas arose out of a commemorative moment. From the *Fort Griffin Fandangle* in Albany, Texas, which opened in 1939 and bills itself as the oldest outdoor musical in Texas, to Lake George, New York's *Last of the Mo-hicans*, which opened in 2010, the stories and histories told in these dramas are painted and promoted as unique to their particular place.

Pendleton, Cherokee, and Chillicothe

This book is arranged chronologically based on when the productions pre-miered: Happy Canyon is first, followed by *Unto These Hills*, and *Tecumseh!* is last. The Happy Canyon Indian Pageant and Wild West Show began as night-time entertainment for audiences at the Pendleton Round-Up in Pendleton, Oregon, in the 1910s. In 1916, Round-Up founder J. Roy Raley added an "Indian portion" to the show with the help of Anna Minthorn Wannassay, a Carlisle graduate from the Confederated Tribes of the Umatilla Indian Reservation. Now, in the twenty-first century, more than 500 Native and non-Native volunteers participate each year. They pride themselves on their long-standing familial participation and the pageant's century-old script. The production takes audiences through Native and non-Native history in the region through the Treaty of 1855, wherein the Cayuse, Umatilla, and Walla Walla ceded 6.4 million acres of land and moved to the reservation. Chapter 1 dissects the early twentieth-century West that gave birth to the Round-Up and Happy Canyon in the 1910s. Chapter 2 examines Pendleton's contemporary tourism industry, juxtaposing the CTUIR's relationship to the Round-Up and Happy Canyon alongside the tribes cultural and economic developments.

Unto These Hills debuted in Cherokee, North Carolina, in 1950 after the creation of the Great Smoky Mountains National Park and after several decades of small-scale, tourist-centered enterprises developed by non-Natives that involved the Eastern Band of Cherokee Indians. *Unto These Hills* tells a romanticized story of Cherokee history through the Eastern Band's resistance to removal, centering on the near-mythic character of Tsali and his decision to die so that his people could remain in their homelands. The Eastern Band rejected this overly sentimentalized, exaggerated production, along with its paternalistic overtones. After several successive attempts to revise the production in the early twenty-first century, the drama still struggles to sustain worthwhile attendance numbers as it tries to draw more Eastern Band and other Indigenous actors into the production as performers, but changing ideas of tourism have led to diminishing ticket sales and revenue. Chapter 3 examines the region's long history of tourism and economic development and the shifts in federal Indian policy that gave rise to the drama. In chapter 4, I follow the drama's numerous revisions alongside Eastern Band economic growth on the Qualla Boundary, demonstrating the shifts in salvage tourism since the 1950s.

Tecumseh! premiered in 1973. A Chillicothe, Ohio, civic organization, the Scioto Society, hoped to capitalize on the American fascination with the famous Shawnee leader's life and tragic demise in the Battle of the Thames in the War of 1812. By inviting tourists into ceded Shawnee territory to see a theatrical retelling of a critical point in Shawnee history, the drama situates Tecumseh's tragic downfall at the hands of his brother, coupled with his star-crossed love for the daughter of a Scottish immigrant, as the emotional crux of the plot. It relegates his resistance against the United States to a secondary story line. Tecumseh looms large in many facets of American mythology and the American imagination, and his life—and perhaps more so his death—occupies a complicated space in the narrative of early American history. This drama attempts to reclaim the imposition of the settler-colonial state onto Indians and Indian lands by turning Tecumseh into a near-mythic character, a man driven by love of his country and his people. In chapter 5, I place *Tecumseh!* among the plans for the nation's bicentennial to explain the drama's creation. In chapter 6, I unpack how—and why—the Shawnee leader's life and legacy have been repackaged and repurposed as a tribute to an imagined American identity through the lens of salvage tourism.

At first glance, these three productions have little, if anything, in common: Happy Canyon and *Tecumseh!* enjoy relative economic prosperity, while *Unto These Hills* fights to remain afloat. *Tecumseh!* and *Unto These Hills* both employ professional actors for a summer-long commitment, while Happy Canyon's four-day run prides itself on its lack of rehearsal and its use of Native and non-Native descendants of earlier residents. Happy Canyon and *Unto These Hills* have always used Native actors (albeit in a range of roles and not always without conflict), while *Tecumseh!* traditionally hires non-Native actors to play the predominantly Indian cast. They have a wide geographic and chronological range: Happy Canyon premiered in the West in the 1910s, *Unto These Hills* opened in the Southeast in 1950, and the Midwestern *Tecumseh!* debuted in 1973. All three began in a particular moment of regional economic uncertainty that pushed local residents and business owners to find an economic impetus or stimulus to revive their economies. All three turned to Native history in order to make this happen. All three productions are marketed toward non-Native tourists, and the theatrical decisions—from the story line to the casting, costuming, and promotion—have been made with this particular audience in mind.

The pull of this faux nostalgia—or "fauxstalgia," if you will—requires a creative reinterpretation of the past in order to recapture those particular feelings. In the same vein as salvage ethnography, these productions aim to rescue and reclaim Indigenous histories. As tourist enterprises, these productions repossess and re-center the narrative through their focus on the authenticity that comes with traveling. But we would be remiss to dismiss them as camp, as mere spectacle. They lay bare the fascinating roots of American claims to national identity, and their staying power underscores a multifaceted need in the American psyche. Their performative component is a central tenet, revealing deeply embedded and ingrained notions of what Americans think about Indians. It's all imaginary, of course, but it's rooted in particular moments and particular movements, enveloping their audiences in romanticism, nostalgia, and sentimentalism. It's about salvaging and creating a usable past by performing indigeneity.

I am often asked how the Native nations portrayed in these productions react or respond to these representations, or how the productions engage with these tribes. It depends. Happy Canyon has always used Native actors, even as some do not believe the pageant accurately represents the region's history. Those who do participate often see it as a place to celebrate their history and culture. The Eastern Band's relationship with the Cherokee Historical Association (CHA) has shifted since the 1950s, particularly as *Unto These Hills* casts more and more Native and local actors and as members of the Eastern Band join the board of the CHA. *Tecumseh!*, however, has hired few Native actors in its nearly fifty-year run. The Happy Canyon arena is ten minutes from the Confederated Tribes of the Umatilla Indian Reservation, and *Unto These Hills* is performed on the Qualla Boundary. But the Shawnee, forced out of the region in the early nineteenth century, now have three reservations in Oklahoma. Newspaper articles and promotional materials in Ohio boast of the Shawnees' 1970s approval of the production, but the contemporary dissonance between the drama and the Shawnee is not surprising.

This, then, is why I consider these productions to be salvage tourism instead of heritage tourism which, to cite the National Trust for Historic Preservation, means "traveling to experience the places, artifacts and activities that authentically represent the stories and people of the past." Despite claims to the contrary, these are not necessarily historically accurate representations. As a reminder, salvage tourism, like salvage ethnography, is not about saving the "vanishing Indian." Instead, it centers on saving unrealistic Euro-American ideas about Indians. By using snapshots of what they consider to be expressions of Indianness in its purest form, salvage tourism underpins the notion that Indian cultures and Indian people are static and unchanging; when they inevitably change, they are no longer considered Indian. Like salvage ethnography, salvage tourism hopes to reenact these moments, to recapture that purity. These historical pageants and outdoor dramas convey this history in a way that seeks to secure the unadulterated and uncontaminated past. The appeal of Indianness relies on non-Natives' desire to find themselves in history, to salvage their ideas of the past by re-creating their ideas of Indigenous pasts and calling it authentic.

I had no idea that a reluctant trip to my reservation during one of the busi-est tourist weekends of the year would lead me down this path. My research has taken me from the Great Smoky Mountains to the slowly rolling hills of northeastern Oregon to south central Ohio. I have sat backstage at the Moun-tainside Theatre in Cherokee, watching the cogs of an aging, albeit well-oiled, drama prepare for a performance. I've traveled from Columbus to Chilli-cothe, watching freeways and the industrial feel of the capital give way to bu-colic farmlands and two-lane highways. I've walked miles in cowboy boots in Pendleton, watching proud descendants of cowboys, Indians, and pioneers reenact their popularized version of history. Despite their many differences, one constant remains. American Indian historical pageantry and outdoor drama are a lens for the past and the present, the historic and the dramatic. And, in the spirit of the historic and the dramatic, I end with the words of William Shakespeare: "All the world's a stage, / And all the men and women merely players; / They have their exits and their entrances, / And one man in his time plays many parts . . . / Last scene of all, / That ends this strange eventful history."[84]

CHAPTER ONE

Days of Old West Are Lived Again

The Happy Canyon Indian Pageant and Wild West Show

It is all a chapter taken out of the history of the old West—a chapter which every American with red blood in his veins should read in the real before it passes by and, like the old West, forever disappears on the horizon of time. But to understand, one must look with one's own eyes on these things. Then you will feel the stir and the thrill of life of these golden lands of hopes and achievements, where man extends a generous and hospitable welcome to those who cross his trails; it is a spectacle which makes you go away with a bigger, finer feeling toward life, and a genuine respect and appreciation for [those] who have "taken chances," have risked limb and even life at times in their sports of daring and skill, that you may see how their fathers once struggled in earnest against unequal odds in order to attain the Winning of the West.

—Charles Wellington Furlong, "The Epic Drama of the West," 1916

Happy Canyon is the result of the overworked condition of the Roundup directors. The Roundup could entertain the people in the afternoon, but there was nothing for them to do in the evening.

"Put on a night show," everyone advised.

"Put on a nightcap," the directors answered. "We don't even have the time to do that. If we attempted it we'd be putting on a night show in the asylum down here."

—*Sunday Oregonian*, September 12, 1915

According to local legend, a handful of men, including a businessman from Pendleton, Oregon, along with a former Indian superintendent, rode out to a council on the nearby home of the Confederated Tribes of the Umatilla Indian Reservation (CTUIR) in the summer of 1910. The Treaty of 1855 had forcibly removed the Cayuse, Umatilla, and Walla Walla Indians to the reservation, which had only exacerbated long-simmering tensions between the Indians and the white residents of Pendleton. But in 1910, boosters and businessmen in Pendleton were planning a round-up—akin to what we would now consider a rodeo—for that September, and they wanted to invite the Indians to town for the events. They promoted the round-up as a time for the Indians to gather at one of their former salmon camps, trade with the whites, participate in parades, and dance for the crowds in the arena. After the council, the delegates, unsure of the Indians' willingness to participate, turned for home and went back to Pendleton. As legend has it, they saw a cloud of dust rising on the horizon as they stood on the loading docks of the Pendleton Woolen Mills on the first morning of the round-up. The tribe had accepted the invitation, and they set up their round-up camp where they had set up their salmon camps so many decades earlier. And so the Pendleton Round-Up was born, a celebration of Western life and livelihoods that has become an iconic pilgrimage for generations of locals and tourists.[1]

It's a great story. But, like all great stories, there's more to it than that. The push to revive the woolen mills and, in turn, Pendleton's economy meant finding ways to put Pendleton on the map. Its railroad connections certainly helped. But Pendleton wasn't Portland, and it wasn't Seattle. It didn't have the luxury of a diversified economy or easy port access. Some scholars and Pendleton organizers argue that a visit from Buffalo Bill Cody and his Wild West show pushed Pendletonians to put on their own show. Others who examine the events focus on the Bishop brothers, the men who resurrected the struggling Pendleton Woolen Mills, and their friendship with Lee Moorhouse, a local photographer and former Indian agent at a nearby reservation. There are those who claim that the switch from a cattle-driven economy to a sheep-focused economy was the catalyst for the Round-Up. Still more recall the region's long history of commemorative and civic celebrations, such as the Portland Rose Festival or Pendleton's 1909 Fourth of July celebration.[2]

Organizers and promoters of the Round-Up and Happy Canyon have long championed these events as real and raw, the epitome of the Western experience and the most authentic portrayal of Western history. The first Round-Up, hastily cobbled together in 1910, not only established Pendleton's claim to authenticity but validated it through the ease with which the production came together. As Charles Wellington Furlong, who counted writing for *Harper's Monthly Magazine* among his many endeavors, noted, a visitor to Pendleton in September would "rub elbows with many an old Indian fighter." Thanks to Happy Canyon, "you are in a little frontier world of fifty years ago," a place where "many of these players are in reality the characters they portray. . . . Not even a rehearsal is held. The 'boys' are simply told what is expected of them and when they are to do it. . . . You see bad men and vigilantes come riding through town; the bar-room has its shooting scrape, and cowboy and cowgirl gracefully reel through their dances on horseback and take part in ranch and town games of various kinds."[3] For Furlong and the thousands who flocked to Pendleton, the frontier world of yore was more than just the stuff of books

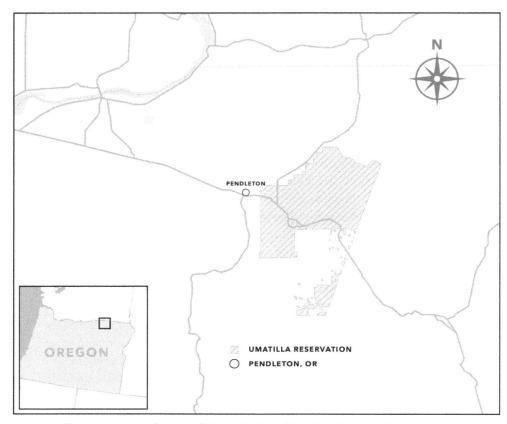

PENDLETON

N

UMATILLA RESERVATION
PENDLETON, OR

OREGON

Pendleton, Oregon, and the Confederated Tribes of the Umatilla Indian Reservation.
Map by Josiah Donat.

and magazines. Like Lerner and Loewe's musical *Brigadoon*, the charming, anachronistic ideal of a sleepy small town came to life for those who truly believed.[4] Unlike the slick, polished Wild West shows that required extensive rehearsals before appearing before their audiences, the Round-Up and Happy Canyon seemingly sprang up overnight. A local newspaper described the scene in 1914: "The town of 'Happy Canyon' has grown from nothing to a thriving frontier metropolis and, commencing Wednesday evening, will be a scene of commercial activity and hilarious festivity."[5]

As a production and a re-created frontier town, Happy Canyon intended to capitalize on the proven draw of the West. From the first Round-Up in 1910 and the first night show in 1913 to the 1914 development of a Wild West–type of vaudeville entertainment and the 1916 addition of an Indian pageant, unraveling the history of these events reveals the multilayered appeal and function of Pendleton's claim to Wild Western history. The Round-Up founders created a commodity structured around its insistent portrayal of itself and its residents, both Native and white, as the personification of the West, and they designed a celebration to appeal to its own residents as well as outsiders.

Pendleton employed a rhetoric of disappearance through the development of the Round-Up and Happy Canyon. Salvage tourism functioned as a catalyst for tourists who believed that the taming of the West made Pendleton itself a vanishing commodity. Promotional materials centered on the Round-Up and Happy Canyon as a means of salvaging the wildness of the West in the wake of the seemingly inevitable march of progress. The tourists (and locals) who flooded Pendleton demonstrate that, even in this Western state in the early twentieth century, the cowboys-and-Indians motif of the West was a powerful draw. In one trip, tourists could witness a multitude of Western-themed events within the rodeo arena and throughout Pendleton.

The addition of Happy Canyon offered the chance to fully experience life in the Wild West. The first few years of the Happy Canyon pavilion included banks, saloons, stores and shops, a hotel, a post office, gambling houses, and "other institutions such as flourished in the 'days of '49.'"[6] Additionally, each institution was "in actual operation" with play money currency called "ten-buck bills," where one buck equaled one penny, and they were the only accepted currency within the pavilion. Before allowing for general merriment, organizers planned for an hour-long program whose features would "be remindful of the early pioneer days."[7] By re-creating a Western town within an already decidedly Western town, Happy Canyon served as a kind of time machine for tourists. The cultivation of Happy Canyon as an immersive experience, coupled with the growing popularity of the Round-Up and the demonstrated appeal of Western-themed entertainment, developed from a flourishing focus on the disappearing Western ideal as propagated through history and period popular culture.

The West, as they say, is history.

"A Long and Colorful History": Oregon's Indians and the Round-Up

Major Lee Moorhouse, whose vast photograph collection includes thousands of images of life on the Umatilla Indian Reservation, took a few photos of a Cayuse man named Paul Showaway in the early 1900s. Showaway, the *East Oregonian* proclaimed in 1904, was "perhaps the most widely advertised American Indian alive, not even excepting Chief Joseph, of the Nez Perce."[8]

Moorhouse's photos of Showaway, who was clad in "one of the gaudiest Indian robes" produced by the Pendleton Woolen Mills, were part of the company's advertising campaign. Not "a single civilized country under the sun," the newspaper boasted, had escaped the onslaught of postcards sent from Pendleton's post office.[9]

Like many men of his era, Moorhouse wore many hats throughout his career. In 1878, he served as the governor's field secretary during the Bannock-Paiute War.[10] Elected mayor of Pendleton in 1885, he became the Indian agent on the Umatilla Indian Reservation in 1889.[11] The Treaty of 1855 had created the reservation through the cession of 6.4 million acres of land a mere fifty-five years before the first Round-Up, and the federal policy of allotment opened up 140,000 acres of the Umatilla Indian Reservation for settlement. The Pendleton Notch Act authorized the sale of tribal lands to the city, and part of the city was built on the reservation.[12] In 1891, Moorhouse oversaw the reservation's allotment and the subsequent auction of "surplus" lands to non-Native ranchers, farmers, and land speculators.[13] Twenty years before the first Round-Up, Indians still needed permission from Indian agents like Moorhouse in order to leave the reservation, and only after revealing "the destination, duration, and purpose" of the trip.[14]

The creation of the reservation had not fully alleviated the tensions between Natives and non-Natives. Indeed, many point to these hostilities—and the need to salvage the relationship between townsfolk and the CTUIR—as the reason why Round-Up organizers invited Indians to participate.[15] When Roy Bishop and his brothers, whose retail merchant father had married the daughter of a prominent Oregon textile mill owner, bought the then-defunct Pendleton Woolen Mills in 1909, they began manufacturing blankets based on the color and design preferences of both local and Southwest Indians.[16] As plans for the Round-Up began to fall into place the following summer, Bishop, thanks to his "personal acquaintance with the Indians" through the Woolen Mills, and Moorhouse rode out to the reservation to invite them.[17] Moorhouse and the Bishop brothers were not planning to use Native participants in the same way Buffalo Bill Cody and other Wild West show proprietors did. Natives who worked in Wild West shows, while still marketed as authentically Indian, usually participated in historical reenactments centered on stagecoach attacks and military skirmishes that painted them as the antithesis of modernity and Euro-American civilization. But the Round-Up organizers wanted to celebrate their history without highlighting the hostilities, especially after, according to author William Willingham, the CTUIR refused to participate in a staged battle if they were not allowed to shoot back.[18]

The Native participants who came to town for the first Round-Up—and every Round-Up since—created an "inspiring spectacle," and their "encampment, dramatic war dances, and daring horsemanship in the races added 'color and novelty'" to the Round-Up.[19] They set up camp and demonstrated horsemanship, dancing, beadwork, leatherwork, weaving, and basket making. They could celebrate their Native heritage without, as Willingham contends, "emphasizing hostilities between themselves and whites."[20] Mildred Allison, writing in 1951, proudly proclaimed, "The Round-Up would not be the Round-Up without Indians. They have gathered here since the 1910 show. It would still be a rodeo, but certainly one lacking in the color and pageantry that the Indians provide." She continued, noting, "They come each year to put up their teepees behind the arena, dance on the turf, participate in the Westward Ho! parade and show their style and grace to the thousands of visitors."[21]

It may seem odd that Pendleton's former-mayor-turned-Indian-agent (and photographer of American Indians) would encourage local Indians to openly act like Indians at the height of the assimilation era. But men like Moorhouse, whom Steven Grafe describes as "Pendleton mayor, Pendleton Round-Up booster, local merchant, and an agricultural and insurance broker," were deeply invested in regional development.[22] In an age when white Americans saw Indians when they traveled to world's fairs, when Wild West shows came to town, and when Indians participated in contests at local fairs, Native involvement in these events was almost always brokered through Indian agents on reservations—a position Moorhouse held in Pendleton for several years. Instead of leasing Indian performers to other fairs and events, the Round-Up directors used Indians from the Umatilla Reservation in economic pursuits intended to publicize the region and hopefully line their own pockets.

It is thus unsurprising that the men behind Pendleton's economy were the most invested in the Round-Up. The Bishop brothers, who had asked Pendleton residents to support the resurrection of the mill, had a lot riding on the success of the Round-Up. Another founder, J. Roy Raley, is immortalized on Happy Canyon's website as "a lawyer, legislator, cattleman, banker, surveyor, engineer, Indian fighter, sportsman, businessman, and creator of community celebrations." Moorhouse's son, a local real estate agent and insurance salesman, is also remembered as a Round-Up founder. Mark Moorhouse volunteered as the first exhibition manager, and he was the director of competitive events until his early death in 1914.[23] Despite local narratives that paint the Round-Up as a spur-of-the-moment manifestation of Pendleton's Western cachet, the Round-Up was deliberately established to put Pendleton on the map—and make their founders rich.

Rosalie Tashwick Kanine and three unidentified boys in front of a number of tipis. According to staff members at the Tamástslikt Cultural Institute of the Confederated Tribes of the Umatilla Indian Reservation, this photograph was likely taken at the Pendleton Round-Up. Courtesy of *The Oregonian*.

Citizenship, Commemoration, and Commerce in Oregon

"Oregon," William Cronon writes, "is central to some of the deepest and most fiercely held narratives of American frontier history."[24] The region's contested settlement, economic growth, struggles over land and citizenship, and the development of local and statewide civic celebrations highlight the environment that gave rise to the Round-Up and Happy Canyon. In Pendleton proper, treaty cessions and arguments over Asian immigrant workers arose alongside Fourth of July celebrations and debates about how to boost the slumping woolen industry. Thousands of Americans made their way west in the 1840s, but the Oregon dream was not open to all who hoped for a better life in the West.[25] As former Oregon representative Tom Marsh bluntly writes, "Oregonians did not want people of color here, free or slave."[26] However, Oregon still needed more white settlers if it was going to make the jump from territory to state. The 1850 Oregon Donation Land Law—wherein land was literally given away for free—sparked what Marsh calls "a human stampede" to Oregon.[27] As Patricia Nelson Limerick argues, this legislation invited settlers to "spread into territory that had not been cleared for occupation" and subsequently infringed on Native rights.[28]

The territory was home to more than 35,000 settlers by the end of 1853, nearly tripling its 1850 population of about 13,000.[29] The flood of eager settlers led to increased hostilities with Native nations. Led by Isaac Stevens, Washington's territorial governor, and Joel Palmer, the Oregon superintendent of Indian affairs, a series of treaties signed in the Walla Walla Valley in 1855 created three Indian reservations. One of those treaties, the Treaty of 1855, ceded 6.4 million acres of land and forced the Cayuse, Umatilla, and Walla Walla onto a reservation outside Pendleton.[30] In the wake of the treaty, the *Oregon Arbus*, a newspaper in Oregon City, published a notice of the treaty in more than half a dozen issues from July to October. The notice listed the boundaries of the cessions, warning readers that those hoping to locate claims on the land should pay attention to "the provisions protecting the Indians in the possession of their improvements."[31] The massive land cessions the government forced on Oregon's Native nations contributed to the almost astronomical growth in settlement that pushed Oregon to apply for statehood in 1857.[32] Oregon, with its exclusionary policies intact, became the thirty-third state in 1859. Its constitution refused suffrage—and citizenship—to both African Americans and those of Chinese heritage.[33]

Barely a decade after achieving statehood, contestations over race-based exclusion continued—this time around Chinese immigration. Industries like mining had brought Chinese immigrants to the state, prompting an 1866 act prohibiting intermarriage between whites and "any negro, Chinese, or any person having one-fourth or more negro, Chinese, or Kanaka blood, or any person having more than one-half Indian blood."[34] In November 1901, residents of Pendleton called for an extension of the Chinese Exclusion Act, and a circulated petition garnered more than 100 signatures in less than two hours. "In fact," the *East Oregonian* reported, "the petition is meeting the hearty approval of almost everyone approached on the subject and is being unanimously signed."[35] A few months later, in February 1902, the paper itself called for the act's extension, arguing that it was the only way to prevent racial strife. "We do not want a renewal of agitation against the Chinese," the editorial noted, "and the only way to prevent it is to keep the Chinese out."[36] Pendleton's rejection of Asian immigrant workers extended to Japanese workers as well. In June 1905, the *East Oregonian* warned its readers about "a menace to the standard of labor as now established!" The war department had decided on an "experimental" importation of 3,000 Chinese and 3,000 Japanese laborers

Capitalism wins

to the Panama strip. But what, the paper howled, "is to prevent this cheap labor drifting into the United States?"[37] The Gentlemen's Agreement between the United States and Japan was not signed until 1907, but anti-Japanese sentiment in Oregon and elsewhere continued to build.

Battles for land also meant squabbles over resources. Early settlement reached as far west as possible, and few cared—or dared—to stop in eastern or central Oregon, preferring to keep going until they got to the Willamette Valley. The valley was, as William Robbins demonstrates, far more attractive to settler-farmers than the arid interior.[38] Cities like Portland quickly became leading centers for trade and industry, attracting mercantile establishments, sawmills, and manufacturers as early as the 1850s.[39] The territory-turned-state continued to diversify what Tom Marsh calls its "manufacturing-industrial base" as the flour milling, lumbering, salmon canning and packing, and wool spinning and weaving industries grew alongside the continuing agricultural and pastoral industries.[40] Its relative isolation spurred the expansion of its transportation system, although it would take several decades before the coast and the eastern part of the state were fully connected to the Willamette Valley.[41]

Many of the early settlers, of course, quickly gobbled up the most attractive lands west of the Cascades. Those who followed later had to settle for lands that seemed less desirable. While many settlers hoped to find enough land to farm, some of the emigrants who made their way to central and eastern Oregon in the 1860s focused their energy on raising cattle and, later, sheep.[42] Umatilla County's first sheep arrived in 1865, and Pendleton businessmen financed a wool-scouring mill in 1893.[43] While pastoralism started to give way to wheat cultivation in the 1880s, pastoralism and agriculture arose as parallel industries in Pendleton and the broader Umatilla County, due in large part to the simultaneous development of the railroad that increased farmers' abilities to transport their products.[44] The railroad reached what is now known as Umatilla, which sits on the Columbia River, in 1881, and it reached Pendleton shortly thereafter.[45] Sherman and Umatilla Counties would lead the state in wheat production by the time of the 1890 federal census with nearly a third of the state's fifteen-million-bushel yield, and Pendleton's wool-scouring mill added looms and textile machinery in 1895 in order to facilitate the manufacturing of shawls and Indian blankets.[46]

While Pendleton got its start later than Portland did, it soon rose to its own prominence. Writing in 1894, Edward Gardner Jones claimed, "Few towns in the state enjoy equal opportunities in shipping facilities which the Pendleton merchants are able to avail themselves of," noting that the town sat on the

Union Pacific line about 230 miles east of Portland and 44 miles south of Umatilla.[47] It was the county's shipping hub, sending out two-thirds of the 1,750,000 pounds of wool harvested in 1892. The county's top industry, according to Jones, was wheat, followed by wool.[48] The county was one of the "greatest grain-producing sections of the state," he crowed, averaging exports between 2 and 3.5 million bushels of wheat since 1885.[49] Jones also noted that the expansion of the wheat industry had restricted cattle-grazing grounds, leading to the decline of the stock-raising interests of the county. By 1904, the *East Oregonian* bemoaned the fact that "it has been but a short time since thousands of cattle roamed over the western hills." But now, the paper wrote, farms were taking the place of big ranges, leaving no place for the herds to run.[50] Others, like Charles Cunningham, who had founded the Cunningham sheep company in 1878, feared the sheep industry would succumb to the same fate as the cattle industry.[51] In 1907, he warned the *East Oregonian* that Oregon's sheep industry, which he claimed brought in $10,000,000 per year, was "in serious danger of being wiped out within the next five years."[52]

As men like Jones and Cunningham bragged and brooded over the fate of Pendleton's economy, cities closer to the coast turned toward tourism and commemoration to help publicize the region, broaden their appeal, and diversify their economies. Towns farther inland, like Pendleton, soon followed suit. From touring productions and world's fairs to festivals and pageants, Oregonians used public commemoration to mold and manipulate their memories and, in the economic spirit of the times, to line city coffers and, perhaps, their own pockets. These narratives of a shared identity and collective belonging have shaped Oregon's history and the subsequent collective, commemorative, and civic celebrations. The Round-Up and Happy Canyon emerged in an era of boosterism, tourism, and economic ingenuity. Round-Up founders sent envoys to other events, like the Portland Rose Festival, and likely hosted delegates from the same organizations. Oregon's Indians, though, were rarely part of these civic celebrations. If they *were* included, it was usually as oppositional figures to American progress and expansion.[53]

Oregon's racially charged history of Asian and African American exclusion and wars with Native nations was not exactly fodder for public celebrations. Instead, the Fourth of July, the Lewis and Clark expedition, the Oregon Trail, and generalized Western narratives took center stage, like when Buffalo Bill Cody brought his show to Pendleton in 1902. Billed as his "first, last and only visit" due to a tour of Europe, an advertisement in the *East Oregonian* promised "The Great Wild West and Wild East Now United Hand-In-Hand."[54] An accompanying article praised Cody's career, noting, "In the years to come, when Cody has passed away, hundreds of imitators will arise to scramble and strive for a semblance of his marvelous force, but he cannot be approached for history has marked him as one of her children."[55]

Locals were less impressed. According to Randy Thomas, the 2014 Round-Up publicity director, "The people in Pendleton, who were both Indians and authentic cowboys, they kind of yawned and said, 'We can do that, but with real cowboys and real Indians.'"[56] In 1902, another writer for the *East Oregonian* boasted that it took "little observation" to see that Pendleton was "every bit as 'wild westy' as the show."[57] Pendleton was not the only stop on Buffalo Bill's tour, and it was not the only Oregon town to plan civic and commemorative events in the late nineteenth and early twentieth centuries. The Fourth of July, as Renee M. Laegreid demonstrates, was cause for a Pendleton celebration as early as the 1870s. Once the railroad reached Pendleton, the Fourth of July celebrations started moving from local affairs to booster events, bringing in special excursion trains that carried visitors into Pendleton.[58]

Small towns and big cities across the state staged civic and commemorative celebrations throughout the era, especially for the centennial of the Meriwether Lewis and William Clark Expedition. President Theodore Roosevelt traveled to Portland in 1903 as the cornerstone of a monument to Lewis and Clark was laid in City Park.[59] Two years later, the Lewis and Clark Centennial Exposition opened in Portland. As Lisa Blee has shown, the Lewis and Clark Exposition aimed to help the United States define itself in the global marketplace.[60] Portland's economy, which was still in a slump following the late 1890s economic woes, could certainly benefit from its own world's fair.[61] Carl Abbott contends that more than 1.5 million people visited the exposition, making it one of the most economically successful American world's fairs of the era, and Blee notes that the exposition pulled nearly $8 million into the local economy.[62]

While the 1903 and 1905 events were designed as one-time-only celebrations, others hoped to bring tourists back year after year. The Portland Rose Festival premiered in 1907, two years after the Lewis and Clark Exposition and four years after Teddy Roosevelt laid the cornerstone in City Park. Most sources credit Portland mayor Harry Lane, who gave a speech at the exposition's closing ceremony calling for a "permanent rose carnival," as the impetus behind the Rose Festival.[63] Lane dreamed of making Portland "the summer capital of the world," and his desire for an annual event, as opposed to the one-time exposition, highlights the cultural and commercial appeal of commemorative celebrations.[64]

While many of the early twentieth-century celebrations centered on Lewis and Clark, a man named Ezra Meeker worked to ensure that the nation would remember the Oregon Trail. Meeker and his wife had traveled on the Oregon Trail in 1851, but by the early 1900s Meeker feared that America was forgetting about its history.[65] He had taken an ox team and wagon to Portland in 1905 to participate in the Lewis and Clark Exposition, and in 1906 he made the first of what would be several trips back along the Oregon Trail in hopes of encouraging the development of a collection of commemorative markers.[66] Meeker took his ox team east, not west, and stopped in a number of towns along the way. He reached Pendleton in late March, and the *East Oregonian* noted that the old pioneer was deeply invested in his patriotic work. The paper excitedly announced that Meeker would give a lecture and a stereopticon entertainment the following night.[67] It would not be Meeker's last trip, but his subsequent trips would highlight the changing nature of American tourism and commemoration.

Back in Pendleton, the commemorative and celebratory aura was a little dim. The woolen mill, a key element of the local and regional economy, faced bankruptcy by 1905. A man named J. Sheuerman and his son, Arnold, leased the mill for one year in 1906 but did not renew their lease.[68] In the fall of 1908, a pessimistic Pendleton Commercial Association met to decide the mill's fate. Despite its rundown condition and questions about the mill's profitability, the association decided to try to save the mill.[69] Revitalizing the mill was about more than sheep and blankets, and it was about more than just the city of Pendleton. In early December of 1908, the *East Oregonian* recognized the high stakes involved in the attempt to restore the mill. A working mill, the paper argued, meant well-paid workers who would have their homes in Pendleton. Well-paid workers meant more business for merchants and more tenants for property owners, which meant an increased population for the town. "If Pendleton wishes to be something more than a good country town," the paper wheedled, "it must be built up from within as well as from without." Pendleton was on the cusp of a period of development, the paper declared, and reestablishing the mill was the first step toward the town and the county's industrial and commercial advancement. But there was a lot at stake: if the attempts to revive the mill failed, fewer investors would be interested in future developments. "If a woolen mill cannot be operated here, what type of industry can?" the paper argued. "This is a wool town."[70]

As the decade continued, so did the struggle to save the woolen mill.[71] If this was a good ol' Western film, this is when the camera would pan to the left and we'd see the Bishop brothers for the first time. The Bishop brothers—Clarence, Roy, and Chauncey—were the grandsons of Thomas Kay, who had established the Thomas Kay Woolen Mill in Salem in 1889. Kay's daughter, Fannie, had been her father's apprentice, learning mill management and operations. Fannie's marriage to C. P. Bishop, a retail merchant who had invited her to a Fourth of July celebration in 1874, meant that their three sons grew up in the industry.[72] But Fannie's brother was chosen to be the president and general manager of the mill after Kay's death, even though Fannie had been the sibling helping Kay run the mill. The Bishop branch of the family resigned their positions and focused on running stores in Salem and Portland. When Pendleton's Commercial Association started looking for someone to bring the defunct woolen mill back to life, Fannie Kay Bishop pushed her sons to buy the mill. She saw the potential in the old building, its proximity to the river, and the nearby supply from local sheep ranchers.[73]

By late 1908, the Commercial Association reckoned it needed $30,000 to make the mill fully operational. Despite the mind-boggling sum, Roy Bishop seemed confident in the people of Pendleton. "I am told by the local business men," Bishop said, "that they will raise the money needed without much difficulty."[74] Bishop's assurance came through—as did the necessary funds—by February of 1909.[75] Once the Pendleton Woolen Mill was fully operational once again, the Bishops knew that they needed to draw customers from outside Pendleton and Umatilla County. They sent Major Lee Moorhouse to the Portland Rose Festival in 1910 as the head of the mill's exhibit, and Moorhouse traveled to the Astorian Centennial in 1911.[76] The collective efforts to resurrect the mill, coupled with Pendleton's shifting agricultural focus and the Bishops' exhibits at other regional celebrations, help explain the rise of the Round-Up. By 1912, locals celebrated the Round-Up—and the mill—as community affairs.[77] Roy Bishop was the first director of Indians for the Round-Up, a position he would hold for a number of years, and his brother Chauncey also served as one of the directors for the first Round-Up.[78] The convergence of the local economy, increasing tourism and commemoration enterprises, the Bishop brothers, Moorhouse's role on the reservation, and of the Indians themselves laid the groundwork for more than a century's worth of celebrations in Pendleton.

Selling the West: Building the Round-Up from the Ground Up

The development of the Pendleton Round-Up and the Happy Canyon Indian Pageant and Wild West Show underscore the widespread desire to simultaneously celebrate and commodify the popular narratives of the West. As legend has it, plans for the Round-Up went into motion shortly before it opened: "For two months the amateur crew of rodeo producers knocked on doors, wrote letters and traveled the early West of the twentieth century. They borrowed money, begged stock and moon-lighted equipment from every rancher on the open range."[79] Some supervised the construction of the rodeo grounds and grandstands, while others organized a parade and arranged for reduced train fares on railroads throughout the Northwest.[80]

The success of the first Round-Up in 1910 was practically instantaneous, much to the delight of the city's businesses and residents alike. More than 7,000 spectators showed up on the opening day, forcing organizers to turn many away and then, overnight, build enough bleachers to hold a few thousand more.[81] The event was billed as "A Frontier Exhibition of Picturesque Pastimes, Indian and Military Spectacles and Cowboy Racing and Bronco Busting for the Championship of the Northwest," and the *East Oregonian* attributed much of its success to its participants:

> The Round-Up has been called a pastoral drama but the implication of
> that name is deceptive. . . . The men before the gaze of the audience in the
> daily exhibits are not actors, they are real characters, and there is nothing
> theatrical, "stagy" or melodramatic in their performances. . . . The actor's
> is the realm of fiction, the Round-Up performer's the province of truth,
> and the cowboy's audience never experiences the disappointment of
> dropping from an imaginary to the actual world at the falling of a curtain, is
> never forced to sigh and say, when it is all over, "After all, it was not real."[82]

The day after opening night, the *East Oregonian* smugly noted, "Most people with red blood in them like horses and they like races and rough riding. This is a fact that has been demonstrated often. It has been well demonstrated by the general interest that has been aroused over the holding of the Round-up."[83] There were cowboys and Indians everywhere, according to the newspaper. Every available place to sit or stand was filled, and hundreds of people were still waiting outside for their chance to enter. The fables of the frontier were enticing and alluring—even in the West itself. The fact that Pendleton, a town of less than 5,000 people, could draw that many attendees for a single day of the Round-Up reveals the appeal of salvage tourism in the West. Despite the changing social and economic structures, Pendleton successfully presented itself as the embodiment of the Western ideal.

The Round-Up's early years drew talented horsemen and women whose skills created the environment that, as the *East Oregonian* gloated, authenticated and legitimated the Round-Up events, the Round-Up, and Pendleton itself. As Furlong later noted, "Many an actor who carried the principal parts against the background of this greatest of national melodramas still stalks in the flesh. There are yet to be found," he bragged, "tucked away in stray corners, the cattle rancher, cowboy, sheriff, horse-thief, ranger, road agent, trapper and trader, the old stage driver, freighter, gambler, canoeman, the missionary, pioneer woman, old-time scout, the placer-miner, the Indian—all pioneer types, primeval actors in this dramatic Odyssey of American adventure and development, the building of the West."[84] The *East Oregonian* quickly recognized the appeal of the Round-Up's old-West aura, noting in 1911 that "the spectacular old West of our forefather's days is rapidly being settled and converted into thriving farms and peaceful cities." Therefore, the people of Pendleton "built one of the finest stadiums in the Northwest, with the idea of holding a grand three-days entertainment each year, at which time cowboys and cowgirls from the ranges and Indians from the reservation of the Northwest will participate in a hairraising Round-Up."[85] By 1913, the *East Oregonian* confidently asserted that the Round-Up had, in its short life, "improved year by year until now it is unquestionably the peer of all outdoor entertainments in the world."[86]

After three years of successful rodeo events, Round-Up organizers decided to offer evening entertainment for the ever-growing number of people who came to Pendleton for the Round-Up. They had been thoroughly unimpressed with that year's Umatilla-Morrow District Fair, which started in 1912 in nearby Hermiston, about twenty miles northwest of Pendleton. They also scoffed at the fact that admission had gone from twenty-five to fifty cents without what they considered an equal increase in entertainment value.[87] The 1912 District Fair, also known as the Hermiston Hog and Dairy Show, was the last of several collaborations between the counties, as legislation passed in 1913 no longer permitted a bi-county fair.[88] Once again convinced they could do better than the local fairs, Round-Up organizers debuted the first night show in 1913, calling it "The Pageant of the West—an Outdoor Dramatic Production, Symbolizing the History and Development of the Great West."[89]

The committee had bigger and better ideas the next year. The Pendleton Commercial Association, according to the *East Oregonian*, had taken on the job of entertaining visitors in the evening, promoting excursions to other fairs to boost Pendleton's visibility, and encouraging local businesses to close early during Round-Up so everyone could participate.[90] On September 2, 1914, the paper announced the newest addition to the Round-Up. "'Happy Canyon' will be the name of the frontier town in the fair pavilion where the Round-up crowds will find entertainment during the evenings of the big carnival week," the paper proclaimed. "It has been thus christened and the name, while suggesting the days of a romantic past, is also indicative of the gayety which will prevail there."[91] The Round-Up crowds, which grew larger every year, had created a demand for entertainment after each day's rodeo events. The enormity of the crowds pushed Pendleton's streets and establishments to their limits, and the potential inability to contain the rowdy throngs dogged the Round-Up leaders. More than 15,000 spectators had packed into the arena to see the first day's events in 1914, making it the largest opening night in the Round-Up's still-young history.[92]

A few days later, Charles Wellington Furlong stepped off the No. 17 train in Pendleton, "full of enthusiasm for the cowboy carnival" and ready to "again tell the world of it in the magazines for which he writes."[93] Furlong, a world traveler, explorer, and author, had traveled west from Boston in order to see the fifth annual Pendleton Round-Up, which was turning Pendleton into a place renowned for its "superiority in cowboy pastimes."[94] Furlong was entranced by Pendleton's rodeo and Pendleton's people, whom he considered to be the "pioneer winners of the West, the protectors and sponsors for a more effete and thinner-blooded civilization which followed in their wake."[95] Furlong had "become so enthusiastic that he even tried to ride one of the bucking bulls" on one of his earlier trips to the Round-Up, much to the delight of his hosts.[96] Unlike the East Coasters who breathlessly read his thrilling tales from the comfort of their homes, Furlong traveled to Pendleton to be part of the Round-Up experience. He wanted to try his hand at a bucking bull, to "feel the touch and sense the romance of the Old West" as cowboys and Indians and townsfolk alike converged on Pendleton to participate in this epic re-creation of a mythic past.[97]

Roy Raley, Lee Moorhouse, the Bishop brothers, and their counterparts had recognized the potential economic boon to be found in reliving the Old West—even if the Old West no longer existed, even in Pendleton. Local newspapers furiously promoted the Round-Up's new evening entertainment. "Not only will they be entertained each afternoon with the thrilling pastimes of the cowboy and Indian," the *East Oregonian* announced, "but in the evening too they will have an opportunity to revel in the picturesque and romantic life of frontier days."[98] The Happy Canyon committee purposely refused to publicize many specifics regarding the pavilion and the show, but they were positive that "the visitor at the Round-up this year will not go away feeling that nothing had been provided to amuse him in the evening."[99] A few days before the Round-Up opened, rodeo headlines in the *East Oregonian* were only overshadowed by headlines on recent World War I battles overseas. The paper announced that advance ticket sales for the rodeo were the biggest in its history, noting that every train brought more visitors to an already congested Pendleton. Special delegations came from Washington cities, and the paper warned locals and visitors to be on the lookout for potential robbers and pickpockets.[100]

A flurry of activity preceded the 1914 Round-Up and Happy Canyon. As the Commercial Association had hoped, businesses closed at 1 P.M. so Pendletonians could head down for the festivities.[101] The *East Oregonian* was positively giddy with excitement, predicting that the crowds would be just as large as they had been the year before, as the director of accommodations was already scrambling to find rooms to rent out to visitors.[102] The society pages gleefully noted that local residents were so excited about the prospective fun to be had at Happy Canyon that "a number of social affairs planned for guests during Round-up evenings have been cancelled and parties are being formed to attend the festivities downtown."[103] The committee, as coy as ever, promised that the show would contain "some peculiarly frontier stunts that promise to create a few ripples of merriment" as well as "a few dramatic scenes significant of frontier life" that would live up to its name.[104]

When the doors to Happy Canyon swung open for the first time, visitors were privy to "a glimpse of towns as they used to be in this section in an early day."[105] There was room for 3,000 spectators in the bleachers with standing room for another 1,000.[106] The committee had named the staged town after an earlier settlement on the Umatilla River about twenty miles west of Pendleton. After a particularly lively meeting of the settlers' dancing club in the winter of 1868, as the story goes, one of the men had moved to christen their community "Happy Canyon." By attaching the name to the Round-Up's "pseudo-frontier town," organizers capitalized on the historical legitimacy of a town built "when civilization was young here."[107] Similarly, the continued success of the Round-Up, as well as the prospective economic boost from Happy Canyon, depended largely on whether or not the organizers could create a satisfyingly authentic Western experience through the rodeo and subsequent evening entertainment.

Around 15,000 people came to town for the Round-Up on September 23, 1914, and 3,000 spectators "crammed and jammed their way" into the Happy Canyon pavilion that night.[108] The *East Oregonian* called it "some great town," noting the audience's unanimous approval. The show not only entertained the Round-Up crowds but was "in harmony with the big wild West show and . . . will add to the fame of Pendleton as the 'Let 'er Buck' town."[109] Carpenters quickly built more seating and enlarged the entrance to alleviate the congestion that hampered the previous night's production. Nobody, including the committee that produced the show, had expected such a tremendous response from the colossal crowd. By its fifth year, the Round-Up's visitors temporarily tripled the population of Pendleton.

The Happy Canyon show included a performance by the town band, a heroic rescue from a fire at the "Stagger Inn," a cowgirl-costumed young lady who sang on horseback, "bad men" shooting up the "town," a stagecoach drive, a mounted quadrille, and "a dozen other events [that] were pulled off with rapidity and dash." The bullfight, done only "as the American cowboy does it," was the biggest hit. The meanest, maddest longhorn in the Round-Up herd was turned loose, followed by cowboys who teased the steer into a fury. Ten cowboys, including Furlong in disguise, recklessly ducked and dodged the steer as the audience thrilled at the sight, cheering for the cowboys with wild applause once the mighty beast had been contained. This was the real live manifestation of the winning of the West, the taming of the unforgiving, uncultivated frontier at the brawny hands of none other but the white American men whose power and rise to the top were only enhanced by the strength of their opponents. Audiences duly praised Happy Canyon's authenticity.[110] Its legitimacy, of course, was based in the careful representations depicted in Pendleton. The romanticized (and tongue-in-cheek) storefronts, saloons, gambling halls, and dance pavilion, coupled with the tricks, thrills, and spills of the spectacle, showcased a West that resonated with its audiences.

After the show, the audience was turned loose in the "town" to enjoy soft drinks in the four saloons. Happy Canyon was built to control potentially rowdy crowds, so nonalcoholic beverages helped contain the boisterous visitors. Besides the saloons, those lucky enough to get a ticket could visit stores, the bank, the gambling hall, and other institutions, all ready to accept the town's ten-buck bills.[111] The saloons and gambling parlors were particularly popular, and the dancing hall was so crowded that dancing was nearly impossible. Old fiddlers played at the Red Dog Saloon as they had decades earlier, the "Western spirit" charging "the very air with its contagion." The *Daily East Oregonian* called Happy Canyon a pronounced success, one that made for a "merry-mad throng" who all went home, of course, quite happy.[112] The harried carpenters could not keep pace with the thousands of people clamoring to experience Happy Canyon. Thursday's crowds were even larger, and every single seat and space filled up long before the show started. Hundreds more had to wait outside for the program to conclude so they could try claiming a spot in the make-believe town. Happy Canyon was so full of people, they said, "They could hardly be stirred with a stick."[113] The third performance elicited similar responses, as a "crowded mass of humanity" filled the seats and the streets. It was received with "wild delight by the spectators, every number being applauded vociferously." The fictitious businesses of Happy Canyon closed well after midnight, and, apparently, "in this it was typical of the old West, too."[114]

The unprecedented and unexpected success of Happy Canyon demonstrates that the Wild West was alive and well in Pendleton. This commodification of the magical, mystical, mythical West sated the desires of Pendletonians and other residents of the West who sought to assure themselves of their continued presence and relevance in the region. They had successfully salvaged their identity as "the quiet, modest, manhood and womanhood who have 'taken chances,' have risked limb and even life at times," having "struggled in earnest against unequal odds in order to attain the winning of the West."[115] The key lay in the realism of the participants. The *Daily East Oregonian* called it "one of the most realistic depictions of a frontier town" that caused its audience to "forget you are sitting on the soft side of a board."[116] These were not actors who had to be carefully coached in the mannerisms of the cowboy, who had to learn to walk and talk and dress convincingly. No, these were the men who never thought twice about wrestling an angry longhorn, men who could bring the West to life with their fiddles in 1914 the way men had done forty years earlier. They were the people of Pendleton, the legitimate people of the West.

The 1914 Happy Canyon was a rousing success. It took in nearly $6,000 before expenses (which totaled nearly $5,000, including a hefty construction bill, leaving a net balance of $875), and it filled a desperate need to entertain the crowds after the days' rodeo events.[117] Pendleton basked in its success, even after the "cowboys, cowgirls and Indians who provided the entertainment" went back to the "range, cowcamp or reservation or to some other city."[118] The town had proved itself worthy of its Western heritage, and the committee kept the admission price at twenty-five cents "even though a five dollar show is prepared."[119] A retired range rider who had "camped on the ground where Pendleton now stands before there was a shack built" wrote to the *East Oregonian* to praise the Round-Up for providing such an entertaining spectacle that he planned to return the next year.[120]

The momentum that drove Happy Canyon to its initial success continued the following year. The Commercial Association planned to make the 1915 production bigger and better than the inaugural show, and the *East Oregonian* reminded its readers that Happy Canyon was to the Round-Up "what the dessert is to a well prepared dinner."[121] The committee again declined to reveal many details, although it did promise "bucking horses, bulls and burros ... cowboys and cowgirls to do all kinds of stunts ... painted Indians ... comedy stuff ... singing and—most exciting of all—a fighting steer that will make the animal used last year seem lame."[122] Once again, the crowds flocked to Happy Canyon. More than 3,000 crammed into the pavilion, and the entertainment portion certainly delivered.[123] The entertainment quality and performative elements in Happy Canyon seemed to increase exponentially in the first few years. Part vaudevillian sketch comedy and part history, Happy Canyon created a production that was at once organic and scripted, raw and polished, real and imagined. Tourists and locals alike packed the pavilion for the show and the subsequent entertainment, clamoring for a glimpse of the terrifying longhorns or for a chance to win big at the gambling hall. Happy Canyon deliberately commodified its history and its people, successfully capitalizing on the characteristics that had fashioned Pendleton back in the days of the Old West and were reborn again every September.

Despite the thunderous applause that greeted Native participants in the parade or after their dances in the arena during Round-Up Week, they were not billed as participants in Happy Canyon's frontier skits in 1914 and 1915. In 1916, Raley added a "sequence of Indian life before the coming of the white man" to the Happy Canyon show. Raley, who had "all of the family background necessary to write an accurate and entertaining account of the history of development of this region," collaborated with local tribal members, including Anna Minthorn Wannassay, on the Indian portion of the pageant. Wannassay was Cayuse, and she had "participated in dramatic arts" during her time at Carlisle Indian Industrial School before she graduated in 1906.[124]

As Roberta Conner, a well-known representative from the CTUIR who has served as executive director of the reservation's Tamástslikt Cultural Institute, has written, "For many in the audience, this pageant and the Indian roles in the Round-Up were undoubtedly their only education about these tribes."[125] In 1917, Happy Canyon promoters noted,

> In a clearing among the trees just above the rocky wall will be an Indian village with real Indians lying about or doing the tasks customary to tribal villagers. The peaceful life will give way to excitement upon the arrival of a scout with news of the passing of an emigrant train. In a moment the braves will don their war paint and feathers and do the war dance. They will then ride away only to return with a white girl captive whom they will tie to a stake. Just as they prepare to burn her, a cowboy will affect

a daring rescue and dash with her up the mountain trail pursued by Indians. To escape they will plunge over the waterfall into the rapids below at the moment a band of cowboys below open fire on their pursuers.[126]

Even as souvenir programs continually insisted that "relations between tribes and with emigrants were generally extremely peaceful," although there were occasional "misunderstandings" due to "conflicts of culture," performances of Happy Canyon included implicit and explicit depictions of violence.[127] The pageant depicts "the settling of the American West, beginning with a portrayal of the Native American way of life prior to the arrival of Europeans, continuing with the arrival of Lewis and Clark, followed by the prairie schooners of the pioneers of the Oregon Trail and concluding with a reenactment of a frontier town's rollicking main street mishaps."[128]

The Legacy of Commerce: The Round-Up and Beyond

In 1911, the year after the first Pendleton Round-Up, the *Sunday Oregonian* promoted the upcoming Astorian Centennial, a monthlong celebration commemorating John Jacob Astor's 1811 founding of Fort Astoria. There were plans for fireworks, displays of naval vessels in the river, swimming races, a military parade, and a speech by the governor. The committee planned "30 days of pageantry" to celebrate "the first settlement of the Pacific Northwest."[129] Another attraction was the premiere of Miss Mabel Ferris's dramatization of "The Bridge of the Gods," which the paper billed as "Oregon's Indian Legend." The paper emphasized the pageant's "strong love story" that had been woven into the plot, and it promised audiences "stirring Indian dances and ceremonies in which real redskins will participate to give it the action."[130]

The rise of civic celebrations in Oregon was emblematic of early twentieth-century endeavors across the country, which were partially due to the proliferation of the automobile and the "See America First" campaign. The Festivals Association of the Pacific Coast, created in 1912, hoped to expand and encourage regional tourism. More than a dozen cities along the coast, from Victoria, British Columbia, to San Diego, California, joined the organization. As part of the "See America First" campaign, the association used railroad booklets, travel bureaus, magazines, and other forms of media to draw attention to events up and down the coast. Marguerite Shaffer has demonstrated how tourism became "a form of geographical consumption that centered on the sights and scenes of the American nation" around the turn of the century, and the Festivals Association was among the operators behind the scenes.[131]

Like other cities, towns, and areas across the country, the Festivals Association hoped to keep American tourists in America at a time when Europe was still seen as home to the most alluring vacation spots. The association, according to the *Sunday Oregonian*, hoped to lay before the pleasure-seeker "a wonderfully picturesque series of celebrations and entertainment features, as a stimulus to the scenic and climatic wonders as yet practically unknown to the great army of American tourists that annually turns a solid and unbroken front toward foreign lands."[132] It publicized events like the Panama-Pacific Exposition of 1915 and the "Tournament of Roses" parade in Pasadena, California, hoping that these host cities could stake a claim to the purported $500,000,000 that American tourists annually spent abroad. An article in the May 18, 1913 issue of the *Sunday Oregonian* included advertisements for the Portland Rose Festival and the Pendleton Round-Up, announcing, "Nowhere in the world is there to be found a more striking, more interesting or more impressive celebration" than in Pendleton.

Soon it seemed that almost any event required performances and parades. The 1915 opening of the Dalles-Celilo Canal in Lewiston, for instance, included a parade wherein "the various historical events of this interior country were presented in allegorical form on floats." More than 200 Nez Perce participated, followed by representations of Lewis and Clark, Sacagawea, and President Jefferson. The celebratory exercises also included a history of transportation in the region, from early freight boats and steamboats to pack trains.[133] This celebration of transportation technology even permeated Ezra Meeker's missions. While he had used ox-teams on his first few trips, he made his 1916 trek in an automobile—a "12-cylinder Pathfinder" outfitted with "the best tires manufactured by the Goodrich Company," to be exact. Meeker scoffed at the new mode of transportation, claiming that it was no more comfortable than the wagon. Additionally, according to the *Sunday Oregonian*, Meeker argued that the use of a car actually hindered his goal. "The ox train, he says, touches the sentiment of the people and is more apt to induce them to prevail upon their representatives in Congress," the paper noted, "to make a permanent military highway of the famous Oregon trail."[134]

In Pendleton, the Round-Up and Happy Canyon drew in bigger and bigger crowds, leading other towns throughout the state to follow suit in hopes of producing similar results. Happy Canyon would soon be one of several pageants staged in Oregon in the 1910s and 1920s. Salem's Willamette University staged a pageant in 1919 to simultaneously celebrate the school's seventy-fifth anniversary and raise money for the university. More than 3,000 people gathered to watch professor Della Crowder Miller's three-hour-long pageant, which included twenty-two episodes (not including the prologue and epilogue). In addition to the pageant, nearly 100 students from the nearby Chemawa Indian School, dressed in full regalia, participated in an Indian fair. Major Lee Moorhouse, who played a role in brokering the Round-Up's deal with the Confederated Tribes of the Umatilla Indian Reservation, supplied costumes and his makeup expertise.[135] The university's newspaper swooned over the production, claiming, "Nothing ever given in Oregon equaled the stupendous historical pageant presented on the campus of Willamette during commencement week."[136]

Two years later, in 1921, residents of The Dalles, a town almost halfway between Portland and Pendleton, created their own pageant inspired by the success of the Round-Up and Happy Canyon. Organizers hoped their pageant would, like the events in Pendleton and Portland, attract visitors from all over the Northwest. "The historical material which centers around this city is so abundant," the *Dalles Daily Chronicle* claimed, "it would be difficult to exhaust the supply."[137] In an April 1921 article, the newspaper echoed Meeker's fears from several decades earlier. "The Old Days may have been rough days, yet they were fraught with decency, fairness and good-dealing," the paper announced. "It was a time when men were strong and women nervy. . . . But the old west when the Dalles was the end of the Oregon trail is gone. Its romance and its legend is being forgotten. Its wholesomeness is being overlooked." Like the Round-Up and the Rose Festival, pageant boosters hoped their production would become "a permanent annual institution."[138] *The Playground*, a publication for the Playground and Recreation Association of America, included a blurb on the Dalles pageant in its April 1921 issue. Thanks to the participation of Indians from the Warm Springs Reservation, who brought "their best equipment and their finest ponies," the pageant "was colorful as a spectacle and convincing as history."[139]

Like all tourism endeavors, some in Oregon were more successful and longer lasting than others. Ezra Meeker would die in 1928 at the age of ninety-seven. In 1924, having retraced the Oregon Trail by ox team and automobile, he took his final trip from Seattle to the nation's capital in an airplane. He had the distinction, crowed the *Athena Press*, of being the only person to have traveled the trail by ox team and by air.[140] Howard R. Diggs, who assumed the presidency of the Old Oregon Trail Association after Meeker's death, proclaimed that the organization's work was meant to save "one of the most thrilling of the epics in the great story of the making of America. The cause is all-American in its scope and spirit. It touches closely every part of our country North, South, East, and West."[141]

A man dressed as a cowboy and Native people from the Umatilla reservation ride in a pageant in Meacham, Oregon, on July 3, 1923. The pageant was part of events commemorating the anniversary of the first wagon train crossing of the Blue Mountains. President Warren G. Harding and First Lady Florence Harding were among those in attendance. Courtesy of *The Oregonian*.

This chapter has highlighted numerous factors that led to the creation of the Pendleton Round-Up in 1910 and the addition of the Happy Canyon Indian Pageant and Wild West Show a few years later. While countless pageants and Wild West shows met their demise before the middle of the century, the Round-Up and Happy Canyon are still going strong. The following chapter moves to the present to examine Pendleton in the twenty-first century, demonstrating how Pendleton is still able to capitalize on tourist expectations of the Wild West. At the same time, the relationship between the Round-Up, Happy Canyon, and the Confederated Tribes of the Umatilla Indian Reservation has shifted over the years as the CTUIR continues to diversify its own economy, due in large part to the Wildhorse Resort & Casino. The Round-Up and Happy Canyon play a different role than they used to, and changing forms of salvage tourism and heritage tourism offer contesting images of the impact on the citizens of the CTUIR.

CHAPTER TWO

It's a Part of Us
The Continued Allure of Pendleton

Even now, however, one could feel the touch and sense the romance of the Old West, for along every trail and road which converged to Pendleton . . . came the Indians from their reservations . . . over half a thousand strong, these red men of mountain and plain soon had their lodge-poles pointing skyward, and, like mushrooms in the night, a white tepee village had sprung up in the picturesque cottonwoods near the Pendleton ford of the old Oregon Trail.
—Charles Wellington Furlong, 1916

There is no better way to understand the history and culture of the Western United States than by traveling to Pendleton the second week of September.
—Former U.S. Senator Gordon Smith, 2009

Unlike Charles Wellington Furlong, I did not step off the No. 17 train in Pendleton. Nearly a century after Furlong traveled west to Pendleton, I fly from Minneapolis to Seattle, hop in a rental car, and drive about five hours southeast to Pendleton. The pine and hemlock trees stubbornly clinging to impossibly steep mountainsides give way to gently sloping, treeless hills as fences and wide-open plains stretched for miles in all directions. Eastern Oregon looks nothing like the coast. There are none of what Emily Brock calls "lush temperate rain forests" out here.[1] Pendleton sits in northeastern Oregon, about an hour southwest of Walla Walla, Washington. Hotel rooms run more than $300 a night in Pendleton during Round-Up Week and sell out quickly, so I stay in Walla Walla when I head west for Round-Up.[2]

I have to admit that I have yet to go to Pendleton for something other than Round-Up, so I have to trust the newspapers that have long described how Pendleton comes alive during Round-Up Week. During the second week of September, the usually quiet streets are jammed with cowboys and tourists playing cowboy, made possible in part by the clothing vendors that conveniently line the road to the arena. Rodeo participants, their numbers carefully pinned to their backs, patiently wait in line for a table at the restaurant or a spot at the bar. Vendor booths take over most of the city streets, and bars and restaurants compete for tourist dollars by posting their deals and specials on chalkboards and signs in front of their respective establishments.

The performative aura permeates Pendleton. In order to get press credentials, I needed to follow rodeo sanctions and, quite literally, dress the part. While I had packed jeans and my cowboy boots, I had neither a Western shirt nor a cowboy hat. So, I did my part and contributed to the local economy of Pendleton, buying the required attire at one of the pop-up shops and returning to the press trailer. An older Pendletonian gentleman, the one with the power to give me the credentials, looked me up and down and shrugged his shoulders, unimpressed by my costume change. "We all have a part to play in Pendleton," he said, handing me my badge. Later, after determining that my go-to ponytail did not fit under my brand-new cowboy hat, I put two braids in my hair as a way to combat the unseasonably warm weather. I passed another Pendletonian gentleman, who commented that my hair made me look "like an Indian." As a Lake Superior Ojibwe dressed up as a cowboy—and feeling decidedly out of place—I decided to take it as a compliment as I made my way to the grandstand for the rodeo.

The Round-Up and Happy Canyon stand as a tangible and, perhaps most importantly, *live* depiction of the Wild West more than a century after their respective inceptions. This chapter highlights the contemporary application of salvage tourism at Happy Canyon alongside the growth and development of the Confederated Tribes of the Umatilla Indian Reservation (CTUIR), largely driven by revenue from the Wildhorse Resort & Casino. The reservation is just a few minutes east of Pendleton, but during Round-Up Week it might as well be on the other side of the world. Native participation in the Round-Up and Happy Canyon varies from year to year and from family to family. As Roberta Conner writes, "Many tribal families participate and enjoy; some avoid, endure, or are indifferent; and others detest Round-Up time."[3]

This is the question that has dogged me ever since I first went to Pendleton: why do members of the CTUIR continue to participate in Round-Up Week? Numerous scholars have tackled the question of late nineteenth- and early twentieth-century Indigenous participation in performative arenas, from small-town events to world's fairs and Wild West shows. But here I am, solidly situated in the twenty-first century, watching Indians waving as they ride horses down the Westward Ho! parade route, as they sit still as statues during the beauty pageant, and as they dance in the arena during the Round-Up. This is not an indictment of those who participate in Round-Up events. Instead, I seek to understand how Indigenous agency functions within the constraints and confines of the Round-Up and Happy Canyon. Indeed, as Laura Peers argues, "Cultural performers have always been perfectly capable

A man photographs a contestant during the American Indian Beauty Contest, 2014. The contest takes place every year as part of the week-long Pendleton Round-Up. Photograph by author.

of distinguishing between overtly constructed cultural representations for tourists and the culture of everyday lived experience."[4]

In this chapter, I question what it means for Indigenous people to reenact scenes from their histories for non-Native tourist audiences, what is at stake for these performers and their communities, and how memory and authenticity function within these commodified spaces. Even as Pendleton becomes purposely and proudly anachronistic every September, it is still seeking to preserve traditions and a lifestyle that were already vanishing by time the Round-Up gates first opened. (The difference, of course, is that the changes for white Pendletonians were due to economic shifts and the changes for the CTUIR were a direct result of assimilation-focused federal Indian policies.) At their core, the Round-Up and Happy Canyon rely on the CTUIR's continued participation in order to maintain their connection to an authentic account of the American West. The key, however, lies in *performances* of authenticity: decades-old regalia for the Indians and boots, hats, jeans, and Western shirts for the cowboys, coupled with multigenerational participation and a strong sense of community volunteerism. Some participants, such as 2014 Happy Canyon Princesses Jory Spencer and Marissa Baumgartner, see Round-Up Week as an opportunity to showcase tribal traditions. "It's about expressing your individuality and the part you play in this traditional show and this community," Spencer said, "and how you have carried on your family's traditions and the parts *they've* always played. It's kind of a pride thing: proud of who you are, proud of what you represent, proud of your community, and how they've made it all this way since 1910."[5]

In Pendleton, salvage tourism is no longer driven by the fears of a vanishing people or a seemingly vanishing identity—indeed, the opposite is true. Happy Canyon is a proud demonstration of the strength of Pendleton's history, of the story told by its Native and non-Native residents. Happy Canyon continues to thrive, demonstrating that the power of salvage tourism may lie in faith as well as fear. Pendleton no longer needs to prove itself as a personification of the West, due in large part to the enduring and endearing legacy of the Round-Up and Happy Canyon, which are still main economic factors in the region.

After salvaging the nineteenth century in the early twentieth century, Happy Canyon's role in the twenty-first century has become a comfortable, comforting commemoration of the past in the present. There are Native families in Pendleton, on the reservation, and throughout the area who have participated since the inaugural Round-Up in 1910, families who have camped in the same spots for generations, families who wear the regalia of their ancestors, and families who have handed down the same roles in the pageant from mothers to daughters to granddaughters. Every September in Pendleton, salvage tourism becomes a reclamation of history and identity, an opportunity to collectively perform a dramatic rendering of a dramatic past.

The Pendleton Round-Up premiered in 1910. After a few years of a vaudeville-type Wild West show, organizers added an opening act depicting Native history in the region until the Treaty of 1855, wherein the Umatilla, Walla Walla, and Cayuse tribes ceded 6.4 million acres to the United States and agreed to become the Confederated Tribes of the Umatilla Indian Reservation.[6] The production, now called the Happy Canyon Indian Pageant and Wild West Show, premiered in 1916 and now includes more than 500 Native and non-Native cast members each year. With the exception of a failed attempt at revamping the show in 2001, the plot has remained mostly unchanged—the only major difference is a narrative script that accompanies the silent staging.[7] Since 1916, the Indian pageant has ended with the Treaty of 1855, the Indians' continued movement westward at the behest of the federal government, and their seemingly imminent replacement by non-Natives. For four nights every September, as the lights dim and the audience members find their seats, a celebrated narrative of American western history comes to life in a dusty arena just a few steps from paved roads and big-box stores.

The Round-Up celebrated its centennial in 2010, and Happy Canyon reached that milestone in 2016. While their collective longevity is indeed remarkable given the fickle nature of tourism, I am not interested in analyzing the year-to-year productions. Instead, these two chapters work together to highlight, in this instance, the contestations and continuities of these lingering performances of "cowboys and Indians." This chapter shifts from the historical framework of chapter 1 to offer an "on the ground" analysis of Round-Up Week by using oral interviews and ethnographic research conducted during the 2012 and 2014 Round-Ups.

Location, Location, Location: Situating Pendleton in the West

Originally established as a trading post on the Oregon Trail in 1851 and officially incorporated in 1880, Pendleton is intensely proud of its Western identity.[8] "This is a historic spot," 2014 Round-Up Publicity Director Randy Thomas said, gesturing to the rodeo arena and Indian village, "because this is where it began. The tribe came to town, and they camped right here in this spot. The first rodeo was right here in this spot." He turned and motioned to SW Court Avenue, which brings visitors to the Round-Up and Happy Canyon arenas. "The street out in front where you were sitting by the bucking horse is the actual location of the Oregon Trail as it came through Pendleton."[9] As one might expect, the town's claim to the Oregon Trail, now paved over, adds to its Western reputation. The town's motto is "The Real West," and Pendleton aims to live up to it every September.[10] The idea of place is integral to the Round-Up and Happy Canyon, and Pendleton can back up this claim as a mainstay of Western history.

The town has an unshakable Western aura during Round-Up Week. Souvenir programs that hold information about the week's events and contestants have long called Pendleton a "Western Brigadoon," a small town that comes alive the second full week in September every year as cowboys, Indians, and tourists flock to the town for the rodeo and the pageant. Pendleton becomes an unabashedly and unapologetically historical version of its current self, staging a celebration of a distinctly Western America dripping in nostalgia. What began as a small-town round-up, whose large crowds required evening entertainment, has morphed into a weeklong manifestation of the Old West with an exhaustive number of events and participants: there are Indian beauty pageants, a parade, dance contests, live music, carnival rides, and day-long rodeo events. Vendors cram the sidewalks, parks, parking lots, and even city streets, selling food and beverages, souvenirs, and Western apparel.

The *Let 'er Buck* statue that welcomes visitors and participants to the Round-Up arena. The statue, created by Austin Barton, is based on Wallace Smith's now-iconic 1920s drawing that has become synonymous with the Round-Up. Photograph by author.

By the turn of the twenty-first century, the pageant itself boasted nearly 500 participants. The dizzying array blurs the line between commemoration and commodification, capitalizing on the seemingly unending obsession with the American West and the fascination with American Indians.

Since 1910, boosters and business owners in Pendleton have continually cashed in on the town's cachet as a place with a decidedly Western heritage, demonstrating how critical place is to maintaining this singular narrative. Pendleton's rich history lets Round-Up and Happy Canyon capitalize on its legitimated location in the Wild West. It is impossible to ascertain the goals and motivations of the hundreds of participants who combine forces to make Round-Up Week a success year after year. However, I seek to move beyond the binary of exploitation versus agency and offer a nuanced examination of the complicated choices facing the Indigenous peoples and performers who have played key roles in the success of the Round-Up and Happy Canyon for more than a century. The Happy Canyon Indian Pageant and Wild West Show is a performance that invites the audience to witness scenes of Indian life, conflict with white settlers, and a vaudevillian-style comedic rendering of nineteenth-century frontier life. The general scenes of the Indian pageant have not changed since 1916, and I assert that the narrative annually performed at

Happy Canyon centers on Indigenous "disappearance" in the West while simultaneously refuting that disappearance through the use of Native participants. This struggle is most evident in the dramatic apex of the pageant: after
the Treaty of 1855, wherein more than six million acres were ceded to the federal government, hundreds of Indians reenact their ancestors' forced removal
to the reservation. Therefore, it is clear that the American Indian participants
in the Round-Up and Happy Canyon have been—and remain—an "embod-
ied form of history."[11]

As a contemporary tourist environment, the Round-Up and Happy Canyon
present an idealized, romanticized version of Western history, one wherein
the celebratory atmosphere masks an often-violent usurpation of Native lands
through treaties and outright force. This narrative, one wherein the Native
portion of the pageant concludes in the mid-nineteenth century, remains
firmly rooted in the fetishized realm of Manifest Destiny. On the surface, Happy
Canyon smacks of the commodification and commercialization of the "cowboys and Indians" fantasy with Indians marginalized not only within the performance arena but through a nostalgic narrative that has remained relatively
unchanged since 1916. By presenting Native and non-Native history through
simplistic, mid-nineteenth-century terms, it would seem that Happy Canyon
is able to ignore the more troubling aspects of Western history. There is no
mention of the transcontinental railroad and its exploitation of immigrant
Irish and Chinese labor, the gold rush and its devastating effects on California Indians in the latter half of the nineteenth century, the forced internment
of Japanese-Americans during World War II, or the struggle over Mexican
labor in the twentieth century. Happy Canyon can—and does—temporarily
turn back to a simpler time without focusing on the settlement and development that tamed the West by offering a production that resonates with Western mythology. As with *Unto These Hills*, the subject of chapters 3 and 4, and
Tecumseh!, the subject of chapters 5 and 6, the tragic overtones serve to heighten
the audience's emotional response and connection to the pageant.

Happy Canyon and its history are more nuanced than that. The Round-Up
and Happy Canyon are tourist enterprises built on regional connections to
local Indians and Indian history, coupled with the history of non-Native settlers and pioneers. Even though the Round-Up and Happy Canyon proudly
demonstrate the power of tradition, having kept many of the same standards
and scripts in place since their respective inceptions, economic changes and
shifts in federal Indian policies highlight how the CTUIR are telling their
own stories and creating their own tourism endeavors outside of Round-Up
Week. But what would it mean for Happy Canyon, the Round-Up, producers,

participants, investors, local businesses, tourists, and Pendletonians if the pageant's narrative changed? The Happy Canyon Board of Directors attempted to transform the pageant in the early 2000s, but the changes were not particularly well received by the participants, the organizers, or the audience. Some of those modifications remained, most notably those that were considered essential to the pageant's continued goal of educating its audience. At the same time, we must acknowledge what could happen when we measure the production's current economic viability against the expectations of the audiences and the participants, even as the pageant has to reckon with the long shadow of popular constructions of Western history. If Happy Canyon changed its story line, what effects would that have on the local economy? Is it worth telling the truth if nobody comes to the show? Happy Canyon is rooted in Western mythology, which is crucial to its success. Lastly, Happy Canyon features many families—both Native and non-Native—who are descendants of previous participants, and this pride continues to drive Happy Canyon while simultaneously authenticating the production.

Akin to the Round-Up, Happy Canyon prides itself on its "distinctive quality and portrayal of both historic and cultural events during the era of Lewis and Clark and the Oregon Trail."[12] Their collective claim to a genuine depiction of Western history has helped the two organizations survive two world wars—although they were suspended in 1942 and 1943 because of the war effort—the Great Depression, threats of boycotts, grandstand fires, and more.[13] The tensions within these contested notions of pageantry and performance underscore the challenges of performing and perpetuating these local histories, especially with regard to Native histories and Native participants. Indigenous identities have long been challenged, compromised, and contained, and perhaps Round-Up Week truly *does* create an environment wherein American Indians can showcase their tribal traditions and emphasize cultural survival. According to Clay Briscoe, who has served as the court director for Happy Canyon, "It's a real, real privilege for Happy Canyon to have that relationship with the tribes that are here, because we're the cowboys, and we have the Indians, and our Happy Canyon show integrates both of those."[14] Conversely, perhaps the politics of representation and identity mirror the long-held tensions between local Indians and non-Native farmers, ranchers, cowboys, and settlers. While indigeneity is celebrated (and commodified) at Round-Up and Happy Canyon, the fact remains that the events staged in Pendleton require a manageable and marketable form of Indianness.

It is, then, a manifestation of a myth.

"Tradition, Tradition"?: Complicating Constructions of Indigeneity and Modernity

The September sun beat down on the dirt path between the rodeo arena and the Indian village as the Native participants, many dressed in generations-old regalia, gathered for their entrance into the arena. Native participation in Round-Up Week is not limited to Happy Canyon. There are daily dance performances in between Round-Up events along with Indian relay races, which often garner more cheers and applause than some of the rodeo events.[15]

Before the daily dance performance, I saw an older gentleman in a cowboy hat and flannel shirt walk up to a young Native man and gesture to the young man's brilliant-colored headdress. The man in the flannel shirt asked the Native man if he could take a few pictures of the headdress. The Native man nodded and made a quarter-turn to allow the man to see him—and his headdress—in profile. After snapping a couple photos, the man in the flannel shirt handed the camera to his wife so she could take a picture of him posing with the Native man. Satisfied with his souvenirs, the visitor shook hands with the performer and continued down the dusty path behind the arena with his wife. Over the loudspeaker, the rodeo announcer proudly heralded the upcoming Indian performance: "They are our friends; they are our partners," he intoned, reminding the audience that the CTUIR had been part of the Pendleton Round-Up since its inception in 1910.

On what appeared to be a silent cue, the gates to the arena swung open and Native participants streamed into the arena, just as they did in the 1910s when Charles Wellington Furlong traveled to Pendleton on assignment for *Harper's Monthly Magazine*. But today, as they danced and a drum group played and sang, another announcer issued an invitation to the Round-Up attendees: "Come visit the village," he said. "Take pictures, ask all the questions you want." After several songs, the Round-Up queen and her court of princesses joined the Native dancers for a friendship dance. After this final dance, and again as if by a silent cue, the dancers began to make their way out of the arena and back to the Indian village. More than a few tourists and rodeo aficionados followed them back to the encampment. Some carried their cameras, some walked straight into the village, and still others stood uneasily by the gated entrance to the village, unsure of how close was comfortable.[16]

Laura Peers has questioned whether heritage tourism and cultural tourism reinforce what she calls "existing social structure and relations of power between peoples of different social classes and races."[17] In instances like this one, tourists are both the audience and actors.[18] As I stood between the arena and the Indian village, I thought back to what Furlong had written nearly a century earlier during one of his trips to Pendleton: "Swinging out of the arena, the present occupants of the country leave before you its former owners—the red men," he proclaimed. "For a time the vast audience is held spellbound by the marvelous riot of color of the Indian ceremonials—the crowning 'glory' of the Round-Up as one witnesses it within the great open-air stadium—the magnificent pageant of the red man, pulsing with the barbarous rhythmic thrumping of Indian drums."[19] It seemed like little had changed in the presentation, except perhaps the technology involved in the tourists' cameras.

For more than a century, the Pendleton Round-Up and Happy Canyon Indian Pageant and Wild West Show have promoted a plotline that celebrates and commodifies a distinct narrative of the Native and non-Native history of the American West, one wherein Indigenous performers "authenticated the Wild West in ways that no mere cowboy could match."[20] What began as a simple rodeo and night show has become a weeklong celebration of the mythic West and what several Round-Up directors called the single largest economic generator for not only Pendleton but all of Umatilla County. According to Rob Collins, one of the 2014 Round-Up directors, an early 2000s study by the Chamber of Commerce estimated that the Round-Up and Happy Canyon had a $34 million impact on the county, and he expected that that number would continue to rise.[21] Every second week of September, the entire town of Pendleton, not just the rodeo and pageant arenas, transforms into a performance space as Indigenous homelands become a convergence of settler/pioneer/cowboy/Indian histories and the descendants of these narratives.

One of the most potentially troubling constructs for scholars of Indigenous performance and performers lies in the binary of tradition versus modernity. Colleen O'Neill has argued that, while asserting "tradition" may be "a way to maintain cultural and economic sovereignty and to counterbalance the impact of colonialism on American Indian culture, the modern/traditional dichotomy nonetheless remains problematic for those concerned about issues of culture and economic development."[22] Jessica Cattelino has similarly noted that culture and economy cannot be analyzed as separate categories but are instead "mutually constitutive."[23] Adria Imada and Paige Raibmon have investigated the seemingly disparate constructions of commodified indigeneity, most notably how Indigenous performers refuted and reconstructed their audiences' preconceived and anticipated images of indigeneity. It is essential to note that American Indians have long been caught in the impossible trap of assimilation versus authenticity. Those who incorporated elements of Euro-American culture into their lifestyles were then immediately dismissed as inauthentic by Euro-Americans, while those who held tightly to the beliefs of their ancestors were deemed "savage" and "primitive," unable to accept change that was, in the eye of the beholder, essential for survival.

Here, the American Indians in Round-Up Week are simultaneously traditional and modern, blurring the lines of what would stereotypically denote an "authentic" Indian. Less than an hour after the dances in the rodeo arena, teenage boys wander through the Indian village with their skateboards and girls with hair straighteners look for a power source. Some tipi poles are topped with U.S. flags, while Seattle Seahawks flags flutter atop others. Young girls, their hair still pulled tightly into braids decorated with long trappings, have swapped their regalia for shorts and tank tops. A Native man emerges from the village clutching his camera, and a Coleman air mattress peeks out from underneath a tipi. These self-constructions of Indigenous identity are, in the words of Philip Deloria, the "juxtaposition between the expected and the unexpected."[24] These seemingly incongruous pairings offer insight into the narrative encouraged—and perhaps enforced—by the Round-Up and Happy Canyon. Indians in the rodeo arena, Happy Canyon pageant, Westward Ho! parade, Indian dance contest, and junior and senior American Indian beauty pageants, along with the young women chosen to be Happy Canyon princesses, perform their own ideas of Indianness alongside non-Native notions of what supposedly authentic Indians should look like.

The juxtaposition of indigeneity and modernity extends to Natives and the economy. The American system of capitalism has wrongly placed Indigenous people, in the words of David Arnold, as the "unwitting victims of American progress." Their supposed inability or unwillingness to assimilate led to economic as well as cultural inequality, "providing the growing nation with abundant land and resources for industrial exploitation while Indians themselves remained at the margins of these economic developments."[25] These problematic demarcations assume that, as with cultural markers of indigeneity, there is no room for change in how Indigenous people engage in local economies. However, individual economic gain is not likely a primary factor in determining Indigenous participation. Round-Up Week is literally that—a single week. This is not employment akin to the work performed by those who spent weeks or months or years traveling and touring with Wild West shows. Those who dance in the arena during the Round-Up receive a chip which they then exchange for $5 (which is, from the perspective of an Indigenous scholar, intensely problematic, as the line of Native people winding through the village eerily echoes a line for commodities or annuity payments). Those who set up a tipi get $10 which, as David Wolf wryly noted as he sat in the

THESE RULES ARE THE WISHES OF THE
MEMBERS OF THE CONFEDERATED TRIBES

INDIANS ENTERING ARENA DAILY

NO CIVILIAN CLOTHES, SUNGLASSES, COWBOY HATS, LEVIS
OR PANTS OF ANY KIND OTHER THAN LEGGINGS (Indian Style).
NO LOOSE HAIR – ALL LONG HAIR MUST BE BRAIDED.
NO COVER-UPS, SUCH AS SHAWLS, BLANKETS, SCARFS, UNLESS
PROPERLY WORN WITH COSTUMES.
NO GUNNY SACK CLOTH OR CAMPFIRE COSTUMES, WING DRESSES
MUST HAVE BEADS OR SHELLS.
NO CHEWING GUM, CIGARETTES OR TOYS.
NO STROLLERS, BUGGIES, WHITE-MAN BABY BOARDS.
NO DRUNKS ADMITTED TO ARENA.
ALL INDIAN PEOPLE IN ARENA MUST WEAR MOCCASINS.
PLEASE, ALL PARTICIPANTS DANCE & DO NOT LEAVE ARENA
FINAL DRUMBEAT.
THANK YOU ALL FOR A FINE INDIAN SHOW
                                                INDIAN DIRECTOR
NOTICE: ALL INDIAN CONCESSIONS MUST HAVE SIGNED PERMIT CARD
NO DOGS OR CATS ALLOWED IN VILLAGE AREA.

This sign outlines the instructions for Native participants who plan to dance in the Round-Up arena during one of the breaks in the rodeo action. The sign notes that the instructions are the wishes of the Confederated Tribes of the Umatilla Indian Reservation. Photograph by author.

shade of his family's tipi, was barely a fraction of the cost of buying, transporting, and setting up a tipi for the week.[26] Those who act in the pageant itself also receive a modest stipend but, according to 2014 Happy Canyon Properties and Publicity Director Corey Neistadt, "It's not much. It's enough to—if some beading breaks, to get it fixed on their regalia. But it's something to help defray the cost of all the stuff that they do."[27]

This is a marked departure from other forms of commodified indigeneity. Clyde Ellis has argued that economic opportunities for Indians markedly declined after the 1890s. Indeed, the 1928 *Meriam Report* (a government study that showed the devastation caused by nineteenth-century federal Indian policy) noted that per capita income for Indigenous people was $100 to $200, which was vastly below a national average of close to $1,350.[28] Scholars have pointed to numerous conditions on reservations that led Natives to seek employment as performers, including promised wages (regardless of how modest they may have been); the opportunity to travel, potentially overseas in Europe; a temporary chance to escape the reservation; or the chance to make money by simply being Native.[29] A mere $5 payment for dancing at the Round-Up in the 2010s forces this discussion to move past the realm of exploitation.

The Round-Up and Happy Canyon are an anomaly in the realm of Indigenous performance simply because the opportunity for economic gain is not and likely has never been an incentive for Native participants. The absence of a large payday—or any payday at all—for Indigenous participants means that Round-Up Week is not a means of "empowering Indian people to take control of their economic destinies."[30] If money is not a primary motivating factor, are the ties of generations of familial participation strong enough to pull hundreds of Indigenous participants to Round-Up every year? Additionally, if government officials in the late nineteenth and early twentieth centuries routinely banned cultural markers such as songs and dances while simultaneously allowing these to be performed in what they considered to be safe or sanitized realms of performance, does the impetus lie in the opportunities, however potentially confining they may be, to celebrate tribal heritage and cultural survival? Or is there a chance that the answer instead lies in CTUIR's development of its tribal economy and cultural heritage practices? The meaning of and reasons for Indigenous participation in the Round-Up and Happy Canyon have shifted over the years, underscoring the evolving ways Native nations have engaged and continue to engage with tourism.

Tourism in places like Pendleton is about more than just the ticket sales. Tourists need places to sleep, places to eat and drink, and probably some places to shop. The Round-Up brought in more than $1.1 million in ticket sales alone in 2017 and more than $1.3 million in 2018.[31] That's not bad for a week. However, the Round-Up and Happy Canyon are not the only major players in the region's economy. The CTUIR opened the Wildhorse Resort & Casino in 1994, six years after the passage of the Indian Gaming Regulatory Act.[32] Wildhorse was the second-largest employer in Umatilla County by 2000, and it later became the largest employer in the region.[33]

Jessica Cattelino has highlighted multiple ways tribal nations use gaming revenues within their communities and in broader economic endeavors.[34] A 2011 article in the *Oregonian* noted that Wildhorse, which was undergoing its third expansion at the time of publication, was doing more than combating unemployment and boosting the regional economy—it was bringing tribal members back home to the reservation.[35] The complex now houses a casino, a hotel, an RV park, a five-screen movie theater, restaurants, a championship golf course, and the Tamástslikt Cultural Institute. The tribe also created the Wildhorse Foundation in 2001. CTUIR does not publicly share information on its per capita payments to tribal members. But the foundation receives 3 percent of the casino's net gaming revenues for its grants, and it distributed more than $11 million to almost 1,500 community organizations in seven Washington and Oregon counties between 2001 and 2017.[36] Like many Native nations with successful gaming operations, CTUIR continues to diversify its economy. The tribe's enterprises include a travel plaza and a business development firm, among others. CTUIR's operating budget was $227 million in 2016, and it included investments in education, economic development, and natural resource protection.[37]

Tamástslikt Cultural Institute opened in 1998 after many years of planning. It houses three permanent exhibits titled "We Were," "We Are," and "We Will Be," along with additional events and exhibits. According to its website, the institute has three clear goals: "to accurately present the Cayuse, Umatilla, and Walla Walla (these three Tribes comprise the Confederated Tribes of the Umatilla Indian Reservation, or CTUIR) peoples' history, to perpetuate knowledge of their history and culture, and to contribute to the Tribal economy."[38] The institute may not have the same type of financial windfall as the casino, but it is still a critical component of CTUIR's vision for itself, particularly in light of the narrative perpetuated by the Round-Up and Happy Canyon.

Wildhorse's contributions to tribal, city, county, and state economies—and to the development of programs on the reservation—underscore how the role of the Round-Up and Happy Canyon have shifted for the CTUIR in recent years. The Round-Up and Happy Canyon gave the CTUIR an opportunity to, as Roberta Conner writes, "remember a different way of life . . . a time to remember living peaceably."[39] Now, the CTUIR brings people together on its own terms. The tribe celebrated its twenty-fifth annual powwow in 2019, offering more than $90,000 in cash and prizes for the competitors who came to the reservation from across the United States and Canada.[40] But none of this is readily apparent during Round-Up Week. Tourists likely do not take the time to consider the strength of the reservation economy, perhaps preferring to participate in the nostalgic performances one comes to expect during Round-Up. Contemporary heritage tourism practices are ignored in favor of salvage tourism. "Everybody plays their part," to paraphrase the man who gave me my press credentials, and the people who come to Pendleton for the Round-Up and Happy Canyon are whisked back in time as the sun sets and the lights go on in the Happy Canyon arena.

"To Witness Life as It Was": Unwrapping Happy Canyon

As the sun moves toward the horizon, the Happy Canyon arena begins to buzz with anticipation. The Happy Canyon princesses sit atop their regal horses near the entrance, seeming to never tire of the admiration they garner from wide-eyed visitors. Local children in frontier costumes—part of the pioneer cast—chase each other underneath the grandstands. The clang of cowboy boots rings hollow through the metal bleachers as people find their seats. A little boy, likely no more than six years old, grins from ear to ear as he trudges up the steps, stopping occasionally to adjust his chaps or double check his tiny holster for his bright plastic pistol.[41] Happy Canyon is not just a performance for the participants in the arena—it's also a chance for the people in the audience to perform. A souvenir program from 1967 captured the essence of Happy Canyon: "The story of Happy Canyon is one close akin to that of Pendleton; both are part of the same frontier spirit. . . . For those that have participated as characters or as audience . . . Happy Canyon is a reality that awakens for four evenings each September, giving us all an opportunity to assume a new identity with our past."[42]

By 2016, Happy Canyon's centennial year, Round-Up and Happy Canyon had practically cornered the market on Western nostalgia. Former and current participants and organizers of Happy Canyon memorialized its first home on Emigrant Avenue—now home to an auto parts store—with a celebration and commemorative plaque. Home to the pageant from 1916 until 1954, the wooden grandstands were long gone, but the memories remained.[43] Nearly a dozen blocks from its current home next door to the Round-Up, Happy Canyon's original arena held almost 5,000 spectators. In 2015, the current Happy Canyon

. . . . g . p . depicts a scene from the 2012 Happy Canyon Indian Pageant and Wild West Show. The set is designed to easily transition from the Indian Pageant to the Wild West Show. Photograph by author.

arena also underwent a $1.5 million renovation that aimed to address safety and accessibility concerns while additionally ensuring that the arena could serve as a venue for other groups.[44] The iconic backdrop also got a makeover ahead of the 100th anniversary production, a nearly Herculean task for a local painter who, despite several calls for volunteers, often worked alone on the days he made it to the arena.[45]

Happy Canyon is performed outdoors in an enormous arena. One would be hard-pressed to find a theater that could hold a team of longhorn cattle, an attack on a stagecoach, or a two-story waterfall. Once the clock hits 7:45, the metaphorical curtain rises, just as it has since 1916, and invites its audience into the Wild West.[46] As a continued act of public history performed for a largely non-Native audience, Happy Canyon annually reiterates a traditional story line of American Indian history, one wherein the Indian "welcomes all," "signals peace," "signals danger," "dons warpaint," and inevitably "retreats," his lands replaced in a "wink of the eye" by a "rip-snorting Western town."[47]

The production begins with just enough daylight left to illuminate the set. Half a dozen tipis are scattered across the set, which also includes trees and painted scenery. The pageant opens with a tableau of a Native man and a military officer. As the lights dim on the two men, a lone Indigenous rider on a beautiful paint horse enters, followed by others who move toward the tipis or carry a deer across the stage. Native participants enter from every possible part of the stage—some move from the second level of the set down to the dusty main floor, while others enter from behind set pieces. The community is preparing for a wedding, and singing and drumming give way to a dance. The men and women line up across from each other for the dance, and the newlyweds move toward their new home. The narration, added in the early 2000s, offers an educational counterpart to the silent performance.

In the second scene, the paint horse and his rider lead a party of men into the arena, where they use pantomime to tell their tales of victory. While few scenes are delineated with a chronological determinant, the third scene, depicting the arrival of Sacagawea leading Lewis and Clark, places the action around the early 1800s. Several women perform a welcome dance as the men pantomime welcoming the visitors and trading goods. But peace does not last, as the fourth scene demonstrates. A white girl, whose blond hair makes her even more easily distinguishable from her Native captors, is pulled across the stage, her hands tied with a rope held by a woman on horseback. Another Native participant takes the rope and hurries the girl up to the second level of the set where she is surrounded by Natives and tied to a stake. She screams continuously, nearly drowning out the ominous music and the narrator's summary of discord between the Indians and the white traders and settlers.[48]

The Native men return on horseback in the subsequent scene, and a medicine man character moves center stage to treat an injured man. As demonstrated by the capture of the girl, who continues to scream, the audience ascertains that they have returned from fighting settlers. As the medicine man works, he sets off a smoke bomb, which signals the man's recovery. The men sing and dance, and their voices pierce the night sky. Frontiersmen who ride on stage to save the girl interrupt the dance. Once untied from the stake, she jumps nearly two stories down into a pond, pulls herself onto a horse, and rides furiously offstage. The emigrants enter in the sixth scene, some on foot and some riding in a covered wagon pulled by a team of longhorn cattle. The narrator notes that, despite tensions in the region, nearly a quarter million settlers came west in the mid-1800s. Phrases like "divine providence" and "Manifest Destiny" hang in the air. The emigrants remain, as do disease, war, and death. The Indians have momentarily disappeared from sight, and the emigrant cast sings and dances to good old tunes such as "Wagons West Are Rolling," "Home on the Range," and "Skip to My Lou" as the audience starts to clap in time to the music. A man shot by an arrow enters on horseback, indicating that a battle between Natives and emigrants took place offstage. As his fellow travelers help him off his horse, Natives pop up from behind the scenery while others ride in from stage left. The U.S. Cavalry rides in from stage right, and Natives on horseback and the cavalry circle the wagon. The Indigenous participants ride off stage left and the cavalry off stage right, but not before firing a shot at the last Native hiding among the scenery, who drapes himself over a cliff.

The final scene is set in the mid-nineteenth century, the period most non-Natives associate with American Indians, and it is the last we see of the Indian settlement. The Treaty of 1855 intended to prevent war and open the region to non-Native settlement, leading to the historical and emotional crux of the pageant. A narrator explains that the discovery of gold likely led to the government's desire for the 1855 treaty, where more than six million acres were ceded in return for a reservation for the Cayuse, Umatilla, and Walla Walla Indians (now called the Confederated Tribes of the Umatilla Indian Reservation). The Native cast members enter from stage left and move across the stage. The narration continues, informing the audience that the treaty, intended to prevent war, did not: a treaty negotiator who had pushed for a peaceful coexistence was brutally slain, and sixty unarmed women, children, and old men were killed on the banks of the Grand Round River. The treaty was ratified in 1859, a month after Oregon became a state. Continued settlement and increasingly stringent policies suppressed Indigenous peoples' traditional lifeways, leading to near-starvation on the reservation.[49] As the Native cast members move across the stage, their trajectory for the audience is from the east to the west, signaling their continued movement westward. Some cast members, including small children, are on horseback. One woman's horse pulls a travois across the stage as men and women dismantle the tipis. The narration ceases as the action continues, all under the watchful eye of the Native rider.

A packed stagecoach breaks the silence, and its raucous occupants include a handful of whooping can-can girls. Several men on horseback race on stage to rob the stagecoach, which serves as the introduction to a boisterous production of slapstick comedy bits that overlap at a furious pace, leaving the audience breathless by the end of the show. Now that the Indigenous participants have left the arena, a series of lights embedded in the set pieces—aimed directly toward the audience—are turned on, leaving the audience temporarily unable to see what is happening. During the momentary blackout, cast and crew members are unhooking and opening portions of the set that will become the merry frontier town. When the arena lights come up again, the Indian village is no longer there. In its place—both literally and symbolically

This photograph is a close-up of a part of the Happy Canyon set after the scene changes from the Indian Pageant to the Wild West Show. The "businesses" include a photographer, a blacksmith, a mercantile, and a restaurant. Photograph by author.

and in the span of a few short minutes—the Western town of Happy Canyon appears, and the audience is treated to a vaudevillian-like performance of "rattling stage coaches, dance halls, pony express, bank robbery, fires, romance . . . and all the hurdy-gurdy of by gone days of the 1840s."[50]

The remaining action is set against a backdrop of storefronts that outline the frontier industries of Pendleton such as the Woolen Mill, Lee's Laundry, a blacksmith, a mercantile, a saloon with the stereotypical swinging doors, a bank, Goldie's Palace, the Happy Canyon Dance Hall, a jail, and a restaurant, among others. Happy Canyon has created a number of vignettes over the years and could likely stage "a four-hour show, if we wanted."[51] Instead, Happy Canyon rotates through the acts. An Annie Oakley–style act, for instance, was included for a number of years, then shelved, then brought back again. A newer carpenter act called for the cast member to carry a comically long board on stage, intermittently and accidentally whacking other cast members with the board.[52]

The slapstick acts include a man in a red union suit going into the outhouse as a rapscallion tosses some sparklers in after him.[53] The four walls (and the roof) explode, leaving the man exposed on the seat. Two nervous men, guns drawn, each tiptoe backward, inevitably running into each other. The stage begins to fill with characters, including a man in a sombrero and woven poncho. In a notable recent addition, a few Natives come in from the East gate to trade a horse for a saddle. According to Corey Neistadt, the 2014 Happy Canyon properties and publicity director, "We have the 'passing race' scene at the end of the Indian portion before the stagecoach comes on ... [but] the Indians didn't disappear. We really needed to show that they didn't just disappear, they were still part of everything that happened in Pendleton."[54] A crew of young boys race on stage, ignoring the "No Swimming" sign on the fence as they strip down and dive in. They are caught, and the soaking wet boys do their best running back impersonations as they jump and juke out of the grasp of the disapproving adults. Three characters clad in white pants, white shirts, long black braids, and the conical hats typically associated with Chinese laborers enter and interact with several other cast members.

The action continues as a gunfight breaks out between robbers on horseback and the gallant sheriff who, of course, emerges victorious. A man in overalls is wounded, leading to the plaintive inquiry wondering if there is a doctor in the house. A crowd gathers around the man, moving him downstage and placing him on a makeshift operating table. A commotion breaks out in the stands as a white-coat-wearing, suitcase-clutching man races down the stairs into the arena, entering with such speed that he tackles the nurse. He proceeds to wash his hands in a bedpan, sneeze into his gloves, "chop" off one of the man's legs, and "saw" off the other (as the man was moved onto the makeshift table, his legs were hidden in the prop and replaced with fake limbs and shoes). The man, whose overalls are now of course much too long, hoists himself off the table, stumbles for a few steps, and eventually runs into a round-off back handspring.

A covered wagon driven by Dr. Hal A. Tosis rides on stage, promising cures for all ailments. A wild-looking man with a comically long gun enters, swinging the gun from side to side, forcing the other cast members to continually scream and duck for cover. He swings the gun toward the sky and pulls the trigger, causing a fluffy white bird to "fall" from the sky. The actors portraying the Asian characters rush forward to grab the animal, and they scurry back toward the laundry storefront. A young lady emerges at the second-floor window of Goldie's Palace, which has "caught on fire." An old-fashioned and hilariously inept firefighting crew runs on stage. They rescue the girl, and an older man in nothing but a red union suit also emerges. He may be safely on the ground, but a buxom woman—presumably his wife—begins to chase him with a broom, and he dives into the pond to escape her ire. Another group on horseback rides into the arena, including well-dressed, sidesaddle-riding ladies and a preacher, who struggles to avert his eyes when the dance hall girls break into the can-can. The Happy Canyon Band performs, and four couples on horseback execute a mounted quadrille that shows off incredibly intricate choreography and horsemanship. The band's rendition of "The Star-Spangled Banner" interrupts the applause, and the audience members leap to their feet as the lead rider on the beautiful paint horse appears, one hand on the reins and the other holding the American flag. The lights, save for the lone spotlight, dim once the horse and its rider have made their way to the top of the stage.

From the dance hall and can-can girls to the preachers, gunfighters, and sheriffs, Happy Canyon continually centers on the romanticized and nostalgic, albeit often comedic, elements of popular Western culture and history. Richard White has argued that the West is what happened when "people of Indian, European, Asian, and African ancestry began to meet within the territories West of the Missouri."[55] Happy Canyon's simplistic and easily relatable narrative allows its audiences to be thoroughly entertained with the story line they likely expect to see. Philip Deloria contends that Wild West performances and public relations materials told "three broad stories of expectation about Indian people." The first, for Deloria, was Indian violence and American character. The second story focused on pacification. The third, rarely popularized, dealt with Natives as modern people. "Even when such stories emerged," Deloria argues, "they focused crudely on the Wild West's role as an engine of assimilation and social progress."[56] Marita Sturken contends that the self-image of America as "innocent" has been key to national identity throughout much of American history, and Happy Canyon's chronicle of history must rely on that sense of innocence in order to succeed.[57]

"You Always Have This Tradition You Can Come Back To": Native Participation in Happy Canyon

The *East Oregonian* published numerous articles about the Round-Up and Happy Canyon in the weeks leading up to the 2016 events, and many happily promoted Happy Canyon's centennial. One article proudly highlighted families who were on their fourth generation of Happy Canyon participants, while another heralded the pageant's designation as an Oregon Heritage Tradition, thanks to the opportunities it afforded to community members and to its "public profile and reputation" that helped distinguish it from "more routine events."[58] The paper's editorial board found it hard to believe that the pageant had survived the eras of silent films, 3D films, and IMAX movies. It boasted that the production was thriving, due in large part to its ability to "keep both volunteers and audiences engaged for generations, even as tastes and politics changed."[59]

The Round-Up and Happy Canyon have never shied away from the fact that neither would be viable without the hundreds of volunteers who donate their time every year. Native participation in the Round-Up economy provides gains for vendors, restaurants, local businesses, hotels, grocers, gas stations, and innumerable other businesses, but the Native participants themselves do not receive a payment for their salary that is in any way commensurate with what they contribute to Round-Up Week. In fact, most incur numerous expenditures leading up to and during Round-Up Week. Many take vacation time from their jobs, and buying a tipi for the Indian village can run upwards of $400.[60]

CTUIR member and Tamástslikt Cultural Institute Executive Director Roberta Conner contends that the Native encampment at Round-Up is the single largest encampment of tribal people locally and the largest on the professional rodeo circuit.[61] There is no doubt that the Round-Up and Happy Canyon boards of directors are well aware of the importance of Natives to their respective events. Happy Canyon President Jason Hill once traveled to Chillicothe, Ohio, to see *Tecumseh!*, the subject of chapters 5 and 6. Hill, failing to contain his smile, proudly noted his Ohio host's awe at Happy Canyon's use of "real" Natives.[62] The emphasis on a culture of volunteerism ultimately precludes the boards from needing to pay participants anything more than a small token of their appreciation. According to local legends that are near-universally accepted as the truth, some of the businessmen behind the first Round-Up rode out to the reservation with an offer: if the Indians came to town for the Round-Up, they'd be allowed to "do [their] music, to do [their] dancing, to trade with everybody."[63]

But Round-Up and Happy Canyon are about more than sheer exploitation of Indians and Indianness. Numerous scholars have examined the reasons and meanings behind Indigenous participation in what might appear to be purely exploitive practices and performances. Adria Imada has asserted that hula dancers throughout the U.S. empire "negotiated with colonization and tourist commodification as self-aware agents, brokers, and political actors," and I argue that the Indians who participate in Round-Up events do the same.[64] The interviews I conducted push past the confining binaries of traditional and modern, exploitation and agency, and commercialism and capitulation into the space where Indigenous actors were—and are—neither oppositional nor accommodating.[65] It is impossible and irresponsible to generally confer a sense of motivation to these Indigenous participants. However, as Conner slyly writes, "Perhaps one of the great legacies of Round-Up is that one week a year, we have permission to once again be a little fierce."[66] While the Round-Up and Happy Canyon continually promote their traditional, unchanging narrative, the range of individual motivations changes over time. These motivations are often different and perhaps conflicting, yet organizers still promote Round-Up Week as a celebration of Western frontier history.

Rayne Spencer sat on the grass under her family's tent. Her mother, Bobby, sat on a lawn chair behind her, twisting and pulling Rayne's hair into two braids. At nineteen, Rayne had participated in several Round-Up events as a child, including the junior beauty pageant, although as she grew older she became more involved in sports. Her family had returned to the Round-Up, and her sister, Jory, was one of the 2014 Happy Canyon princesses. As Bobby braided Rayne's hair under the watchful eye of Rayne's grandmother, the women explained their decision to partake in the events of Round-Up Week. "I think it's really cool and it's just something unique that we do here," Bobby said. "Even though we don't actually work in Happy Canyon—at least, we're not in the show—and I see Rayne . . . now she's like, 'Look, mom, I'm making moccasins!' It kind of helps—you always have this tradition you can come back to. It incites kind of a spark, I think." She fiddled with Rayne's hair as she spoke, working until Rayne's braids were perfect.

"Even if I'm not participating, I just take pride in what it's like to be an Indian because people put so much time and effort into everything they do here," Rayne added. "Also, since a lot of kids are growing up not being engulfed in the traditions, that . . . even if it's little, like riding in the arena, the kids will start learning to do that. They see other people doing that and that's what they're going to want to do. It helps keep the traditions going."[67] For the Spencers, Jory and Rayne's interest in tribal culture brought them back to the Round-Up, not Happy Canyon. Rayne's work on the reservation allowed her to see daily applications of language and culture, even among younger children. Her tangible pride in her tribal traditions was demonstrated by the three women's lengthy discussion regarding proper braiding technique, and it established her belief in the positive components of Round-Up and Happy Canyon.

For Viola Minthorn, whose family has been part of the Round-Up and Happy Canyon since their respective inceptions, the pageant was an opportunity "to tell people *our* story . . . and they can see that transition, you know— that we had the land but then you can see what the white people did."[68] Minthorn, who has participated in the marriage scene and the finale, which she called "the sad scene," echoed Rayne Spencer's enthusiasm and proudly outlined her young niece's participation: "It's kind of awesome to see that next generation," she said. "We get to dress them up and they have to do what we used to do, so we get to teach them that. . . . I like keeping our traditions alive. I speak to her in our language and dress her, and she's so little that she catches on really quick. It's really cool to see."

As young women, Minthorn and Rayne Spencer may be indicative of their generation's approach to the Round-Up and Happy Canyon. It is not my intent to use these interviews to generalize the motivations of nearly 500 participants. However, both clearly summarized not only their own education in tribal history and culture but that of their younger family members. Minthorn and Spencer recognized that Round-Up was a place for Natives, non-Natives, and tourists to come together and celebrate this history. "We have the cowboys' sides and we have our Native American sides," Minthorn said, "and it's good for the tourists to see both sides."

Tessie Williams, who was inducted into the Pendleton Round-Up and Happy Canyon Hall of Fame in 1991, took a break from preparing the evening's meal for more than a dozen rodeo courts. A longtime cultural leader for the Confederated Tribes of the Umatilla Indian Reservation, she gestured around the village. "Look at all these people," she said. "They all dress the way they enjoy themselves, they respect themselves. And that's the way the pride in them shows." She did not hesitate when asked how she felt about the Native history portrayed in Happy Canyon: "A lot of people have been a part of it, and I think more acts have been fabulous and changing and making things right and portraying the people that they portray. They feel it, and they're part of it. So they enjoy what they do."[69]

Chief Carl Sampson sat outside his tent with several family members. Like Minthorn, his family traced their participation to the first Round-Up. "I've been doing this all my life," he said. "It's a part of us. Meeting and greeting old families and getting to know them again." He boasted about his nine-year-old grandson, a champion fancy dancer and mutton buster. As far as Happy Canyon was concerned, he conceded that "some parts aren't really what they should be, but they've done a pretty good job." While he, like the others, believed that the traditions of Round-Up and Happy Canyon would continue to succeed, he also alluded to what he considered to be the decline of Pendleton outside of Round-Up Week.[70] "We were one of the poorest tribes . . . and some of the others were well-off because they had a lot of good economy. But now *we're* one of the strongest because of the Wildhorse Casino. We're getting even with the white man," he laughed. "Taking all his money away from him."

It was evident that for Sampson, as well as the other Native participants I interviewed, Round-Up Week was not key to personal or tribal economic gain. Unlike Minthorn, Williams, and the Spencers, Sampson clearly pointed to the decades of violent unrest in the region:

When the treaty was made and signed in 1855 over in Walla Walla—that's my part of the country right there—my leader, Pio-Pio, was murdered by the Oregon militia. They don't like to call it that, they like to call it a big defeat . . . but that's not what happened. They murdered my leader. . . . The militiamen cut off his ears, they cut strips off his back . . . they cut both his hands off, both of his feet, and they scalped him. When they scalped him they made buttons out of his skull and gave them to those soldiers also. When they cut off his ears they put his ears in whiskey to kind of maintain it and they took it to the Oregon state capital. And they put him on display down there, right in front of God and everyone to look at. . . . But it seems like . . . there's hard feelings a lot of times between us and these good old cowboys down here. I kind of resent them a lot of times. Growing up here, I know how they felt.[71]

The murder of the Walla Walla leader is, not surprisingly, absent from the narrative of Happy Canyon. The juxtaposition of the silent Natives in the arena against the backdrop of the Indian Village creates a startling contrast, one that enhances and exacerbates the pageant's tensions.

Happy Canyon's collective cast of Natives and non-Natives is a testament to not only its economic power but its role as familial tradition, as many of those who participate each year have inherited their roles from parents, grandparents, and even great-grandparents.[72] Participation varies within the tribe and even within families.[73] But Round-Up and Happy Canyon are still performances, which elicits questions as to how to reconcile performing historical elements with contemporary indigeneity, and how to compare pride in retaining tribal knowledge while performing the historical narratives that mostly non-Native audiences want to see. As with the Round-Up, Happy Canyon reiterates its authenticity by promoting its lack of rehearsals. The 1967 souvenir program, for instance, announced that Happy Canyon allowed audiences to "unfold a glimpse of the past—the children following in the moccasined footsteps of their elders without rehearsal or advanced direction."[74]

The fallacy of Happy Canyon, of course, lies in the fact that after decades, if not centuries, of government meddling, the lifestyles depicted in Happy Canyon no longer exist as they once did. But again, we must question what these depictions mean for the participants as opposed to the audience. While the influx of tourist dollars certainly helps—although exactly *who* it helps might be debatable—the fact remains that Round-Up and Happy Canyon continue to serve as an outlet for these elements of performative culture. Despite the focus on the commodified (and continually commodifiable) past, the Round-Up and Happy Canyon may have served as a boon for their Indigenous participants because they became a space, albeit one created by and for non-Natives, for the practices of Indigenous ways of life that were prohibited by the government. Coupled with the CTUIR's economic growth, the Round-Up and Happy Canyon still serve as a gathering place for those who choose to come.

I've learned that I need to remember that the Round-Up and Happy Canyon is just one week of the year. Yes, it's an important week for Pendleton's economy, but the CTUIR doesn't need to rely on it as much as it might have in the past. The specter of the Indian agent no longer haunts the reservation, and it no longer needs to dedicate a single week to protecting and preserving cultural heritage. On the surface, Happy Canyon is not broken—it has a narrative that has worked since the 1910s. That is not necessarily the case for *Unto These Hills*. As chapters 3 and 4 demonstrate, salvage tourism does more than simply define a tangible place or commodify a particular people. We will now move from Oregon in the 1910s to North Carolina in the late 1940s and early 1950s, a time period characterized by a fundamental shift in post–World War II race relations both domestically and abroad. In the next two chapters, I illustrate how salvage tourism functioned—and continues to function—in Cherokee. Playwright Kermit Hunter's desire to present what he considered "authentic" Cherokee Indians pushed organizers to marginalize and exclude members of the Eastern Band from leading roles both on and off the stage. Chapter 3 shows how Hunter's initial production used images of static Indians as the basis for the salvage tourism production of *Unto These Hills* that played for more than fifty years. Chapter 4 examines the production in the twenty-first century as the drama has gone through numerous revisions since 2005—including a return to the original production in 2017 amid continually declining attendance. Like the CTUIR, the Eastern Band of Cherokee Indians now runs an incredibly successful gaming enterprise, and its relationship with the production has shifted over the decades. While Pendleton has successfully salvaged its history and repackaged it for tourists, the struggles in Cherokee exemplify the contested and unpredictable nature of salvage tourism.

CHAPTER THREE

Out of the Darkness of Tragedy
The Creation of Unto These Hills

The Cherokee story looms large in this country's heritage as a great lesson.
In a world unable to reconcile differences between races, nations, and the
hemispheres, it takes on vast meaning. Its echoes resound over present day
conflicts. On the broad canvas of history it stands out as a great lesson,
speaking with Biblical simplicity of things close to men's hearts.

—Cherokee Historical Association promotional brochure, 1951

In late October 1949, the *Waynesville Mountaineer*, a newspaper in western
North Carolina, published an editorial bemoaning the title of an outdoor
drama set to premiere the following summer in nearby Cherokee, North Carolina. Cherokee sat on the Qualla Boundary, the reservation of the Eastern
Band of Cherokee Indians. The editorialist wrote,

> For many years, the citizens of this area have looked forward to the time
> when an outdoor Indian pageant could be staged each summer season
> at Cherokee.
>
> The dream of over a decade is destined to become a reality next sum-
> mer as present plans are being pushed to have everything in readiness
> for the event which is destined to attract thousands of people from far
> and near.
>
> The shocking bombshell which has been thrown into the whole
> scheme, is the name which in our opinion will be as a wet blanket cast
> over the event. The original name for the pageant was "The Cherokee
> Trail." This was the name which identified the event, and certainly the
> word trail is as typical an Indian name as it is possible to get.
>
> Now the plans are, as we understand those in charge of writing the
> pageant, the title will be—"Unto These Hills."
>
> What is there about such a title to set it apart from being in Piedmont
> Carolina, or the red clay hills of Georgia, or even the sandhills of the
> coast?
>
> Where is there any Indian identification in such a title?
>
> It seems that the pageant will start out with two strikes against it if it
> has to struggle under such a name as "Unto These Hills."[1]

According to the newspaper, this decision spelled doom for the drama. The editorial's author firmly believed that tourists would be unable to distinguish the Indianness of the drama or its placement in western North Carolina without any distinct identification in the moniker and would be utterly unenthused. The decision not to use the word "trail"—which the paper deemed "as typical an Indian name as it is possible to get"—was the metaphorical nail in the coffin.[2]

The author begged the drama's author and organizers to reconsider, noting that residents around the region had raised a large sum of money for the drama based on their civic pride as well as their "affection for the Cherokee Indians who are our neighbors."[3] The paper was not alone in its unfavorable reception of the drama's title. Members of the Western North Carolina Associated Communities (WNCAC), a local community organization focused on economic and cultural development, were also unimpressed.[4] WNCAC, along with local trader Ross Caldwell, had poured hours of their time into the upcoming production, and they also struggled to understand the title's appeal.

Less than two weeks later, the paper published a letter to the editor from Kermit Hunter, a graduate student at the University of North Carolina at Chapel Hill and the author of the script, who wrote to the paper to defend the drama's name. He explained that they thought there was a copyright for a song called "The Cherokee Trail," and organizers felt that attempting to circumvent that or having to pay to use the name was disadvantageous.[5] They had created nearly 100 potential titles for the drama, using "every word we could find which had some semblance of connection with the theme of the play" and trying each word "in every combination we could think of." It was hard to come up with the right name for an outdoor drama.

Hunter had suggested *Sunrise Drum*, *Drums in the Dawn*, *Dark Triumph*, and *Morning Drums* as possible titles. While "drums" most certainly would have evoked Indigenous imagery, it also seemed too stereotypical. Hunter felt that "the whole story of the tribe was one of sheer, unmitigated tragedy," and something like *Sunrise Drum* might offset the heartbreak of the drama.[6] Later possible titles included *Drums across the Mountain* and, of course, *The Cherokee Trail*. But *Unto These Hills*, they believed, most closely matched "the real idea involved. It has dignity, it carries the idea of the play, and it is different."[7] The title came from the 121st Psalm in the King James Bible, "I will lift up mine eyes unto these hills, from whence cometh my help," and the literal correlation to Cherokee's position in the foothills of the Great Smoky Mountains likely seemed ideal.

Hunter declared that organizers had received countless letters praising them for their "good taste." The *Mountaineer*'s dissent, he claimed, was the first

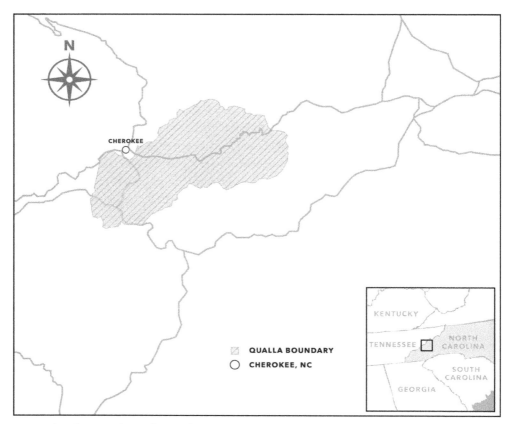

Cherokee, North Carolina, and the Qualla Boundary, the reservation of the Eastern Band of Cherokee Indians. Map by Josiah Donat.

"adverse mention" he had seen. He suggested that, "as we see it, the full title, in newspapers, posters, pamphlets, and elsewhere, would read: Unto These Hills, A Drama of the Cherokee, In the Heart of the Great Smokies. If people call it The Cherokee Pageant, or 'that pageant over at Cherokee,' or anything else, we certainly cannot prevent it."[8] Hunter's assertion that he had had favorable responses to the name from as far away as Alabama did not soothe the wounded feelings of the *Mountaineer*'s staff. Many still believed that the drama had no defining characteristics that would encourage tourists to travel specifically to the towns within and along the Great Smoky Mountains. "This fact bears out what we said in our first editorial on the subject," the paper argued in early November, noting that "the adopted name could well apply to the hills of the Piedmont, or the red clay hills of Georgia (or Alabama)."[9]

A local letter writer agreed, calling the title "meaningless and inappropriate for a pageant portraying the tragic life of the Cherokees."[10]

Their fears were not unfounded. *Unto These Hills* was one of more than thirty outdoor dramas that would open in the 1950s, according to the records of the Institute of Outdoor Drama, now known as the Institute of Outdoor Theatre. From North Carolina to North Dakota, organizations across the country were turning to outdoor dramas as a means of increasing regional tourism. Spurred by the success of *The Lost Colony*, the 1937 drama on Roanoke Island that purportedly told the story of the 1587 English settlement, the post–World War II boom of outdoor dramas stretched from Alaska to Florida and in nearly every state in between. Those who questioned the name of the Cherokee drama likely wondered: what would make *Unto These Hills* stand out from a drama called *Prologue to Glory*, staged in Illinois, or *The Common Glory* in Williamsburg, Virginia? What about *Faith of Our Fathers* in the District of Columbia? How would it be distinguishable from other 1950s dramas, like Selinsgrove, Pennsylvania's *Out of This Wilderness* or Berea, Kentucky's *Wilderness Road*?[11] What would make tourists come to Cherokee, North Carolina, to see a drama about the Trail of Tears?

But the *Waynesville Mountaineer* conceded by early February 1950. "The controversy over the title for the Cherokee pageant is at an end," the newspaper noted, after a meeting of the executive committee of the Cherokee Historical Association (CHA), which was the organization dedicated to the drama's development. The paper joined the rest of Western North Carolina in looking forward to the production, believing that it would "attract visitors by the thousands, and be the beginning of a new era for the tourist business in this entire section."[12] This exchange of letters published in the local newspaper acknowledges the power and allure of the commodification of Native people, Native places, and Native history. The dispute between the paper and the playwright over the name of the drama captures the motivations and incentives driving the numerous parties who hoped to capitalize on one of the most infamous narratives in American history—the nineteenth-century removal of the Cherokee from their homelands into Indian Territory. While most of the Cherokee were forced to move from their homes in Georgia to what is now Oklahoma, a small band of outliers in North Carolina continued to resist removal. They became a separate band, now known as the Eastern Band of Cherokee Indians. The decision to use this narrative to stage an outdoor drama on the Qualla Boundary—the heart of the Eastern Band—with the hopes of increasing tourist activity highlights the region's long history of using local Natives and Native history for economic benefits.

This undated photograph shows the entrance to the Mountainside Theatre on the Qualla Boundary in Cherokee, North Carolina. *Unto These Hills* premiered in 1950 and quickly became a popular tourist destination. Courtesy of the Institute of Outdoor Drama/ Institute of Outdoor Theatre Archives, J. Y. Joyner Library, East Carolina University, Greenville, North Carolina.

Produced in Cherokee since 1950, *Unto These Hills* has been alternately a boon and a burden to the western portion of the state and its Indian inhabitants.[13] While the ebb and flow of tourist dollars to the region has proven to be a financial benefit, it has come at the cost of decades' worth of misinterpreted and misappropriated Indigenous history. This chapter examines the drama's creation—the seeds of which were planted in the early twentieth century—through the lens of salvage tourism. The organizers and producers of *Unto These Hills* wanted to capitalize on the postwar tourism boom. Even though the Eastern Band had a previous history of engagement with tourism, *Unto These Hills* crystallized a narrative of static Cherokee history while marginalizing local Natives.

As with Happy Canyon, the creators of the drama did not concern themselves with actual Natives. Matthew D. Thompson has argued that, in Cherokee, the predominantly non-Native audience wished "to be catered to through certain narratives of history," while local whites "stood to benefit from their proximity to the Cherokee too."[14] Within *Unto These Hills*, and the Cherokee tourism industry more broadly, salvage tourism serves to publicly depict a narrative of Natives and Native history as truly authentic, even as the Eastern Band was continually pushed to the sidelines and behind the scenes, away from the spotlight. The inaugural drama, for instance, listed only three members of the Eastern Band in its cast of characters. The vast majority of the leading roles went to non-Native students from the University of North Carolina at Chapel Hill who were part of the Carolina Playmakers program. The history of the Eastern Band, including those who vigorously fought the violent hand of federal Indian removal in the early parts of the nineteenth century, became fodder for an outdoor historical drama initially conceived as a means to "illuminate regional history while bringing in coveted tourism dollars" to the region.[15] Examining the history of the Eastern Band underscores the decades-long contestations over many elements of the initial staging, such as the script, casting, housing, and the tenuous relationship between the Eastern Band and the CHA, as well as the subsequent revisions and the recent decision to return to Hunter's script.

The drama premiered in the early years of the Cold War, which also explains some of Hunter's dramatic decisions. Numerous scholars have demonstrated that the Cold War left the ugly truth of American race relations and Jim Crow segregationist policies at the mercy not only of Communist nations but of those who had fought to free themselves from colonial and imperial rule. As Thomas Borstelmann argues, "Race formed a prominent contour of world history during the second half of the twentieth century," especially in the United States, whose greatest weaknesses during the Cold War were "inequality and discrimination."[16] The Cold War struggles for national and racial equality in America and around the world—and the accompanying violence and outrage—have come to define the era.[17] The creation of *Unto These Hills*, including the fierce contestations over Hunter's script, highlights the convergence of questions of race and citizenship, shifting economic developments, and federal Indian policy.

"An Authentic Saga": The History of the Eastern Band

The history of the Eastern Band must have seemed both profoundly tragic and wonderfully romantic to midcentury tourism promoters, making it the perfect combination to draw tourists to Cherokee after World War II. According to historian John Finger, Cherokee removal is "one of the most familiar—and distressing—stories in the annals of Indian-white relations."[18] Cherokee homelands had initially covered what are now North Carolina, South Carolina, Tennessee, Georgia, and eventually Alabama; at their peak, the Cherokee claimed about 40,000 square miles of land.[19] By the early 1820s, tensions in and around Cherokee country became what War Department clerk Thomas McKinney called a "crisis in Indian affairs."[20] Georgia passed several acts that severely infringed upon the rights of the Cherokee Nation beginning in 1828, and Georgia and the federal government redoubled their efforts to evict the Cherokee after the 1829 discovery of gold on Cherokee lands. It no longer mattered that the Cherokee had borrowed "political systems and racial ideologies from the United States to avoid being colonized by the United States."[21] Congress passed the Indian Removal Act in 1830, three years after the ratification of the Cherokee Constitution.[22] A trio of Supreme Court decisions, including *Cherokee Nation v. Georgia* (1831) and *Worcester v. Georgia* (1832), would become the foundation of federal Indian law in the United States.[23]

The Indian Removal Act fractured the Cherokee nation. Some Cherokee sided with Principal Chief John Ross, who vehemently opposed removal. Other influential Cherokee, including Elias Boudinot; his brother, Stand Watie; their cousin, John Ridge; and their uncle, Major Ridge, became the core of the "treaty party," who argued that voluntary removal was necessary for the survival of the Cherokee Nation.[24] President Jackson appointed John Schermerhorn, a retired minister, to deal with the Cherokee in 1835. Schermerhorn called for a council at New Echota, a little bit south and west of the borders between Tennessee and North Carolina, and just north of Georgia. New Echota had ceased to be the capital in 1830, which made it an illogical place for Cherokees to meet. Out of the thousands of members of the Cherokee Nation, maybe 500 people, including women and children, met at New Echota. Out of those 500, eighty-six men voted. Out of those eighty-six, seventy-nine approved the treaty and seven opposed it.[25] The treaty—and the means by which it was approved—was hotly contested. Under the terms of the treaty, the Cherokee would surrender all their lands in the East and move to the West within two years of the treaty's ratification.[26] The Senate approved the Treaty of New Echota in May of 1836, and President Andrew Jackson claimed it ratified on May 23, 1836, meaning that the Cherokee were to leave Georgia by May 23, 1838.

The Cherokees' forced removal out of Georgia has come to stand as a symbol of the federal government's horrific treatment of American Indians.[27] Those who remained in North Carolina after removal "clung tightly as lichens to the cliffs of the Great Smokies" and eventually found themselves at the gateway to Great Smoky Mountains National Park, America's most visited

Likely a promotional photo of the Eagle Dance from *Unto These Hills*, 1963. Playwright Kermit Hunter's use of the Eagle Dance was one of the most controversial elements of the drama and elicited a range of responses from the Eastern Band of Cherokee Indians. Courtesy of the Institute of Outdoor Drama/Institute of Outdoor Theatre Archives, J. Y. Joyner Library, East Carolina University, Greenville, North Carolina.

national park.[28] The Eastern Band is composed of the descendants of the Cherokee who, "during the removal west, refused to leave their native hills and took refuge in the Great Smoky Mountains."[29] They had been living in North Carolina, not Georgia, at the signing of the Treaty of New Echota. Qualla Town was already outside the boundaries of the Cherokee Nation. The Cherokee had ceded that land in the 1810s, but some Cherokee had chosen to stay. William Holland Thomas was among those who argued that the Treaty of New Echota should not apply to the Cherokee in Qualla Town, since they had already separated from the Cherokee Nation. Additionally, according to Article 12 of the treaty, those who opposed removal could remain in North Carolina, Tennessee, or Alabama if they agreed to become citizens of their respective state.[30] While North Carolina did not necessarily embrace the Cherokee, the state was not nearly as aggressive as Georgia in demanding Indian removal.[31]

This is where history and myth merge in the telling of the Cherokee story, and where we meet a man named Tsali. Major General Winfield Scott, the officer charged with carrying out removal, believed it would be best to move all the Cherokees west.[32] James Mooney, an ethnographer who studied the Cherokee, included his version of the story of Tsali in his 1891 *Myths of the Cherokee*. According to Mooney, soldiers had prodded Tsali's wife with their bayonets to make her walk faster. When Tsali gave a command in Cherokee, he was among several men who attacked the soldiers and killed one. The families fled to the mountains, joining others who had escaped. General Scott, frustrated at the Cherokee refusal to obey government orders, sent word that the Cherokee hiding in the mountains could stay in their homelands if Tsali and his family surrendered. In Mooney's words, "On hearing of the proposition, Charley [Tsali] voluntarily came in with his sons, offering himself as a sacrifice for his people. By command of General Scott, Charley, his brother, and the two elder sons were shot. . . . From those fugitives thus permitted to remain originated the present Eastern band of Cherokee."[33]

However, some scholars question the validity of this narrative. Finger argues that no documentary evidence supports the charges of soldiers mistreating Tsali and his family, and he claims that Tsali did not surrender. Rather, he was tracked down, apprehended, and executed by other Cherokees, suggesting "there was no noble sacrifice."[34] Similarly, Duane King contends that "the account cherished by the majority of the Eastern Band and accepted by the several million tourists who have witnessed the play is at best a romanticized version of an important period in Cherokee history."[35] In his analysis of Hunter's script, Gregory Smithers argues that Hunter chose "the most dramatic version of a confusing and contested story" and relied heavily on Mooney's writings while working on his script.[36]

At the same time, Finger acknowledges that Tsali remains a legitimate symbol for the Eastern Band and affirms their attachment to their homelands. Paul Kutsche similarly argues that the question of fact versus fiction is irrelevant. The tale of Tsali was integral to "the Cherokee Indians who were eager to escape exile . . . to the United States Army troops and other White Americans who were responsible for rounding up the whole tribe, and to Whites who came later to study the remnants of the tribe who remained in the Southern Appalachians."[37] Christina Beard-Moose questions whether these factors were even relevant for drama organizers in 1949, especially since "the sole purpose . . . was to give the passing tourist a glimpse of a Cherokee story. Artistic license is, after all, an accepted excuse for taking liberties with historical 'fact.'"[38] This history, coupled with growing national and international tensions after World War II, created the perfect environment for a drama that would publicize the horrors of Indian removal and simultaneously attempt to atone for it.

Unraveling the Relationship between
Local Tourism and Federal Indian Policy

Citizens of the Eastern Band had been participating in the tourist landscape in the town of Cherokee and the surrounding areas for decades by the time *Unto These Hills* premiered.[39] *Unto These Hills* was neither the first nor the last twentieth-century tourism endeavor to emerge in western North Carolina or to engage the history of the Eastern Band. The subsequent rise of automobile ownership, coupled with statewide road developments and improvements, added to the number of tourists who came to the Qualla Boundary, and the Eastern Band became "the most visited American Indian group in the United States" by the 1920s.[40] Tourism, as we might expect, became a double-edged sword for the Eastern Band.[41] As Annette Bird Saunooke argues, "Co-existence might be the best way to describe modern Cherokee culture and a tourist economy," even if it has not always been an easy relationship.[42] However, she also contends that even though the reliance on and promotion of what she calls "false historical tourism" in Cherokee might appear to be cultural degradation, it has also led to cultural preservation.[43]

Eastern Band craftspeople started selling their wares at regional fairs in the early twentieth century, and the somewhat-nearby town of Asheville was also becoming a marketplace for Native-made items.[44] In 1912, Commissioner of Indian Affairs Cato Sells went to Cherokee to meet with the agency's superintendent and farm agent about promoting and sponsoring an Indian fair.[45] Sells authorized the Cherokee Indian Fair two years later. When the fair opened on the Boundary, it was originally designed both as a tourist attraction for non-Native communities around the Boundary and to give Eastern Band farmers the opportunity to show their harvests.[46] The 1925 Cherokee Indian Fair, for instance, promised Indian arts and crafts exhibits and agricultural displays, an Indian ball game, an archery contest, and an Indian baby show— alongside hot air balloons and a parachute jump.[47] The fair, which drew visitors from hundreds of miles away, was advertised as an effort to "stimulate and encourage among the Eastern Band of Cherokee Indians a keener interest in farming and to promote a greater desire for better homes and better living."[48] Twelve thousand people visited the fair each day of its 1928 run, and the 1929 fair pulled in 50,000 visitors in just two days.[49]

The Cherokee Indian Fair opened four years after the first Pendleton Round-Up. Federal Indian policy still centered on allotment and assimilation. The 1924 passage of the Indian Citizenship Act, signed into law by President Calvin Coolidge, unilaterally granted U.S. citizenship to all Indigenous peoples residing within the United States.[50] As with most federal Indian policies, the Indian Citizenship Act (ICA) sought to reduce what Kevin Bruyneel calls "the corruption and inefficiency of the Department of the Interior and the Bureau of Indian Affairs [BIA]" but simply led to more confusion. The ICA, according to Bruyneel, created and confirmed a form of citizenship that "affirmed dual citizenship status as well as citizen-ward status."[51]

On the Qualla Boundary, questions of citizenship and sovereignty collided with the goals of the Indian agents and tourism promoters. It might seem strange that North Carolinians would use the Eastern Band and the Trail of Tears as a means to lure tourists to the region in the era of segregation, just as it seemed strange that Moorhouse and the Bishop brothers would encourage the CTUIR to set up an Indian village at the height of the assimilation era. However, as Andrew Denson argues, the commemoration of Cherokee removal "is a southern tradition, not a recent innovation."[52] Recognizing the Trail of Tears allowed North Carolinians to keep Indians in the past—removal, after all, meant that most Indians no longer existed. Those who were still there, meaning the Eastern Band, were just an anomaly. African Americans in the South were a present challenge to Jim Crow's racial order, but some institutions that tried to keep them out of the public memory were just as willing to recognize the Trail of Tears. Indians were exotic and unexpected—the perfect tourism hook.[53]

Federal Indian policy slowly shifted away from allotment and assimilation when John Collier became commissioner of Indian Affairs in 1933. Collier's Indian Reorganization Act (IRA), passed in 1934, aimed to rebuild Indian societies, rehabilitate and enlarge Indian land bases, reconstitute or create Indian governments, and preserve and promote Indian cultures. Collier wanted to erase the repressive legislation that had heretofore characterized federal Indian policy, restore the powers of political and cultural self-determination, and restore Indian economies on a communal and cooperative basis.[54] The Eastern Band ratified the IRA in 1934, but opponents succeeded in blocking attempts to create a tribal constitution under the legislation.[55] John Finger and Courtney Lewis have both argued that this was a rejection of BIA imposition over the Qualla Boundary.[56] However, subsequent shifts in federal policies threatened to undermine the Eastern Band's sovereignty and its economy. Despite Collier's zeal and best intentions, the uneven application of the legislation was not the legacy Collier hoped to leave.

Throughout the lurching, stumbling attempts at reorganizing tribal governments, members of the Eastern Band kept participating in the local and regional tourism industries. They had been "playing Indian" for tourists for decades before *Unto These Hills* opened. While the Indian Fair and other opportunities offered a yearly bump in tourist travel, they were not the only avenue open to the Eastern Band. As Beard-Moose has shown, tourists had been buying Cherokee-made pots and baskets since the early 1920s—meaning that the Eastern Band, like Indigenous people around the country, had a similar history of creating craft items for sale. Eastern Band artisans and the tribal government formed the Qualla Arts & Crafts Mutual, commonly called the Co-Op, in 1946 to sell and promote Eastern Band crafts.[57] Numerous scholars have examined how non-Native tourists traveled to see Indians acting like Indians, from the Southwest and the Pacific Northwest to the Midwest, so it made sense that tourists would travel to Cherokee.[58]

"Craft shops" opened in and around Cherokee in 1930, the same year that "chiefing" became established as a profession. Older Eastern Band men, usually over the age of thirty-five, participated in this enterprise, which has become the "most visually prominent" tourist industry on the Qualla Boundary. Tourists were encouraged to stop and take a picture with the "chief"—for a small fee, of course—as a memento.[59] Numerous scholars, including Saunooke, Lewis, and Heidi L. Nees, have noted the inherent irony in this practice of using Plains Indian imagery, but it aligns with tourist expectations of what "real" Indians look like.[60] "Chief" Henry Lambert, one of the most well-known chiefers, once experimented with Plains regalia and Cherokee clothing. He earned about $80 a day when he wore Plains regalia or a war bonnet, but he only made about $3 when he wore proper Cherokee clothes.[61] The historical framework of Native crafts and performance, coupled with the larger economic shifts, demonstrates how Indians have capitalized on these methods as a means of survival.

The Great Smoky Mountains National Park was established in 1934, and the Blue Ridge Parkway followed suit in 1936. The Qualla Boundary served as the eastern entrance to the park, which also led to an increase in tourists who came through the reservation.[62] In fact, Michael Frome contends that the land for the park was partly chosen *because* of its proximity to the Boundary.[63] The federal government gave the Eastern Band "official reservation status" in 1934 under the Indian Reorganization Act, but the status depended upon, according to Laurence French and Jim Hornbuckle, the development of the Tennessee Valley Authority, the Blue Ridge Parkway, Great Smoky Mountains National Park, the Boundary, and a number of towns as tourist attractions in relation to the park.[64] Bureau of Indian Affairs agents in Cherokee, for instance, saw tourism as the best means of economic stability for the Eastern Band.[65]

As tourists kept coming to western North Carolina, Indian Agent R. L. Spalsbury began collecting information for "enacting a pageant of Cherokee history here, which . . . we hope to make an annual feature during the height of the tourist season."[66] His successor, Harold Foght, produced a small show in 1934 before announcing the premier of a 1935 production called "Spirit of the Great Smokies: a pageant commemorating the one-hundredth anniversary of the Great Removal, 1835–1935" that would reveal "something of the Cherokee ancient religious life," as well as other parts of Indian life "which we cannot afford to lose."[67] In Cherokee and around the country, Indians and Indian history were seen as novelties and curiosities, "snapshots of a disappearing primitive past," even as they engaged in what Paige Raibmon calls "calculated, competitive business transactions."[68] Staged for two days in early October, the pageant included a Cherokee cast, Cherokee music, and Cherokee dances.[69] The pageant's script may have served as inspiration for Kermit Hunter's 1950 script for *Unto These Hills*, since the same historical characters made appearances in both productions, demonstrating that "there was already some consensus among Whites about what aspects of Cherokee history should be presented."[70]

By 1935, the Cherokee Indian Fair's twenty-second year and the first year of "Spirit of the Great Smokies," its program included an exhaustive list of activities. The Cherokee Indian Fair Association boasted that it had "become renowned over the nation at large for the excellence of its programs and its thrilling Indian games and pageantry" and that it would attract especially large crowds that year due to its "splendid Indian programs." There were agricultural and arts and crafts exhibits, numerous contests for everything from archery to square dancing, a midway with rides and sideshow amusements, and a performance of American Indian lore by the Dramatics Club of the Chilocco Indian School.[71]

Coupled with Indian dances and ball games, the fair was a whirlwind production of history, culture, and economics. The focus on Native-made crafts, especially those made on the grounds, added a layer of authenticity to these products that created an even greater demand and allowed Indigenous crafters to capitalize on their own Indianness, despite the rigid constructions of indigeneity expected by event promoters.[72] The pageant, though, was the highlight. Written by Margaret Pearson Speelman, who had what Andrew Denson calls "substantial experience creating Indian-themed dramas," the plot focused on persistence rather than progress.[73] Performed three out of the fair's four nights in a "rustic, open-air stadium," the pageant depicted "the struggles between the Cherokee and the encroaching whites."[74] The pageant, for Denson, balanced the needs of the tourism economy and the Indian Reorganization Act's policy goals.[75] A newspaper from nearby Sylva announced that an estimated 15,000 people had visited the four-day fair.[76] The pageant reappeared for six performances in 1937, but that was the end of the "Spirit of the Great Smokies."[77] As the Indian agent on the Boundary, Foght had hoped to make it an annual feature of the fair, but Finger argues that the internal Eastern Band battle over the Indian Reorganization Act doomed the pageant.[78]

The participation of the Eastern Band was critical to the fair's success, but the shifting tide of salvage tourism in Cherokee reveals dissonance between the Eastern Band and non-Native constructions of authenticity in the subsequent creation of *Unto These Hills*. The Eastern Band cast in "Spirit of the Great Smokies" was not replicated in *Unto These Hills*, especially in regard to the leading roles, and this decision strained the relationship between the Eastern Band and the CHA, the organization that would produce *Unto These Hills*. The decisions over how to tell the story of the Eastern Band—and who would tell that story—led to animosity and anxiety both on and off the Qualla Boundary. The rise in tourism and the drama's financial returns had a clear economic impact on the region, but the question—at what cost—deserves a closer look. At the same time, rumblings of changes to federal Indian policies, coupled with the end of World War II and the onset of the Cold War, created an environment on the Boundary and across the country that highlights the tug-of-war over citizenship, sovereignty, and local economies.

From the Page to the Stage: Bringing *Unto These Hills* to Life

The *Ruralite*'s 1935 assessment of widespread non-Native interest in Indians, most notably what Clyde Ellis calls their "perceived primitivism," would hold true in North Carolina and around the country for decades.[79] In 1941, the same year the United States would enter World War II, a non-Native trader in Cherokee named Ross Caldwell talked to several friends about producing a pageant of Eastern Band history.[80] Tourism was not high on anybody's list of priorities during the war years, so Caldwell's idea remained just that. Once the war ended in 1945, Caldwell broached the subject with Indian Agent Joe Jennings, who agreed that such a production would be "an asset to the area." The large scale of the project would have required professional advice and assistance, as well as deep pockets, and the plan died.[81] Caldwell's interest and Jennings's enthusiasm in using Cherokee history as the basis for boosting regional tourism demonstrates the continued potential economic benefits that could be attained through the commodification of local Indigenous history.

While the Round-Up and Happy Canyon were born amid turn-of-the-century commemorative practices, *Unto These Hills* premiered several decades into the region's burgeoning tourism industry. Andrew Denson contends that removal commemoration began in the 1920s and the 1930s as tourism promoters used the dramatic story of the Trail of Tears to highlight the landscape of the mountains.[82] The dream of community self-development, despite the region's status as a "land-locked peninsula," rested on the expansion and modernization of the area's transportation and communications systems.[83] The drama's almost overnight success helped drive the continued development of commemorative practices in the region. In 1951, for instance, the Eastern Band and the CHA planned a commemorative walk along the Trail of Tears. Vice Chief MacKinley Ross, listed as a descendant of Principal Chief John Ross, and Joseph Washington, listed as "a great-great-grandson of Esali [sic]," led the delegation. The delegation stopped at forty cities along the 1,200-mile trek, offering traditional white clay calumets to the mayors of the cities that showed sympathy and kindness to the Cherokee on their forced journey west. Lastly, according to the *Carteret County News-Times*, the Eastern Band carried an invitation to the drama to the Cherokee in Oklahoma.[84]

Tourism in the United States took off in the years following World War II. Driven largely by the Tennessee Valley Authority, the folkloric elements of the Great Smokies and the Appalachians became a key factor in tourism endeavors during the Cold War.[85] In western North Carolina, tourism became the clearest path to economic growth and stability as civic leaders in the area worked to establish the region as a tourist economy based on its "mountainous natural beauty."[86] In the summer of 1946, eighteen folks from six communities, the Cherokee Indian Reservation, and the Western North Carolina Teachers College laid the foundation for what would become the Western North Carolina Associated Communities (WNCAC).[87] Their early efforts included improving the North Carolina side of the Great Smoky Mountains National Park, completing the Blue Ridge Parkway, and building tourist accommodations in Cherokee.[88] For some, the creation of the national park meant involving Indians in the business of tourism, as park visitors would likely want to "see 'real' Indians, buy their wares, and perhaps be photographed with one."[89] The Indian agent believed that the Eastern Band's presence at the park would be a "valuable asset" and that the Indians would be "a big drawing card for it."[90]

Another project centered on the creation of a "western North Carolina drama, similar to THE LOST COLONY of Roanoke Island." WNCAC members, many of whom had had a similar desire over the years, wanted to develop a nationally recognized production.[91] They believed that this could be the golden ticket to cornering the regional tourism industry. A member of the WNCAC Projects Committee knew Paul Green, the author of *The Lost Colony*, and asked him for advice and invited him to join them in the project's development. Green declined, and recommended Samuel Selden. Selden was the longtime director of *The Lost Colony* and directed the Carolina Playmakers, the repertory company at the University of North Carolina at Chapel Hill. Students in the Playmakers, founded in 1918, would quite literally play important roles in Cherokee for decades.[92] Selden traveled to Cherokee in late 1947 to meet with Jennings, Caldwell, and George Stephens, another member of WNCAC.

Selden's influence permeated the decision-making process. While the original plan called for a raised stage in the middle of a large level area, Selden had other ideas. He dismissed the three potential sites for the amphitheater. Overwhelmed by the mountains around Cherokee, he insisted on staging the production there.[93] He suggested a playwright: a graduate student at UNC named Kermit Hunter. He suggested a director: Harry Davis, the associate director of the Carolina Playmakers. He suggested an architect for the amphitheater: Albert Bell, who had designed the Manteo Waterside Theatre for *The Lost Colony*.[94] WNCAC was all in, as were Hunter, Davis, and Bell. A flurry of correspondence started flying in and out of Cherokee, and the CHA was incorporated in February 1948.[95]

Caldwell wanted to set up a meeting in early 1948 with Bell, Davis, and other key people to determine a final plan.[96] Despite the overall enthusiasm, the goal of opening in the summer of 1948 was dashed by April. Davis was, like the others, disappointed, but he wrote to Bell that "there may be a bright side to the disappointment."[97] Construction on the amphitheater had started that spring, but it took longer than anticipated. It would take nearly two years to build the Mountainside Theatre, even as Ross Caldwell received help from Eastern Band workmen "employed between crops and their own handicraft production schedules." Caldwell supervised the construction, and the Indian Service partnered with the CHA to provide Eastern Band workers in a "construction-training project."[98] Since historical pageants and outdoor dramas pride themselves on their regionally specific settings, the construction of a theater for *Unto These Hills* was of the utmost importance. Promoters needed to publicize and demonstrate the authenticity of these productions by building a theater in the same place where these dramatic, thrilling, and historical events had originally occurred.

Hunter plugged away at the script. Since the CHA had already spent several years and several thousands of dollars on the drama, the script needed to be exciting and dramatic, capable of consistently drawing large crowds while still maintaining some sense of historical accuracy to the events depicted in the drama. Hunter apparently struggled to write a script that remained "reasonably true to a complex history." Even more critically, the production "was expected to convey to diverse audiences a patriotic message concerning Indian dispossession, the common man, and the American Dream."[99] The seemingly incongruous connections among these disparate elements—especially in the context of a "patriotic message"—underscore the application of salvage tourism as *Unto These Hills* painted the Eastern Band as a static people submerged in the past.

Hunter was writing in the late 1940s and early 1950s, a time when the majority of Americans were well acquainted with the stereotypical portrayals of American Indians—usually Plains Indians—in movies and television. In a letter to Selden, Hunter bemoaned the fact that authentic Eastern Band performers, with their "breechcloths, scalplocks, and turbans," would look "decidedly plain in contrast to what the average theatre-goer conceives of as being American Indian."[100] Hunter's theatrical concerns can also be traced to the decades-old portrayals of American Indians in film and Wild West shows. According to Jacquelyn Kilpatrick, much of the Hollywood Indian's outfit was based on a costumer's interpretation of the well-known Plains Indians, which usually consisted of "a long, flowing, feathered headdress, a breech cloth . . . and moccasins."[101] A photograph from the June 29, 1950 edition of the *Waynesville Mountaineer*, for instance, shows Carl Standingdeer and Epps Welch, both clad in slacks, button-down shirts, and Plains-style headdresses, who were said to be "ready to welcome [visitors] to the Reservation and 'Unto These Hills.'"[102] Hunter was not alone in his reluctance to accept traditional Cherokee dress in favor of the more well-known style of the Plains Indians.[103] Director Harry Davis's wife, Suzanne, was in charge of costumes for the drama, and students in the homemaking department at the Indian School at Cherokee created most of the costumes.[104]

While Hunter felt that "a strictly accurate drama probably would not be much of a drama at all," members of the Eastern Band fought for a story line that was accurate and authentic to their history. Some who were privy to an early draft of the script offered "harsh criticism" because of the drama's historical inaccuracies.[105] Davis wrote to Harry Buchanan in August 1949 asking how the script would be approved. "After your approval as President," Davis wrote, "I do not know just what procedure you plan to use in getting the play indorsed [*sic*] by the Indians themselves."[106] He suggested having Hunter come up and read the play to some (but not all) of the Eastern Band leaders, but he also admitted that Buchanan and Joe Jennings, the agent on the reservation, might have a better idea as to how to handle it.

The Eastern Band was outraged at Hunter's usurpation of the sacred Eagle Dance, not only because of his trivialization of the ritual but because he used non–Eastern Band dancers in the staging.[107] Tellingly, Selden wrote to Buchanan that Hunter had worked out "a pretty good compromise—something which is true to the *spirit* of Cherokee history and is at the same time quite actable."[108] The contestations over what was authentic to the Eastern Band and what non-Native audiences would consider authentic demonstrate that, as Thompson notes, "the art of displaying culture and history for tourists is anything but straight-forward."[109] According to Wallace Umberger, a large number "continued to demand strict historical veracity."[110] However, as Andrew Denson argues, the drama would be "a non-Indian entertainment produced for a predominantly white audience, its authors more concerned with telling a story about the United States than about the Cherokees."[111]

The contestations over authenticity show that the CHA was more focused on what would be the most appealing to its audience. *Unto These Hills* was, above all, centered on the commodification of a particular narrative, one that not everyone felt was an accurate representation of historical events and figures. Some of Hunter's most vocal non-Native critics levied their critiques at his apparently unsympathetic characterization of Andrew Jackson. The governor of Tennessee even wrote to the governor of North Carolina, calling the drama "a travesty on American history." Hunter politely acknowledged the controversy but also insisted he was "writing creative drama, not history lessons."[112] Hunter, like Paul Green and other authors of outdoor dramas, believed that the artistic license afforded to him as a playwright allowed him to draw inspiration from history rather than creating an authentic drama.

Hunter's script was not particularly faithful to the history of the Eastern Band, despite their push for accuracy: "As is common in such pageants, historical nuances succumbed to broad generalizations and stereotypical characterization," according to John Finger. "Even more questionable were the characterizations of Indians like Sequoyah, Tecumseh, Drowning Bear, and unfortunately Tsali, who as an unassuming and obscure man would probably find his theatrical sainthood embarrassing. Good history the pageant is not, but it is highly engrossing entertainment."[113] Finger's description of the Eastern Band characters is a telling example of the drama's insistent focus on creating a dramatic narrative.

Hunter, like Paul Green, took a number of liberties with history in order to write a compelling drama. True to the ideas of salvage tourism, this is not really about the Eastern Band—this is about using Eastern Band history to tell a story of American democracy and democratic ideals. Scholars often dismiss *Unto These Hills* because of its historical inaccuracies, but that misses the point. The contestations over the accuracy of the drama are not focused on the overarching themes of these dramas. As the inaugural program for *Unto These Hills* declared,

> The theme of *Unto These Hills* is peculiarly appropriate to the world of today. As the temper of a nation changes and moves in various new directions to meet new problems, there is no better place to look for understanding and clarity than the past, where the temper of the present was born. Perhaps in re-examining the mistakes as well as the accomplishments of our forebears in their effort to establish American democracy, the real meaning of democracy can best be found, and the truths that we have always held to be self-evident can best be defined.[114]

Here, as chapter 5 will also demonstrate for *Tecumseh!*, the ideals of democracy are held to be above reproach, even as the actions of some historical actors are themselves reproachable. The similar treatment of these particular historical moments is not purely coincidental.

The 1950s: Capitalizing on the Cold War

We can apply the program's declaration of "mistakes as well as the accomplishments" to this analysis of the creation of *Unto These Hills*, the Cold War environment, and the development of the federal Indian policy known as Termination, which was euphemistically characterized as a means of liberating Native nations from federal control. In reality, it intended to dissolve reservations and tribal sovereignty and integrate Indians into American society. Hunter's script, like those of Paul Green, focused more on championing democratic ideals and less on historically accurate retellings, and Hunter found an audience ready to hang on his every word in Cold War Cherokee. Mary L. Dudziak has argued that the struggle over the narrative of race and democracy plays a key role in the story of civil rights and the Cold War. In the wake of Soviet propaganda that strove to highlight America's racial hypocrisy, the federal government sought to use the nation's troubling racial history as a means of recognizing its problematic past and its "inexorable march toward justice" through democracy.[115] Hunter's script, coupled with the CHA's promotional materials in the early years of the drama, did not shy away from the government's treatment of the Cherokee—instead, the script and the CHA embraced the horrors of the early nineteenth century.

By revealing—not concealing—America's past failings, the drama painted American history as "a story of redemption."[116] The salvation of the Eastern Band rested on its inclusion in American society, just as the salvation of western North Carolina rested on the inclusion of the Eastern Band's history in the regional tourist economy. On a broader scale, proponents of Termination argued that the inclusion of American Indians in the wider American society was the only means of "saving" Indians—similar to the argument assimilationists made at the turn of the century. Cold War contestations had forced the United States to defend itself against Communist propaganda about American racial discrimination, and the federal government had pushed to tell "a particular story about race and American democracy: a story of progress, a story of the triumph of good over evil, a story of U.S. moral superiority."[117]

Andrew Denson has argued that American government agencies often drew contrasts between "abusive American actions in the past and the generous federal policies of the present" during the Cold War, and the same could be said of North Carolina's Native tourism industry.[118] Indian removal was politically safe and historically distant, as opposed to the continued contemporary racial struggles.[119] Even as *Unto These Hills* quickly became the most popular outdoor drama in the country, Charles Roland notes that a 1960s congressional investigation showed that North Carolina had the most dues-paying members of the Ku Klux Klan.[120] Government entities like the United States Information Agency attempted to show that the government's treatment of American Indians, while regrettable, showed how far the federal government—and the nation—had come in terms of achieving social justice.[121] The American approach to accusations of racially charged discrimination centered on acknowledging a troubled past in the wake of a promising future.

Previous eras of federal Indian policy could be characterized as shameful, but they could also be portrayed as a distinct contrast to the government's then-current good intentions.[122] The projection of this narrative of progress symbolizes the juxtaposition of early discrimination against contemporary democracy. American Cold War propaganda can, on one hand, be seen as an attempt to "hide the nation's blemishes" in order to portray American democracy as the ideal. On the other hand, "of equal interest are the stories the government would *tell* about the American past, including sins that were purposefully exposed."[123] Telling a shameful story like that of the Cherokee through an outdoor drama became a vehicle for national reconciliation.[124]

The movement to "emancipate" Indians from federal oversight began during World War II.[125] Commissioner Collier presented a list to the House Committee on Indian Affairs in 1944, a decade after the Indian Reorganization Act went into effect. Collier's list grouped Native nations into three groups: predominantly acculturated populations, semi-acculturated populations, and predominantly Indian populations. The Eastern Band, listed in the document as the "Eastern Cherokee Agency and Reservation," was in the first group— those considered the most prepared for the withdrawal of federal support.[126] House Concurrent Resolution 108, the innocuous legislative name for Termination, did not become law until 1953, but the wheels of Termination started turning long before *Unto These Hills* premiered. While numerous scholars have highlighted the disastrous effects of Termination, Vine Deloria Jr. offers what might be the most succinct argument against the policy. For Deloria, Termination was "a rationally planned and officially blessed disaster of the United States Congress." In practice, he argued, the policy was "a weapon against the Indian people in a modern war of conquest."[127]

A few years later, Collier's tenure as commissioner had ended and William Zimmerman took over as acting commissioner. Zimmerman submitted his own list to the committee based on his own standards for withdrawal, which included the ability of tribes to make "a decent standard of living." Zimmerman put "Cherokee" in the second group (those he considered "semi-acculturated populations"), but he did not note the particular Cherokee nation.[128] In fact, some scholars have argued that *Unto These Hills* helped save the Eastern Band from Termination. Joe Jennings, the Indian agent in Cherokee, argued, "If the tourist business is properly exploited the possibilities are such that it should provide nearly all of the Cherokees with a good living." But he warned, "These same possibilities make the Cherokees very vulnerable if withdrawal should come without proper safeguards set up by the State and Federal Governments." Jennings's own assessment put the Eastern Band in category four: the least prepared for Termination.[129] The Eastern Band may have escaped the devastation that has come to characterize the Termination experiment, but the Cold War context of replacing Native sovereignty with American citizenship underscores the tension on the stage and on the Boundary.

Unto These Hills Comes to Life

There was a lot at stake in Cherokee as the drama's premiere neared. The National Park Service had reported that 1.5 million tourists had come to the Great Smoky Mountains National Park in 1949 and spent about $10.00 per person per day.[130] Park tourists' proximity to the Qualla Boundary was a potential gold mine for the drama. After the October 1949 disagreement between Kermit Hunter and the *Waynesville Mountaineer*, the paper—along with the community—wholeheartedly threw its support behind the drama. Shortly thereafter, Harry E. Buchanan, the president of the CHA, had named Carol E. White the general manager and E. Carl Sink the publicity director.[131] By mid-March of 1950, Harry Davis was on his way to Cherokee with a casting crew to select Eastern Band Indians for the drama's ensemble—but not necessarily for many leading roles. Davis also traveled throughout western North Carolina and eastern Tennessee in search of actors.[132] In addition to the drama, the CHA announced the creation of a school of arts and crafts, where classes would be offered "under Indian School supervision."[133]

In April 1950, just months before *Unto These Hills* was set to premiere, the CHA president admitted that the drama was $20,000 short. He noted with pride that all of the money "had been raised in the counties comprising the western 12th Congressional District, and 'not one dime'" had come from outside the district.[134] By May, business manager White had the "unenvied task" of finding the remaining funds to finish the Mountainside Theatre. If all else failed, he had access to "a mere $10,000, already guaranteed as a loan by personal credit notes" by the trustees of the historical association.[135] By the time *Unto These Hills* opened in July, the initial budget of $30,000 had tripled.[136] At a Chamber of Commerce banquet at the end of April, Buchanan told the assembled guests that visitors would "know they're in North Carolina" before the drama's inaugural season ended. One of the biggest issues that plagued tourism proponents centered on the Great Smoky Mountains National Park, as visitors were apparently unclear as to when they were in western North Carolina and when they were in eastern Tennessee.[137] By mid-May, White had set up his office in the Cherokee American Legion building and the Mountainside Theatre, "already dubbed 'America's spectacular outdoor theatre' by visiting writers," was nearly complete. His office was "'the most complete information center in the South' by joint effort of the state of North Carolina and the U.S. Indian Service," and they were already receiving reservations for opening night.[138] A nearby public library sponsored an essay contest for students in county and town schools. Tasked with writing essays about the Cherokee, the top five student writers would win tickets to the drama.[139] Despite the growing enthusiasm, the drama was still $8,000 short: the state had invested $35,000 and the citizens of western North Carolina—both privately and through the WNCAC and the Western North Carolina Tourist Association—had raised nearly the same amount. The Cherokee Indian Council had chipped in $5,000, while the U.S. Indian Service spent $15,000 on the construction of roads leading to the theater.[140] Other contributions came from private donation to the CHA, including from a Catholic bishop in Raleigh who gave $300 on "behalf of the Catholics of North Carolina."[141]

The widespread interest in the drama pushed the CHA to announce eight consecutive performances beginning July 1, and the show would then play Wednesday through Sunday evenings through Labor Day.[142] Less than three weeks before the show opened, Davis called for around-the-clock rehearsals.[143] By June 23, he was confident the drama would be "a fitting presentation for this magnificent Theatre."[144] By the end of June, the *Waynesville Mountaineer* joyously noted that "Cherokee Indians are staging the biggest new attraction in the Great Smoky Mountains this summer," sponsored by the state of North Carolina and the U.S. Indian Service. Indians had been hard at work since last summer, the paper explained, and the village of Cherokee had become a boomtown. Eastern Band handicrafts were on display, while "Braves in full regalia" greeted tourists and posed for pictures—"animated cigar store Indians," as one visitor dubbed them.[145] A few weeks before the show opened, a small blurb in the *Waynesville Mountaineer* announced that the CHA had invited every Indian in North America to the final dress rehearsal. Chief MacKinley Ross extended the invitation to the Cherokee in Oklahoma, while Indian superintendent Joe Jennings did so through the Bureau of Indian Affairs. "Even the Eskimos have been invited," the newspaper claimed.[146]

This is where the application of salvage tourism becomes clear. The Eastern Band's lengthy history of engagement with regional tourism, from crafts and chiefing to performing and dancing, makes their exclusion from the opening years of the drama that much more evident. Despite the Eastern Band's attempts to push Hunter toward a historically accurate portrayal of their history, the script presented a highly romanticized plot. Historical hindsight, coupled with the impulse for a dramatic production, leaves much to be desired from Hunter's script. The theme of inevitability, one of the most pertinent problems in American Indian history, is evident not only in the script but in "The Story of the Cherokee," which Hunter wrote for the 1950 souvenir program. "It should be noted," Hunter proclaimed, that "the Indians, simple and plain-spoken as all primitive people are, were continually disappointed, confused, and angered by constant treachery, greed, and unscrupulousness on the part of white explorers and colonizers." He contended that, while the facts may not be entirely accurate, "many efforts were made officially to establish peace between the two races, [but] friction was increasingly aggravated by persons on both sides who had no vision of the future and little concern for peace or progress."[147]

The creation, production, and early success of *Unto These Hills* reveal the contested nature of authenticity, indigeneity, and history, as well as their confluence with salvage tourism. If Native people could theoretically forgive the federal government for the horrific policies directed toward them, then the possibilities of equality and equal participation in the nation were end-less. According to George Myers Stephens, writing in 1951, the drama was "part of the Cherokee story, the reward for the character and tolerance of a people who preserved the white man of Western North Carolina as their friend."[148] But this "Cherokee story" lacked a critical element: Eastern Band actors in leading roles. While Happy Canyon and "Spirit of the Great Smok-ies" drew heavily on local Native actors, *Unto These Hills* did not. According to CHA Executive Director John Tissue, the first casts were predominantly "a bunch of white kids from Chapel Hill," meaning the Carolina Playmakers.[149] The 1950 souvenir program, for example, lists only "three native-born Chero-kee in the cast": Ethelyn Saloli, who played Tsali's daughter, Nundayeli; Ar-sene Thompson, who would play Elias Boudinot for many years; and Cain Saunooke as "the Indian leader who greeted DeSoto on his historic expedi-tion in 1540."[150] The rest of the major players were either members of the Carolina Playmakers or established local actors, a pattern that continued for decades.[151]

The distinct omission of Cherokee Indians in a drama about Cherokee Indians is striking but not surprising. Perhaps the organizers used trained ac-tors in order to create a professional production akin to the already-well-known *The Lost Colony*, and they may have feared that American Indians would not perform as well on stage. The casting decisions also reflected popu-lar midcentury opinions of American Indians. Philip Deloria has argued that non-Native expectations in this era centered on constructions of Indians as having "almost dropped out of history itself."[152] The *Waynesville Mountaineer* ran a photo of Ethelyn Saloli and her young daughter in August 1950. The caption read, in part, "Cherokee Indian women have become so modern in appearance that they have to use make-up—to make them look like Indians—for roles in the drama, 'Unto These Hills.'"[153] Audiences at *Unto These Hills* likely would not have considered Native performers like Saloli to be authen-tic Indians, despite the paper's description of her as "a full-blooded Chero-kee." That honor would go to the non-Native actors who would have infused their performance with the elements of apparently authentic Cherokees.

Saloli, Thompson, and Saunooke were not the only Eastern Band partici-pants in the drama. One newspaper noted that these three were joined by "some 25 Cherokee young people" in unnamed roles, such as dancers, archers, and participants in crowd scenes and more than fifty "original Americans" who worked as secretaries and stenographers, ushers, concession clerks, traf-fic directors, and costume sewers.[154] The focus here is on Eastern Band labor used in the creation of the drama and, for many audience members, only a passing, cursory interaction at the theater. The construction of Indigenous peoples as industrious workers *for* the drama rather than as leading players in Hunter's reenactment of their own history reflects a distinct shift in non-Native expectations of Indians and Indianness after World War II. The expec-tations surrounding authenticity in Cherokee never focused on producing an accurate portrayal of Eastern Band history. Instead, they centered on what organizers considered their most important variable: the economic opportu-nities that arose by exploiting non-Native constructions of Indianness for non-Native audiences. Salvage tourism in Cherokee in the 1940s and 1950s focused on salvaging imagined Indianness, not the Eastern Band.

"Far Better Than Expectations": *Unto These Hills* Premieres

Set and staged in the Great Smoky Mountains, albeit in the shadow of *The Lost Colony*, those involved in the creation of *Unto These Hills* sought to capitalize on the Indian history that, they argued, had unfolded in their own backyard. This claiming of history by proxy—and geographic proximity—is one of the most critical components of salvage tourism and its use in outdoor dramas. By drawing on the history of the Eastern Band, the CHA hoped to turn one of the most devastating events in American history into an economic windfall. More than 18,000 people saw the drama in the first ten shows, and comments were "unanimous and effusive in praise" of the production and the theater.[155] A writer for the *Waynesville Mountaineer* called it "far better than expectations" and urged readers to plan a trip to see the colorful and "soul-stirring" drama. "Mere words cannot do justice," he swooned, "in describing the drama, its beauty, the music, setting, color, and modernistic lighting that helps make history of centuries long ago live anew."[156] He sighed that one could not watch the show without a pang of remorse and the question "Why wasn't this staged years ago?" But it was worth the wait.[157]

Another Waynesville writer begged his readers not to miss the show. "If war fears sweep over you, carry your family today into the heart of the Blue Ridge and live for a few hours with the first Americans. You will find new strength.

The sweeping majesty of 'Unto These Hills' will overwhelm you and give you new pride in your forerunners."[158] The rush of tourists led other businesses to offer services for visitors to the drama. Smoky Mountain Trailways soon announced an express bus service would stop in five other North Carolina cities, Asheville, Canton, Clyde, Lake Junaluska, and Waynesville, on its way to the theater.[159] By late July, they added tours from Junaluska to Cherokee.[160] At the same time, an overflow of eager audience hopefuls delayed the start of the show, leaving the CHA scrambling to find solutions.[161]

In August, the paper bragged, "Very few dramatic productions in America today, of the size and scope of 'Unto These Hills,' can boast of having three native Cherokee in its cast. And likely none can match the roster of over 50 original Americans on the production staff."[162] A few weeks later, the paper called the drama "truly a Cherokee production," noting the use of Eastern Band members in a variety of roles, including their previous labor in the theater's construction and costume creation. The drama would close on Labor Day after "establishing itself as America's outstanding outdoor drama for 1950." More than 60,000 people had seen the first thirty-five shows, and Buchanan had already announced the drama's return in 1951.[163] Ticket sales would push more than 100,000, if the interest held for the rest of the run.[164]

Unto These Hills was, by all accounts, a runaway hit. The drama brought more than $1 million in tourist dollars to local businesses in its first year, and the Eastern Band earned more than $50,000—quite a return on their $5,000 investment. They paid $20,000 to tribal construction workers and $25,000 to others on the payroll. They earmarked additional money as prizes for exhibits in the agricultural fair that later went into improvements at the school. The CHA had been $30,000 in debt when the show opened, but their $158,000 gross allowed them to allocate more for the next year's production budget.[165] In the weeks that followed, anywhere from 150 to 500 people visited the theater every day "just to 'look it over.'" Ever optimistic, the paper suggested using the theater for other events—perhaps an Easter Sunrise service with "some outstanding speaker such as Billy Graham," who could undoubtedly fill the theater.[166]

Drama critic John Gassner concurred several years later, promising that *Unto These Hills* "suffers from no serious flaws." He noted that the production was "the stirring drama of people who became the victims of history as well as the rapacity of individual culprits . . . held together by the great double theme of justice and the struggle for survival."[167] He praised the stage direction, the lighting, and "the excellent choreography," and remarked that *Unto These Hills* deserved the success it had enjoyed thus far. While *Unto These*

Hills had opened its first season with a sizable debt, it claimed a rather large net profit thanks to the more than 100,000 people—an average of over 2,000 per performance—who saw the drama.[168] Stephens declared that the production "has made a schoolbook subject come alive for the American people."[169]

On the surface, *Unto These Hills* had successfully capitalized on Eastern Band history, using it as the springboard for economic growth in western North Carolina. It sold its one-millionth ticket in 1957, breaking attendance records for any previous production.[170] Hunter, writing in 1955, argued that "the motivating factor in outdoor drama is a small, energetic community determined to revitalize itself through a grand tourist attraction in the form of a permanent outdoor production"—in this case, it was the WNCAC and the CHA.[171] A regionally specific symphonic drama seemed an excellent way to attract tourists to the region, as "pride and prosperity often culminate in historical nostalgia."[172] On paper, *Unto These Hills* soon became the most popular outdoor drama in the country.

There was also plenty of drama behind the scenes. While *Unto These Hills* enjoyed success early on in its run, the narrative that had thrilled non-Native tourist audiences for decades would soon lose its allure—especially for the Eastern Band. The CHA and the Eastern Band rarely agreed on anything: they argued about casting and the use of the Indian school dorms to house cast members, and the Eastern Band sought to remove the superintendent in 1953. The shadow of Termination hung over Native nations, overlapping with the peak years of tourism on the Boundary.[173] Attendance steadily declined by the early years of the twenty-first century, leaving the CHA on the brink of bankruptcy. Its relationship with the Eastern Band was in shambles, due in large part to the association's continued refusal to compensate the tribe, alter the script, or encourage local tribal members to audition for lead roles. While *Unto These Hills* had initially been one of a few regional tourist attractions, subsequent enterprises like Harrah's Cherokee Casino, built on the Boundary in 1997, siphoned away tourists and their dollars.

The following chapter traces the application of salvage tourism in Cherokee since 1950. The association has revised the drama four times since 2005 (most recently in 2017), frantically searching for a way to salvage the production as a viable element of the tourist economy. The association has also been working to repair its strained relationship with the tribe in the wake of decades of contestations surrounding the drama and tourism on and around the Qualla Boundary. The initial revision, spearheaded by Hanay Geiogamah of the American Indian Dance Theatre, provided such a staunch refusal of the narrative of salvage tourism that the drama garnered a slew of responses from angry tourists. Since then, more revisions have sought to give *Unto These Hills* a distinct place within the ever-diversifying regional tourist economy. The latest revision in 2017 saw the CHA revive Hunter's original script—after it was "updated for cultural sensitivity and extra stage drama."[174] The recently renovated Mountainside Theatre is host to what a local tourism website calls a "keep you on the edge of your seat" experience. As I contend in chapter 4, *Unto These Hills* is still struggling to find its place in the contemporary tourism industry on the Qualla Boundary and in western North Carolina.

CHAPTER FOUR

We Are Telling Our Story
Salvaging Unto These Hills

Immerse yourself in the story of the Cherokee people as they strive to maintain their lifestyle and hold on to their ancestral homelands. Many of the local people you see in the production are the descendants of those whose story is told before your eyes. The language you hear and the traditional dances and songs performed are as old as the ages.

—*Unto These Hills* souvenir program, 2019

A lot had changed in the time between my visits to Cherokee. I was a graduate student doing dissertation research when I flew from Minneapolis to Atlanta and from Atlanta to Asheville before driving west to Cherokee. I stayed at the Pageant Inn on Tsali Boulevard, a short walk away from the Museum of the Cherokee Indian, the Qualla Arts & Crafts Mutual, the Cherokee Historical Association, and the Cherokee Indian Fair Grounds, and a short drive to the Mountainside Theatre. By the time I came back several years later, the Pageant Inn was gone. A fire in February of 2014 had engulfed the motel, which was closed for the season and thankfully had no customers in it.[1] Within a few years the former Pageant Inn had been renovated and renamed Rolling Hills Lodge.[2]

The next time I went to Cherokee, I was an assistant professor when I flew from Minneapolis to Atlanta, picked up my rental car, and headed northeast. The means of getting to Cherokee, though, had not changed. Cherokee sits almost an hour and a half west of Asheville, about three hours north of Atlanta, and two hours east of Knoxville. While the larger cities around Cherokee have relatively large airports, the easiest way to get to Cherokee—regardless of where you are coming from—is to drive. As shown in the previous chapter, tourism is not a recent phenomenon in the region. Some tourist enterprises bring in millions of visitors each year. The Great Smoky Mountains National Park, for instance, straddles the North Carolina and Tennessee border and consistently brings in more visitors than any other national park in the country.[3] Dolly Parton's sprawling resort and amusement park, Dollywood, is one of a handful of entertainment options in Pigeon Forge, Tennessee, just on the other side of the mountains. And then, of course, there's Harrah's Cherokee

The former Pageant Inn on the Qualla Boundary in Cherokee, North Carolina, which burned down in 2014 and is now known as the Rolling Hills Lodge. Photograph by author.

Casino, built in the late 1990s on land that used to be home to a theme park called Frontier Land.[4]

But the biggest change in Cherokee was on stage at the Mountainside Theatre. After more than a decade of revising, rewriting, and restaging *Unto These Hills*, the Cherokee Historical Association had brought Kermit Hunter's original script back to life. While promotional materials assured audiences that the production had been updated to reflect cultural sensitivity, the return to Hunter's script is a compelling indication that the Cherokee Historical Association (CHA) is seeking, quite literally, to salvage *Unto These Hills* amid a growing and increasingly diverse regional tourism industry. This chapter follows the drama into the twenty-first century, moving through a series of revisions in the mid-2000s to the 2017 return to the original.

On the surface, things looked rosy in Cherokee after the drama premiered in 1950. It soon became the most popular drama in the nation, even outstripping its inspiration, *The Lost Colony*. Tourists streamed into Cherokee, where the drama tugged at their heartstrings and opened their wallets. But it was a different story behind the scenes. According to John Tissue, the executive director of the Cherokee Historical Association, "The tooth of the Hunter script was a fantastic story, but it wasn't terribly accurate and it was kind of patronizing. The tribe was embarrassed."[5] Today, the CHA struggles to balance audience expectations with the concerns of the Eastern Band, whose members have seen their history misinterpreted for more than half a century.

Unto These Hills enjoyed early financial success, and the region benefited from the subsequent influx of hundreds of thousands of tourist dollars. However, the drama has struggled in recent decades due to declining attendance and the changing nature of tourism in the region. Christina Taylor Beard-Moose's work centers around what she considers to be the "public" and "private" faces of the Eastern Band, comparing the very public tourist industry with private elements of Indianness that are critical to their self-identification and self-determination. Matthew Thompson's dissertation focuses on his firsthand account as an employee of the CHA and participant in *Unto These Hills . . . A Retelling*, the 2006 production of the drama that sought to distance itself from Hunter's script. Beard-Moose and Thompson, who are both anthropologists, each offer compelling, in-depth examinations of the early revision process, and my work builds on theirs by covering the more recent revisions in Cherokee. Historian Gregory D. Smithers's piece on *Unto These Hills* was published in 2015, shortly before the return to the original script. While their fieldwork and scholarly analyses provide indispensable accounts of the contemporary nature of tourism in Cherokee, none of these scholars could have anticipated the uncertainty, unrelenting revisions, and still-declining attendance and revenue that continue to dog the drama.[6]

Salvage tourism manifests itself in an entirely different way through the revised productions of *Unto These Hills*. While the original *Unto These Hills* focused on producing a narrative of salvage tourism through depictions of historically static Cherokee, the current focus in Cherokee centers on the literal attempts to salvage the drama while working against the constructions of salvage tourism. The growth of competing tourist attractions like Harrah's Cherokee Casino, which was built on the Qualla Boundary in 1997, has forced the drama to vie for tourist dollars.[7] At the same time, the CHA struggled to salvage and rebuild its relationship with the Eastern Band after decades of purposeful commodification and exploitation. The initial success of the drama and tourist dollars that supported the local economy created a relationship based on what Thompson calls "guarded ambivalence," thanks in large part to "the context of the drama's story, and the location of the theater on Indian land."[8] The mercurial nature of the tourism industry acknowledges not only the uncertainty surrounding the lifespan of *Unto These Hills* but also the potential for further changes. Like the Confederated Tribes of the Umatilla

Indian Reservation, the Eastern Band continues to build and diversify its economy. The success of these other ventures means that *Unto These Hills* no longer needs, in a sense, to drive tourists to Cherokee.

Dreams and Drama: The CHA versus the Eastern Band

As noted in chapter 3, Hunter's script trumpeted democracy, freedom, and peace. According to the drama's script, the dream of the Cherokee and the hope of all America was full participation in the American democratic system. Despite "the subjugation and destruction of people of color" in early American history, *Unto These Hills* demonstrated the power of democracy to absolve past sins by creating a society based on equality.[9] The Cold War–era rhetoric that permeated Hunter's script proclaimed that the dream of the Cherokee— and the hope of all America—was to choose peace.

Peace, though, did not permeate the off-stage environment, the tensions between the Eastern Band and the CHA, or the broader scope of federal Indian policy. Many members of the Eastern Band continually challenged and disputed CHA activities. In 1951, for instance, the Eastern Band tried to collect 10 percent of the CHA's gross receipts, but the CHA dismissed the attempt. In 1952, CHA president Harry Buchanan sent a strongly worded letter to Mr. Carol White, the drama's general manager. Chief Osley Bird Saunooke had approached White about employment in the drama, but Buchanan informed White that the board of trustees handled these things. "The Board of Trustees has never, at any time, stated or authorized anyone to state that the members of the cast, the employees of the theatre and the office would all be Cherokee Indians," Buchanan wrote. "It has, however, been our policy to employ as many Indians as possible consistent with good sound business judgement [*sic*]." Despite the Eastern Band's repeated attempts to have more control over how the CHA told the tribe's story, Buchanan dismissed their concerns.

"The Board wants to work in harmony with the Indians and wants the cooperation of the Tribal Council and all the Indians," Buchanan continued. "We feel that we have done much for the Indians for the short time in which we have been operating and will do much more for them in the future if they cooperate with us." Buchanan hoped that White and Harry Davis, the drama's director, could employ and train a competent cast and production employees. "We want employees who are courteous, loyal, and cooperative," he said. "We want you to employ as many Indians as in your judgement [*sic*] are competent to do the job for which you employ them."[10] In just a few short years, the CHA's push for an outdoor drama would create almost as much drama off the stage.

The contestations—and construction—continued. In 1951, the CHA created an offshoot called the Tsali Institute for Cherokee Indian Research.[11] Its official purpose was, in brief, to engage in scientific research, to study, collect data and public information, and sponsor projects of "investigation and education" to create a broader public understanding and appreciation of early Cherokee life.[12] The institute, coordinated through departments of anthropology and archaeology at the Universities of North Carolina, Tennessee, and Georgia, hoped to make its information available to students throughout the country.[13] The Oconaluftee Indian Village, a re-created eighteenth-century Cherokee village, opened in 1952.[14] First called the Pioneer Indian Village, the Tsali Institute suggested that "in order to provide an atmosphere of reality, Indian families are expected to live in the village" to fulfill two distinct purposes. The first was to give visiting tourists a glimpse into Cherokee life "shortly after the Cherokees had established permanent contact with the white people." The second was to give present-day Cherokee "an insight into their own past way of life, of which they have now only a vague knowledge."[15]

I pause here not to discuss the irony of initially calling the area a Pioneer Indian Village, nor do I pause to discuss the overwhelming ramifications of the suggestion to force families to live in the village in the same vein as fin de siècle world's fairs and expositions. Rather, in a nod to the previous chapter, these suggestions happened as the Bureau of Indian Affairs (BIA) was moving toward the policy now known as Termination, which would sever the relationship between Native nations and the federal government, dismantling both reservations and tribal sovereignty. Andrew Denson and John Finger have argued that tourism on the Qualla Boundary, and especially *Unto These Hills*, helped the Eastern Band avoid Termination. The CHA, which depended on the popularity of the Eastern Band as a tourist destination, feared that any alterations to the Eastern Band's status would negatively affect the tourism industry—if the Indians were no longer Indian, tourists would have no reason to come looking for Indians.[16] Southern race relations were also a factor. Termination meant to integrate American Indians into American society, but it was not a welcomed prospect in the wake of the Supreme Court's decision in *Brown v. Board of Education*.[17]

In 1953, the same year Congress passed House Concurrent Resolution 108 in support of Termination, Chief Saunooke raised concerns that non-Native cast members housed in the school's dormitories were drinking and throwing raucous parties.[18] Superintendent Joe Jennings had received approval from the BIA in 1950 to allow cast members to stay in the agency dormitories, and correspondence sent to cast members suggests they stayed in the dorms into the 1960s.[19] Saunooke introduced Resolution 3, which sought to remove Jennings from his position on the reservation, at the September 10, 1953 Cherokee Tribal Council meeting.[20] Jennings had started working on the reservation in 1945, and he also served as the treasurer of the CHA.

As tensions between the Eastern Band and the CHA continued to rise, the BIA decided to transfer Jennings on December 1, 1954.[21] It is unclear how much of the decision was based on Termination policy and how much was based on the troubled relationship with the Eastern Band, but the CHA and tourism proponents immediately rose to his defense. Bill Sharpe, a Raleigh magazine publisher who did not believe the Eastern Band could run the drama without Jennings or the CHA, sent a letter to a North Carolina senator. The CHA and local non-Natives, he wrote, "have done more for the Indians' independence than all the efforts of the federal government in 100 years." Sharpe continued, arguing, "Realizing that sooner or later the Cherokees must be cut loose and must stand on their feet . . . I believe this move now is like towing a drowning man half way to the bank and then going off and leaving him in deep water."[22] The CHA also struggled to ease the tension, unveiling a comprehensive program for the Eastern Band that included health benefits, educational facilities, and means of protecting Cherokee lands.[23]

Despite the troubles behind the scenes, by 1954, *Unto These Hills* was the most popular outdoor drama in the nation for the fifth year in a row, and *The Lost Colony* was the third-most popular drama.[24] Throughout it all, the drama promoted itself as a bastion of democracy and a benefactor to the Cherokee. The souvenir program, as shown in chapter 3, for the drama's inaugural season opined,

> The theme of *Unto These Hills* is peculiarly appropriate to the world of today. As the temper of a nation changes and moves in various new directions to meet new problems, there is no better place to look for understanding and clarity than the past, where the temper of the present was born. Perhaps in re-examining the mistakes as well as the accomplishments of our forebears in their effort to establish American democracy, the real meaning of democracy can best be found, and the truths that we have always held to be self-evident can best be defined.[25]

The souvenir programs continued to focus on democracy as the decade progressed. In his introduction to the 1958 program, Buchanan proudly proclaimed that the CHA was not only carrying out its original purpose of perpetuating the history and traditions of the Cherokee, but was also "doing much to raise the living standards of the Cherokee and instill in them a greater appreciation of themselves and their race."[26] The discord in Cherokee was not a by-product of growing pains. Rather, it exemplifies the continued friction between the CHA and the Eastern Band, one that would persist nearly unabated for decades.

From Crafts to Casinos: Changes in Cherokee Tourism

Hunter's script called for peace and love and democracy, but that did not resonate with everyone. In 1961, an anonymous group sent a memorandum to the FBI, the House Un-American Activities Committee, the Senate Internal Security Sub-Committee, and civic leaders around Cherokee charging the drama with promoting Communist psychological warfare. The group suggested the drama end instead with a warning to America to "maintain her guard, protect her freedom and liberties, inform her people, and not reap the harvest of the false promise of 'peaceful co-existence', which is currently high on the list of Communist goals."[27] There is no mention of a response to the memo in the Institute of Outdoor Drama's archives, but the unnamed author's vitriolic reaction to the drama underscores the Cold War tensions that permeated the country and the world. The American tourism industry continued to grow despite the omnipresent shadow of Cold War fears, and North Carolina was no exception. An amusement park called Frontier Land, billed as an authentic re-creation of the Old West, was scheduled to open in Cherokee in 1964.[28] Non-Native entrepreneurs who owned and operated the park leased the land from the Eastern Band. The theme park, with its cowboy-and-Indian motif, midway rides, and games like skeeball, could have been plunked down anywhere in the country since it had no distinctively Eastern Band elements.[29]

The following year, Harry Davis wrote to Mark Sumner at the Institute of Outdoor Drama advising against the development of an outdoor drama in Gatlinburg. While Gatlinburg had staged a drama called *Chucky Jack* for four years in the 1950s, that production had had a detrimental effect on attendance in Cherokee, just on the other side of the Smokies.[30] The 1960s, like the 1950s, saw a rapid growth in outdoor dramas across the country. The Institute of Outdoor Drama (IOD) archives show that at least two dozen dramas cropped up everywhere from Alaska to Alabama, including half a dozen in Kentucky. With subjects ranging from Daniel Boone to the Spanish settlement of Florida, outdoor dramas continued to serve both commemorative and economic purposes. In 1966, Sumner wrote to Margie Douthit, a member of the CHA, anticipating an "epidemic" of outdoor dramas, thanks to the increased national interest in tourism, history, and culture and the federal money available for these productions.[31] The interest was not as widespread on the Qualla Boundary. In 1967, Production Coordinator Anne Davis wrote a letter to an actor who wanted roles in the drama for her children. "Incidentally," Anne Davis wrote, "since the Cherokee kids now have so many poverty programs and so much easy money available, they have become increasingly difficult to hire and hold in the drama." Harry Davis had had a policy against using children of company members in the show, but he was running out of options.[32]

The turmoil continued into the 1970s. The 1971 introduction to the program read, "Perhaps at no time in history has the theme of *Unto These Hills* been more pertinent than now. In a world shaken to its very core with the poisoned fruits of centuries of injustice, reasonable and compassionate men and women everywhere are becoming increasingly aware of the need to look to the past to discover the truths we so desperately need to know in order to survive a perilous future."[33] But the turbulence continued. While Cherokee tourism had done well in the 1960s, the industry dealt with a significant drop in profits by the late 1970s.[34] Attendance in 1974 took a hit due to the oil embargo.[35] The Cherokee Museum and Cultural Center, established in 1948, moved into a new building in 1976 and was now within walking distance of the Qualla Arts and Crafts Mutual, the Oconaluftee Indian Village, and the Mountainside Theatre.[36] Just three years later, the drama expected a 20 percent drop in income for the 1979 season.[37] Some hoped the 1982 World's Fair in Knoxville would be a boon to regional tourism, but Annette Bird Saunooke suggests it may have had the opposite effect. Tourists canceled or changed their vacation plans, and few World's Fair attendees made it all the way to Cherokee.[38] Despite the continued drops in attendance, the North Carolina dramas kept pumping money into the state economy. In 1994, for instance, the dozen outdoor productions had a $75 million economic impact—*The Lost Colony* brought in $22.7 million, while *Unto These Hills* was responsible for $25 million.[39]

Everything changed when Harrah's Cherokee Casino opened in 1997. Scott Parker, the director of the IOD, sent a letter to the management in Cherokee in December. "Normally, I wouldn't write a note such as this because I try not to meddle in other people's business," the letter began. "But, because I consider all three of you guys good friends, and I know you realize how much I care about *Unto These Hills*, I hope you will take this as coming from someone who is family, not an outsider meddling." Parker was worried about the casino's effect on the drama, especially given the number of feasibility studies the IOD had done in communities with casinos. He warned that the casino could negatively affect the drama's attendance for up to five years—and this was on the heels of the all-time worst attendance year on record, due in large part to the 1996 Summer Olympics in Atlanta.[40] He offered a few potential strategic maneuvers, but he encouraged the CHA to "draft a very aggressive campaign as quickly as possible, and seek assistance from influential fronts: state, tribe, etc."[41] Parker also sent a letter to the casino's marketing director the following summer after he took a trip to Cherokee, noting that very few of the casino guests he had talked to even knew about the drama. The director had asked him how the casino could help support the drama, and Parker offered a few suggestions, including a large poster display and a "little show" twice a day. "I expect you have more people there than you may realize who simply don't know about the shows, or know too little to sway them to buy a ticket," he wrote. "I also suspect you could reduce the ticket price a bit and get away with it. Anything is better than 60 people in a 1,500 seat house, right?"[42] Parker and the CHA were not the only ones concerned about Harrah's. The Eastern Band had hosted bingo since 1974, but some concerns went beyond the moral question of gambling. While the Eastern Band would run the casino, Harrah's had required the entire Boundary—all 57,000 acres—as collateral in case the casino failed. Many feared they would lose their land, just as they had in the 1800s. The success and continued expansion of the casino means that the Boundary lands are likely safe, but the fact remains that, for some, the potential loss of the Boundary felt like a very real possibility.[43]

Twenty-First-Century Troubles: Working to Revitalize *Unto These Hills*

The turn of the twenty-first century was not much brighter for the CHA. Parker sent a letter to Barry Hipps, the drama's general manager, in August 2000. "I know you're frustrated on a number of fronts, not the lest [sic] of which is declining attendance, but if there is any consolation to be taken, its [sic] that this is happening to many of the other theatres across the country," Parker wrote. "Once a show goes through the decline you've seen, it's hard to earn your way out of it, especially if the slump continues for several more years. It usually takes some contributed income to get things back on top."[44] Parker sent almost the same letter the following summer, adding, "I wish we had the magic bullet to fire and things would turn around."[45]

The CHA filed for bankruptcy in 2004. The Eastern Band voted to help the association and, by extension, the drama, which now has members of the Eastern Band in more prominent roles both on stage and behind the scenes. Historically run by non-Natives, the CHA had often clashed with the Eastern Band over the script, the casting, the housing arrangements, the financing, and just about everything else.[46] In 2005, Peter Hardy, who had directed the drama for sixteen seasons, wrote to Parker that the CHA decided to hire a Native director for the following season. He wished the production "the best of luck in these changing times," and noted that he was looking forward to exploring other creative avenues.[47] The new director was Hanay Geiogamah, a Native playwright, producer, professor, and the founder of the American Indian Dance Theatre (AIDT). Change was long overdue in Cherokee, but the clashes continued. Harrah's profits kept growing, regional tourism kept diversifying, and the numbers at the Mountainside Theatre continued to decline.[48]

In 2006, the University of North Carolina at Chapel Hill issued a press release regarding the upcoming production of *Unto These Hills*. It promised "an all-new show . . . a celebration of Cherokee history and culture," written and directed by an American Indian for the first time in the show's fifty-seven seasons. It noted that Hunter's original script had "sympathized with the Cherokee in its portrayal of the tragic removal of most of the tribe from its native Great Smoky Mountains to Oklahoma in 1838," although, according to then–CHA Executive Director James Bradley, "it left an impression of the Cherokee as a woeful and broken people."[49] After more than fifty years, the first major overhaul of *Unto These Hills* promised not to reduce the "spectacle" of the show, assuring audiences that the drama would contain "abundant Cherokee music, abundant Cherokee dance and abundant Cherokee ceremony."[50]

The quite-literal dramatic shift from Hunter's well-known (albeit problematic and paternalistic) script to a production that proudly vowed to serve as "a new kind of cultural preservation for the tribe" underscored numerous tensions that had been present in Cherokee since *Unto These Hills* premiered in 1950. The drama had long been a source of friction, most notably among "its multiple audiences who contest each other's authority to authenticate its narratives of the past."[51] The Eastern Band was not the sole factor driving early tourist-driven initiatives, as shown in chapter 3, but many members participated in and profited from these endeavors.[52] The establishment of Great Smoky Mountains National Park and the expansion of roads and highways in the region proved irresistible for Indian agents, park officials, and local entrepreneurs who recognized that the history and culture of the Eastern Band could be used to generate tourist traffic and tourist dollars. Hunter's script for *Unto These Hills* was deeply wedded to salvage tourism's narrative of static indigeneity, most notably in its restoration in the twenty-first century and continued contemporary contestations over the drama. Hunter's depiction of the Cherokee as "stereotypical Indians" eventually led the CHA to dismantle the original in order to produce a drama that the Eastern Band, individually and collectively, could be proud to participate in and publicize. These motivations were simultaneously encouraged and hampered by several decades of declining attendance. As Thompson has noted, "the relationships among tourism, history, authenticity, and the growing cultural revitalization movement complicate any simplistic understanding of the politics of display."[53]

The current staging of Hunter's script, which opened in 2017, is the fifth revision to the drama. In 2006, the Eastern Band brought in Hanay Geiogamah to revamp the production. Geiogamah's reinterpretation was a surprise and a shock to many audience and cast members, and the CHA went in a different direction the following year. Pat Allee and Ben Hurst wrote the script for the 2007 production, and their script was reworked in subsequent years. Linda Squirrel, who was the executive assistant for the CHA, used Hunter's script as the inspiration for her production but made several significant changes. Hunter's drama has, for better or worse, become a defining element of the Eastern Band as well as the local economy, and it has become inextricably intertwined in the lives of the people whose lives it purports to portray. The Eastern Band, like the Confederated Tribes of the Umatilla Indian Reservation, has had to reckon with these productions as markers of memory, economy, and identity.

The years of revisions, coupled with growing tribal participation, a burgeoning tribal economy, and the broader tourism environment, exposes the underlying tensions between these subsequent applications of salvage tourism. Why, we may wonder, would the CHA work so hard to salvage a drama that is so clearly out of step not only with constructions of Indigenous history but with contemporary Natives? Why does the Eastern Band continue to have a stake in the production of *Unto These Hills*? On the other hand, the current staging and casting have become a marketing tool for the drama and the region's tourist economy. According to a local tourist website, *Unto These Hills* is "one of the longest-running outdoor dramas in the U.S." that has "thrilled and entertained more than six million people since 1950. Recently rewritten to better reflect the Cherokee's true history and culture, the play is a 'must-see' when visiting the Smokies."[54] Another calls it "a spectacular reimagining of the Cherokee story . . . an outdoor drama that stirs the soul nightly. With sensational artistry this critically acclaimed production portrays the gripping legacy of the Cherokee people through the zenith of their power, through the heartbreak of the Trail of Tears, and finally culminating in the present day where the Cherokee people continue to rewrite their place in the world: a place based in traditional Cherokee values and modern sensibilities. Thousands of years in the making, *Unto These Hills* covers ritual, betrayal, love, action, suspense, and loss."[55] But these reimaginings of Cherokee history cannot escape the past or ignore the events that, even without dramaturgical interference, create such a heart-wrenching narrative.

More than half a million tourists streamed into Cherokee in just the first five seasons, creating what Thompson calls "a pop culture phenomenon."[56] The heyday for tourism in Cherokee spanned the few decades after World War II, and it was a time when cars were "bumper to bumper through the whole town from May to October."[57] According to Beard-Moose, more than three million people attended *Unto These Hills* between 1950 and 1990, which translated to an average attendance of 2,133 per performance.[58] The drama's best years were from 1950 to 1983 where, with the exception of 1979, yearly attendance well exceeded 100,000 visitors.[59] However, the box office numbers reveal that the first three decades of success gave way to subsequent decades of decline due to economic recessions and the rise of other tourist-centered enterprises. As noted earlier in this chapter, *Unto These Hills* now faces increased competition from Gatlinburg and Pigeon Forge, Tennessee, which sits at the western entrance to the Great Smoky Mountains National Park and houses major attractions like Dolly Parton's Dollywood theme park.[60] The growth of additional tourist venues reveals the surge in and diversification of regional economic and tourist-driven development, all of which serve as competition for the tourists who had previously had few options for this type of entertainment and may have turned to *Unto These Hills* out of habit or lack of other possibilities.

By the turn of the twenty-first century, the future of the drama had not improved. As shown below, attendance had dropped by nearly 18,000 from 2000 to 2004. A slight spike in 2002 gave way to a precipitous drop of almost 10,000 fewer attendees the following year. In 2005, the final year of the first iteration of Hunter's script, attendance rose by about 8,000. While the burst of tourist interest seems incongruous with the decision to close the Hunter production, attendance in 2005 was still nearly 10,000 tickets below the numbers for 2000. As a frame of reference, attendance had been steadily dropping, with minor fluctuations, since the early 1970s: attendance went from around 140,000 in 1970 to around 106,000 in 1980 to around 92,000 in 1990. Tourist interest in *Unto These Hills* was seemingly hurtling toward an inevitable demise. Thompson's work has demonstrated that the CHA took a rather lackadaisical approach to record keeping, and even they may have been unaware of how significant these issues had become.

The extraordinary overall drop in attendance and the subsequent hit to the local economy forced the CHA to recognize that Hunter's version of *Unto These Hills* was not as profitable as it had been in the past, and that its story line was

Unto These Hills, 2000–2005

Year	Attendance	Shows	Average	vs. Year Before
2000	63,715	62	1,028	N/A
2001	60,382	62	974	−3,333
2002	62,421	62	1,007	+2,039
2003	52,952	62	854	−9,469
2004	45,943	62	741	−7,009
2005	54,120	62	873	+8,177

These numbers are based on attendance figures from John Tissue, the 2012 executive director of the Cherokee Historical Association. The numbers in Matthew Thompson's appendix are similar, albeit not identical. Thompson makes numerous references to the CHA's haphazard filing and bookkeeping systems, and these discrepancies are likely a result of those inconsistent methods.

outdated. Thompson, writing in 2009, asserted, "The sun has set on *Unto These Hills'* glory days and its role as the major tourist draw has been usurped by the casino. To the burgeoning cultural revitalization movement in Cherokee the accommodations served by *Unto These Hills* are of less consequence today."[61]

Similarly, as Beard-Moose has argued, many members of the Eastern Band had told tourists to avoid the show, and others refused to take their family and friends. According to James Bradley, a former executive director for the CHA, many tribal members believed that "It's not *us* up there, just white ideas of us."[62] Bradley's succinct explanation of the troubles surrounding contemporary Native aversion toward the drama echoed concerns raised more than a half-century earlier. The drastic distinction between the nineteenth-century Cherokee depicted on stage and the contemporary Eastern Band demonstrates the divide between the historical and cultural accuracy the Cherokee anticipated in the production and what is on stage. Hunter's script, which members of the Eastern Band had deemed problematic *before* it opened in 1950, was a definitive element of the tourist industry in western North Carolina for decades. Here we see the contested nature of these productions in regard to audience expectations against the Native nations whose histories are exploited for touristic desires and local economic gain.

Rather than continuing the narrative of salvage tourism that left the Eastern Band firmly marginalized and inextricably stuck in the past, there was a temporary rejection of the static nature of salvage tourism's take on authenticity in 2006's *Unto These Hills . . . a Retelling*. This production rattled many non-Native audience members who had grown accustomed to the comfortable "authenticity" of Hunter's original script. It also aggravated Eastern Band cast members who felt Geiogamah took too many liberties with their culture and history. Plenty of non-Native audience members held strong personal connections to the Hunter script and were frustrated with the CHA's decision to alter the drama. One woman, for instance, called the CHA and insisted they bring back the Hunter script: "We were at the [2006] show two weeks ago and we didn't like it. Then we heard that you're bringing back the old show. If that's true then we'd like to bring our family back."[63] Subsequently, the multifaceted decision to rework the drama had to reconcile the production's long and often-problematic history both on and off the stage.

"How Did It Begin?": *Unto These Hills . . . A Retelling*

Indigenous opposition to the drama—and, by extension, to the CHA—had long colored the relationship between the CHA and the Eastern Band. The Eastern Band continued to push for a CHA contribution to tribal operating expenses into the 1970s, but it met further refusal. Harrah's Cherokee Casino opened in 1997, and the casino immediately became a major player in the local economy. Its influence in the region quickly spread, and it changed the entire economy of the western North Carolina region. It was the largest tourist destination in the state, and it became the largest regional employer west of Asheville.[64] In contrast, the CHA's foundation was crumbling, and the association filed for bankruptcy in 2004.[65]

The Eastern Band bailed out the CHA, as noted earlier, and tribal members moved into management positions and began to look at revising *Unto These Hills*. Previous appointees to the CHA executive board served for life, leaving little room for additional members. The new system, implemented in 2004, was a nine-member board. Each member of the board served three-year terms. Lastly—and most importantly—the first new board was entirely composed of Eastern Band members. It was the first time that the organization was run by the Eastern Band since the CHA's inception.[66]

According to Beard-Moose, the new CHA management had two main directives for the new *Unto These Hills*. One was that a majority of the Cherokee cast members had been confined to the anonymous, silent roles in crowd scenes, and the CHA reportedly intended to move them into "vital speaking roles." The second was that the new production would seek to "repair and replace errors" in the Hunter script in order to make it "more culturally accurate."[67] To achieve this, the Eastern Band defined six points that would finally pull *Unto These Hills* into the twenty-first century:

1. To tell the story in a Cherokee storytelling tradition instead of as a linear set of vignettes.
2. To add dialogue and songs in the Cherokee language wherever possible.
3. To add actual Cherokee dances and the corresponding chants/songs, and to eliminate the anglicized versions.
4. To replace the key staff positions with Cherokees, where possible, and with other American Indian tribal members everywhere else.
5. To hold only one set of auditions so that all interested Cherokees could audition.
6. To have a Community Review Committee play a large part in the overhaul.[68]

Geiogamah came in to mount the new production of the drama in 2006, which would be called *Unto These Hills . . . a Retelling*.[69] Attaching Geiogamah to the project was likely a coup for the Eastern Band and the CHA, due to his widespread fame and success in various performative arenas.[70] Under Geiogamah's direction, AIDT premiered in 1987 and toured both nationally and internationally. The *New York Times* noted, "The hallmark of this company is authenticity, at least to an extent reasonable within the context of any staged production. These are serious artists conveying basic facts of their lives and cultures. There are no musical-comedy whoops and tomahawks here."[71]

Even here, the overtones of "authenticity" demonstrate the strength of salvage tourism. Geiogamah's work is dynamic, drawing on numerous cultural elements from various tribes in order to create powerful productions that proudly illustrate how American Indians are more than just static historical characters. His revisionism, couched in terms of entertainment and collective indigeneity, shows that contemporary productions of Indians and Indianness are not necessarily bound by historical constructs. Unlike Hunter's script, which featured an unnamed narrator with a "deep baritone voice," Geiogamah used Selu and Kana'ti, two pivotal figures in Cherokee history, as narrators.[72] The new production incorporated the seven Cherokee clans portrayed by actors in masks and costumes. Geiogamah also doubled the number of dances in the production. James Bradley, then-president of the CHA, supported the new production, proclaiming, "The new show has the Cherokee rising up from the ruins" of the past depicted in Hunter's drama.[73]

For Beard-Moose, "it was remarkable to hear the Cherokee language spoken onstage by Cherokee performers. Gone from the old version is the overwhelming sense of morbidity and defeat."[74] Thompson's fieldwork, however, tells a different story. His behind-the-scenes viewpoint examines the nearly insurmountable challenges to retelling *Unto These Hills*. The specter of Hunter's script, and the CHA's approach to the drama and the Eastern Band, still permeated almost every aspect of the 2006 production. The initially optimistic production staff spent two days auditioning local tribal members with the hope of "casting locals as the stars of their own show," but they soon realized that Eastern Band members did not necessarily share their enthusiasm.[75]

Unto These Hills had never been a Cherokee drama. While the production had used Cherokee history, Cherokee land, and famous Cherokees as inspiration, members of the Eastern Band had never been considered integral to the drama.[76] Disputes between performers and the production staff recalled decades-long animosity.[77] Despite Bradley's enthusiasm and Beard-Moose's encouraging review, the 2006 production of *Unto These Hills . . . a Retelling* was not a crowd favorite. Eddie Swimmer, an Eastern Band member and director of the 2012 drama, noted that Geiogamah's production would have done very well as a touring production but that the new production was "way out there" for the drama's returning clientele. "The original idea," according to John Tissue, "was to update the Hunter script with more accurate historical and cultural references . . . but it never developed."[78]

Linda Squirrel, the 2012 CHA executive assistant, agreed: "It was a shock to everyone because it was so far different than what people were accustomed to seeing. It was a great *production*, but not really a play. It was visually stunning, but the story wasn't there." Thompson argued that the 2006 drama was "a fundamentally different way of relating to the past" that offered "an alternate history unbound from the personal memories of the audience and in opposition to the nostalgia that coats the genre of outdoor drama."[79] The varied explanations for audience reactions to *Unto These Hills . . . a Retelling* speaks volumes about the expectations of tourists, especially in regard to the long-outdated story of Cherokee history, culture, and removal that played out on stage in Cherokee.

Writing in 2013, Geiogamah contended that "effective and compelling theater is always just a step or two ahead of the zeitgeist of the community it serves," and his staging of *Unto These Hills . . . a Retelling* appears to have been exactly that.[80] However, this is not what the largely non-Native audience had grown accustomed to seeing every summer in the Mountainside Theatre. Geiogamah's powerful rejection of Indigenous disappearance and static Native culture pulled the depictions of the Eastern Band from the past to the present. The Indians in Geiogamah's drama were meaningful participants, not stoic, static representations of stereotypical Indians. The tensions and failures surrounding this reconceptualization are just as important as whether or not the drama was considered a "success."

Almost 10,000 more visitors came to *Unto These Hills . . . a Retelling* in 2006 than the year before. Beard-Moose's and Thompson's fieldwork both ended in 2006, leaving them unable to predict the subsequent changes that would follow the Geiogamah production. Still, their notes reveal a concerted attempt to rebrand and remarket the drama, even if the audience did not find it as appealing, as entertaining, or perhaps as authentic as the Hunter script. The incorporation of more Cherokee dances and the Cherokee language demonstrates how certain cultural elements of the Eastern Band now have a larger role in the drama revisions than in previous years.

Contestations over authenticity again dogged the show. Thompson highlights several instances where Geiogamah pushed past Cherokee constructs of authenticity for the sake of his aesthetic vision.[81] Thompson spent 2006 working at the CHA and was cast in Geiogamah's staging of *Unto These Hills*. He noted the mixed reactions of the Eastern Band and tourists, as some praised the retelling and others vehemently opposed it. Responses, for Thompson, fell into three categories: "First is ambivalence concerning the notion that the Cherokee should turn a commercial profit over the theatrical display of their culture and history. Second is the belief that the drama should instead answer to a higher calling of educating the American masses as to the tragedy of Indian removal. Third is anger when the desire to see that tragedy acted out on stage is deferred and replaced instead with an uplifting message of perseverance."[82] Thompson's analysis includes the audiences' ambivalence toward the fact that the Eastern Band profited from the drama. Brian Hosmer has advanced what he contends to be the "rather commonsensical proposition that Indian people could understand the workings of the capitalist market system and at least attempt some constructive adaptations," arguing that Indigenous participation in the marketplace simply lends itself toward political and economic independence.[83] One disgruntled audience member wrote to the CHA in 2006, bemoaning how the CHA had "commercialized and re-written the truth. . . . You should be embarrassed to charge money for this version of the history of the Cherokee people."[84]

At the same time, the Eastern Band was increasingly diversifying its interests, most notably with the casino. The purposeful decision to depict a narrative that offered proof of tribal and cultural survival directly opposed the declension narratives that had long defined popular accounts of Indigenous history. Geiogamah's version got mixed reviews, but he likely never intended to create a distinctly and stereotypically "authentic" outdoor drama. His efforts to showcase authentic Indianness unquestionably countered Hunter's focus on static narratives, and his insistence that American Indian participants be more than just anonymous faces in the crowd reveals the contestations behind decades of salvage tourism in Cherokee.

The years that followed the 2006 production were equally dramatic. While the Geiogamah version seems to have focused more on entertainment than portraying a specific, linear, historically dramatic narrative, the CHA moved in another direction for the 2007 production and brought in Pat Allee and Ben Hurst, who had been integral to the updates to the Museum of the Cherokee Indian.[85] *Unto These Hills*, as written by Allee and Hurst, premiered in 2007. "We tried to put the history back into it, but it was too much history," Swimmer said. "Man, if you went to the bathroom, you lost a decade."[86]

Tissue concurred, calling it "a very dry play." While the Hunter script was more drama than history and the Geiogamah show was more dance than history, "the pendulum swung the whole other way" with the Allee and Hurst production. "There was too much going on, and people couldn't follow it," added Squirrel. For Swimmer, Tissue, and Squirrel, the drama struggled to find the balance of history and culture, education and entertainment, and innovation and tradition. Attendance at the 2007 season of *Unto These Hills* was the second lowest since 2000, and nearly 14,000 *fewer* people saw the drama in 2007 versus 2006. The legacy of Hunter's production cast a long shadow over the CHA's tourist economy, which threatened to collapse under the weight of its early success and contemporary inability to mirror that triumph.

Nevertheless, the CHA was undeterred. Squirrel undertook the task of rewriting the show because she wanted to "correct the historical inaccuracies of the initial show, to incorporate Cherokee dances, and to aid in helping the local people be in the show as actors, not just standing in the crowd as they did for so many years."[87] She was not discouraged by the previous revisions that had not lived up to the high expectations of the CHA, the Eastern Band, and the tourist audiences. Using Hunter's script as an imperfect model, Squirrel set out to create the elusive *Unto These Hills* that would educate and entertain its audience while portraying the Eastern Band in a more historically and culturally accurate—and sensitive—manner. The rapid-fire, radical changes to *Unto These Hills* in the early years of the twenty-first century demonstrate numerous issues surrounding contemporary American Indian historical dramas. However, salvage tourism again appears in this moment of uncertainty. The CHA was only resuscitated through the intervention of the Eastern

A member of the 2012 *Unto These Hills* cast warms up backstage. Photograph by author.

Band.[88] After closing the Hunter production and attempting several radically different dramas on the heels of bankruptcy, the CHA had the unenviable task of salvaging its drama, its audience, its cast, and its role in the local and regional tourist economies.

Squirrel's script was loosely based on Hunter's original, but her script, like the two previous revisions, sought to incorporate more cultural elements and correct the historical embellishments. While many elements were similar, if not identical, Squirrel made conscious choices that situated the drama more deeply within the history of the Eastern Band as a people, not a commodity. Hunter and Squirrel's scripts were not, for the most part, drastically different, but Squirrel's ending is noteworthy. Selu and Kana'ti proudly speak of Cherokee survival through removal, through boarding schools, through the federal government's continued efforts to strip the Indians of their culture, language, and religion. As opposed to the generalized, Cold War–era rhetoric that proclaimed that the dream of the Cherokee—and the hope of all America—was "not that a man's skin is black, or red, or white. Choose the way of peace. Take all men as your brother," Squirrel's drama ended with an unmistakable display of Indigenous pride in their survival despite a horrific history.

The More Things Change, the More They Stay the Same: Returning to Cherokee

Of course, the 2017 decision to bring back the Hunter script meant I had to go back to Cherokee. I'd spent years poring over the old script and comparing it with the subsequent revisions, and now I'd actually get to see a version of Hunter's drama. Over the three-and-a-half-hour drive, the roads and the towns kept getting smaller and smaller as I got closer to Cherokee, but the roadsides became increasingly littered with billboards advertising every kind of tourism adventure one could hope for in western North Carolina. There were signs for guided fishing tours and river tubing. There were signs for orchards and fruit stands. There were signs for Santa's Land Fun Park & Zoo, a year-round, Christmas-themed amusement park in Cherokee.

But the region's long history of engagement with the tourism industry was most evident in the wide array of lodging opportunities. Some looked brand new (or recently remodeled), and others showed their age. Even more, like the El Camino Motel, with its "WINNERS STAY HERE" sign on the roadside message board, looked like they belonged in a Quentin Tarantino film. Harrah's Cherokee Casino Resort, though, overshadowed them all. The massive complex sprawled along Paint Town Road was under construction during another expansion. The woman at the check-in desk asked me if this was my first visit to the casino. When I replied that it was, she reached for a map. She drew what felt like an unending line, directing me to the appropriate elevator bay that would take me to my room. I politely took the map, as I had been born and raised in the Midwest, and stuck it in my back pocket once I was out of sight. I admitted defeat a few minutes later and pulled out the map. I'd underestimated the sheer scale of the resort, and I couldn't imagine what the maps would look like once the expansion was done.

The familiar roads brought me back to the Mountainside Theatre, and I sat down in the middle of the last row in the main section. Most of the other attendees had chosen to sit as close to the stage as possible, but I like to sit a little farther back. I did not expect a full house on a Wednesday night, but a generous estimate would say the lower section was about one-third to one-half full—and the upper section was empty. I had purchased a VIP ticket package for three attractions—*Unto These Hills*, the Museum of the Cherokee Indian, and the Oconaluftee Indian Village—so I munched on my free box of popcorn during the pre-show entertainment.

The show started at 8 P.M. The sun hadn't set quite yet, and a few light rain showers prompted audience members to scramble for umbrellas and plastic ponchos. The drama goes on rain or shine—only severe weather, like a thunder-storm, forces a performance to end prematurely. The revised version of Hunter's script is mostly faithful to the original. The drama begins with a dance, which is interrupted by Hernando de Soto and his men. De Soto demands gold and marches off stage. In the original version, one of de Soto's men shot and killed a nameless Indian character before the Spanish exit. That element is gone from the revision, so the bloodshed has to wait a few more scenes. The next scene moves 250 years in the future when Tecumseh travels south in hopes of persuading the Cherokee to join his cause. The Cherokee refuse, and Tecumseh storms off. Next, we meet Tsali as he leaves his wife, Wilani, on his way to war. It's now 1814, and the Cherokee have sided with the Americans. Here, in the Battle of Horseshoe Bend, Junaluska, another major figure in Cherokee history, leads the Cherokee faction. Junaluska and Tsali save Sam Houston from certain death, and the Cherokee argue with Andrew Jackson over the best plan of attack. The Cherokee prevail, and the battle begins. Jackson and Junaluska's combined forces defeat the British and, in one of many moments of dramatic irony in the production, Junaluska saves Jackson at the end of the battle. When the war is over, Tsali returns and meets his newborn daughter, Nundayeli.

The next scene draws on the Cherokee's "primitive past," to quote the voice-over. It features the Eagle Dance, long considered a cornerstone and one of the most controversial components of the drama. The drama moves to 1835 and the discovery of gold on Cherokee lands. A white woman who runs a local establishment protects a young Native boy from drunk miners. We meet Reverend Schermerhorn, who talks about buying lands from Cherokee to move the Indians west. The next scene moves us to Schermerhorn's meeting, and we meet Elias Boudinot, Yonaguska, his adopted son Will Thomas, the missionary Samuel Worcester, and his wife, Ann. The Cherokee and their allies challenge Schermerhorn, asking why their chiefs—including John Ross—are nowhere to be found. The meeting falls apart, and Schermerhorn's mission is left, for the moment at least, unaccomplished.

The drama moves to Washington, D.C., where Sam Houston, Junaluska, and John Ross have arrived for a meeting with Secretary of War Lewis Cass. After a lengthy argument with Cass and Jackson, an angry Junaluska says he should have let Jackson die at Horseshoe Bend. In the final scene before intermission, we see Nundayeli's traditional and church weddings. The ceremonial atmosphere is shattered by gunshots, and Major Davis enters with the order for removal. The lights go down, and the audience awkwardly claps—

not because of the scene's content, but because it's what audiences do at the end of the first act of a show.

It's nearly pitch black when the second act starts. The voice-over talks of equality. Major Davis orders the removal of several American men who claim they need to collect debts from the Cherokee. Davis gives Yonaguska money to give back to people even if they are not on the list. Lest the audience see Davis as a magnanimous character, he then says that any Cherokee found hiding in the hills will be shot on sight. A soldier beats Wilani. Tsali stabs him, and he and his sons run away. Men carry Wilani's body across the stage. Davis says those in the hills will be saved if Tsali and his sons come back. Junaluska and Will Thomas find Tsali and his sons, and they tell him about the service for Wilani and Davis's orders. The next scene is the funeral for Wilani. Mrs. Perkins is the last one there, and she hoots like an owl before she exits. Tsali and his sons run on. Tsali is the last to leave, and he gently places something on Wilani's body.

Worcester says that he and his wife will go with the Cherokee, who call him a "true friend to our people." The stockades open. Tsali and his sons enter, and it is agreed that he and his sons will be executed by his fellow Cherokee. Ann Worcester saves the youngest son. Tsali addresses his people. The Cherokee start singing "Amazing Grace" in Cherokee. Tsali kneels by his youngest son and gives him a necklace. Soldiers lead Tsali and his other two sons offstage. Boudinot kneels center stage and starts reciting Psalm 121—"I will lift up mine eyes unto these hills, from whence cometh my help"—in Cherokee as the voice-over repeats the psalm in English. Shots reverberate offstage. The removal procession starts as the voice-over continues with drumbeat and music under it. Soldiers yell at the Cherokee. A snow shower projects behind them. Shots, screams, and shouts ring out as soldiers violently force the Indians to continue walking. The last to cross is Junaluska, who carries the eternal flame.

The next scene moves to an 1841 meeting between Daniel Webster and President William Henry Harrison. Webster brings in Yonaguska and Will Thomas. Harrison is sick, and his doctor is also there. Webster asks for land and citizenship for the Cherokee, and Will Thomas explains his lease system. As a white man with the ability to buy land, he purchases what he can and then leases it to the Cherokee. Yonaguska asks the president to grant citizenship to the Cherokee and let them stay in North Carolina. Harrison says he will work to protect the Indians, but he cautions them that citizenship will take time. The voice-over tells us that Harrison would be dead two weeks later. The final scene moves back to the village where Tsali's daughter, Nundayeli, is about to have a baby. An aged Junaluska enters right before the baby is born, and he happily says that now Tsali has a grandchild. Junaluska, having returned to his homeland at the end of his life, says his good-byes. As the voice-over repeats Hunter's pleas of choosing the way of peace and taking all men as your brother, the lights dim, and the drama ends. The applause was louder at the end of the show, and the audience members started making their way toward the exits.

After the show, my VIP ticket packet entitled me to a backstage tour, which was led by a few effusive members of the cast. We started on stage left and made our way behind the stage until we came out on stage right. The cast members shared some anecdotes, showed us prop rooms and curtained-off quick-change rooms, and reminded us about the other CHA attractions we should check out while we were in Cherokee. With the drama and the tour over, I headed back to Harrah's. It was easy to find, even in the dark.

I have deliberately chosen not to offer a scene-by-scene analysis and historical breakdown. Even though it pains my historian's heart to say this, I have come to realize that history—meaning the events themselves—does not necessarily matter in outdoor drama. Smithers argues that Hunter sacrificed historical authenticity "for a more politically palatable version of the past," minimizing the role of key prominent Cherokee in a period of transformation.[89] Hunter's own correspondence suggests as much. In a 1996 letter to the Cherokee Heritage Center in Talequah, Oklahoma, Hunter addressed concerns over the *Trail of Tears* drama script he had written several decades earlier and that the Cherokee National Historical Society—which commissioned the first script—now wanted him to revise. The last line of his letter reads, "You must decide between history and show business."[90]

There are numerous historical inaccuracies in *Unto These Hills*, as we might expect. An oft-repeated quip about Hunter's research centers on Hunter's own joke that he spent more time researching *Unto These Hills* than any other script he ever wrote—and he spent five hours in the library at Chapel Hill.[91] In the scene with Tecumseh, for instance, Thompson, citing Raymond Hayes, argues that Hunter employs the method of "telescoping," meaning that the playwright "has taken a group of historical figures who could never have met one another and put them all together in the same place at the same time for reasons of dramaturgical expediency."[92] Akin to Paul Green's dramatic conclusion to *The Lost Colony*, the conflation of places, people, and events demonstrates Hunter's concerted effort to develop a story line that would evoke particular responses from his audience: pride in the Cherokee's alignment with the United States with an underlying note of sympathy based

Finished beadwork pieces adorn one of the stations at the Oconaluftee Indian Village in Cherokee, North Carolina. Photograph by author.

on the Cherokee's eventual fate. Marita Sturken argues that the "consumer culture of memory" helps affirm a culture of innocent victimhood, and Hunter's deliberate construction of the intended response from the audience highlights the continued focus on these notions of innocence.[93]

The next morning, I drove back over to the theater parking lot, which serves visitors to the Oconoluftee Indian Village during the day before serving drama audiences at night. I'd purchased my ticket ahead of time as part of the Gold VIP Triple Package experience, and I was told that a guided tour started every fifteen minutes if I wanted to wait for that. The informal tour group grew to about a dozen by the time our tour guide started. As we walked through the woods, we saw a series of stations. An older woman sat at the first one, working on a weaving. Our tour guide, who appeared to be a high school student from the area, explained the traditional methods and uses for weaving. At the next station, an older woman worked on beadwork. At the third station, an older woman was making pottery.

As our group moved from station to station, the women and the tour guide patiently and graciously answered questions from the audience. As a scholar of Native performance, it was hard to shake the feeling that this was a modern iteration of the world's fair exhibits that put Native people on display for non-Native audiences. However, Laura Peers reminds us that Native interpreters who work at historic sites often work within a tradition of cultural performance, one that "serves as a vehicle for Native agendas and creates an intercultural space which can be controlled by Native performers."[94] Several of the women said they had learned the crafts when they started working at the village, and they were able to sell their creations in the gift shop. As noted in the introduction, scholars have long grappled with the tensions between culture and commodification, between agency and coercion. Oconaluftee had opened in 1952, less than forty years after the first Cherokee Indian Fair and the year before House Concurrent Resolution 108, which codified Termination as the federal Indian policy of the era, went into effect. As in Pendleton, these performative constructs highlight the contestations and contradictions over federal policy and cultural economies. Both Annette Bird Saunooke and Heidi L. Nees, writing in the 2000s, reported instances where visitors at Oconaluftee repeatedly asked where the "*real* Indians" lived or were upset that cotton-clad employees weren't in "full traditional attire" based on their preconceived notions of Indianness.[95]

Our tour was interrupted by the "Time of War" performance staged in the middle of the village. The seven smaller seating areas covered three of the four sides of the small dirt stage, and all seven were nearly full. The short show, set in 1762, focused more on violence than on historical interpretation. But the audience saw a war dance, the villains met their demise, and everyone seemed to enjoy the short break from the educational elements of the village. The "Time of War" cast members worked at *Unto These Hills* or at the village, and some cast members immediately made their way to the food shack once they were out of costume.

There were a few other stations, including woodcarving, blowguns, and basket weaving. The guided tour ended there, and folks were free to wander around the rest of the village. Kids ran up and down the trails, giggling as their parents tried in vain to keep up. Some visitors doubled back to look at stations they had already seen, while others headed to the food shack and the gift shop. I bought a slice of pizza at the food shack and did some people watching—I mean, serious academic research—before heading to the gift shop. The gift shop was a mix of crafts and kitsch, but it seemed to promote the Native crafts over the magnets and T-shirts.

Oconaluftee is set in the 1760s, well before the violence and removal of the early nineteenth century. It's billed as "much more than just a place; it's living history."[96] As in Pendleton, the focus on the past was continually disrupted by the presence of and performances by Eastern Band members. My group's high school–aged tour guide, whether purposely or not, slid back and forth between past and present tense as he described the work done at each station. Their knowledge and skills, as Peers argues, not only strengthens cultural identity but, in the words of James Clifford, plays "a necessary role in current movements around identity and recognition."[97] More than six million people had gone through Oconaluftee by 2000.[98] However, as Beard-Moose contends, only a small portion of the millions of tourists who annually visit the region even make it to the village.[99]

It was a short drive from Oconaluftee to the Museum of the Cherokee Indian, which had opened in a log cabin on the Qualla Boundary in 1948.[100] The death of a local collector in the 1960s and the subsequent donation of an extensive collection, coupled with a 1958 fire at the previous location, prompted the decision to build a more permanent space dedicated to the museum.[101] It was renovated and expanded in 1998.[102] Like the Tamástslikt Cultural Institute in Pendleton, the Museum of the Cherokee Indian balances the past and the present, reminding its visitors that Cherokee people still live on their homelands. A middle school field trip filled most of the museum, but that didn't seem to bother the rest of the visitors. The first stop was a short video in a small auditorium, which led to more exhibits that chronologically followed thousands of years of Cherokee history. The last stop before the gift shop was a new exhibit called "People of the Clay: Contemporary Cherokee Potters." The exhibit opened in April 2019, and it featured more than 100 pieces of pottery created by over sixty Cherokee Nation and Eastern Band members from 1900 to the present.[103] The gift shop at the museum was similarly crowded. I'd bought myself a pair of earrings at the Oconaluftee gift shop, so I grabbed a T-shirt for my older son and a stuffed black bear for my younger one.

As I drove from Cherokee back to Atlanta, the road turned from slowly winding two-lane country roads to multiple-lane freeways. I wondered what the early twentieth-century tourism proponents in North Carolina would think about the contemporary tourist landscape. No longer under the thumb of the BIA and Indian agents, the Eastern Band, like the CTUIR, was diversifying its economy and its tourism industry. Courtney Lewis has highlighted the ingenuity of small business owners on the Qualla Boundary and the resulting "economic sovereignty," a term she uses to define the ability of Native nations to exercise sovereignty through economic self-determination.[104] From the Cherokee Cultural District to bookstores, coffee shops, and a funeral home dedicated to the specific needs of the Eastern Band, the Boundary's development underscores how economic sovereignty has shifted the meanings of salvage tourism and contemporary heritage tourism in Cherokee.[105]

What Does the Future Hold for the Eastern Band and *Unto These Hills*?

Chapter 3 examined the early omission of Eastern Band members from the cast of *Unto These Hills*. In recent years, the CHA, which has also undergone a shift toward Eastern Band leadership, has pushed to include more Native participants in all aspects of the production. Earlier portions of this chapter highlighted the difficulties the association faced in its initial reworking of the drama, such as auditioning Eastern Band members who had long been consigned to the background.[106] Akin to Happy Canyon, the descendants of those who were forcibly removed from their homelands reenact the horrors inflicted on their ancestors. Unlike Happy Canyon, whose authenticity came from its use of potentially charming and rustic characterizations of authentic Indigenous participants, *Unto These Hills* drew many of its early leading players from the Carolina Playmakers.[107] There was no trifecta of Native history told by Native people in a Native place in Cherokee. Rather, *Unto These Hills* organizers likely intended to create a more professional production by casting trained white actors in the leading roles. The drama in Cherokee was competing for the same audience as *The Lost Colony*, other dramas, and other tourist attractions. While earlier historical dramas had often attempted to utilize Indians in order to highlight the authentic nature of the production, the professional element of outdoor dramas pushed many Indians out of the casts.

Despite the renewed tribal interest and participation in the drama, attendance has declined significantly in recent years. Attendance dropped from nearly 64,000 in 2000 to less than 37,000 in 2011. However, the declining attendance and increasing casino activity may not be the death knell for *Unto These Hills*. According to Thompson, cultural performance in Cherokee remains important even as other enterprises such as Harrah's "have since eclipsed older attractions such as the drama, village, and museum." Thompson argues that the casino has become a key player in Cherokee cultural tourism as well as the Eastern Band's "ethnic renewal" by providing the financial resources that allow the tribal government to assume control of the representation of its history and culture.[108] The casino brought in $386 million in revenue in 2010 and continues to expand, and the Eastern Band continues to negotiate and advocate for its citizens. The Eastern Band opened an immersion school in 2004, and it pays the salaries for Cherokee language instructors in the school

A sign at the intersection of Drama Road and US-441 S (also known as Tsali Boulevard) points tourists toward the four main tourist attractions in Cherokee, North Carolina. Photograph by author.

districts in the surrounding three counties. There is now a residential treatment facility, a justice center, and a new school campus. The Eastern Band's renewal contract with Harrah's in 2011 included the purchase and maintenance of a $1.2 million MRI machine for the new Cherokee Indian Hospital.[109] The casino has not replaced heritage or historical tourism enterprises, and the economic diversification goes both ways.

Concentrating on how the Eastern Band has fought to resist Hunter's focus on salvage tourism allows us to see how tourism—from turn-of-the-century endeavors to *Unto These Hills* and Harrah's—has moved from something imposed upon the Eastern Band to something intrinsically tied to its sovereignty. In the early twentieth century, the Eastern Band had to rely more heavily on the small tourist niche created by the drama, "chiefing," and arts and crafts, and federal Indian policies dictated its economic potential and exercise of tribal sovereignty. Now, tribal gaming helps drive economic growth, and the Eastern Band can diversify its own economic interests and tourism practices.

The casino, then, has effectively altered the function of the drama. "We are telling our story," Eddie Swimmer told me in a 2012 interview. "Our history didn't end with the Trail of Tears. We're still here, we're still strong."[110]

The various versions of *Unto These Hills* that have trod the dirt stage at the Mountainside Theatre since 1950 underscore the fickle nature of the region's tourism industry. The next chapters turn to Chillicothe, where, like in Pendleton, the regional drama has remained a steady source of income for the drama's organization and the surrounding area. Ohio's implementation of outdoor dramas in the latter part of the twentieth century—some of which have been more successful than others—highlights not only the continued resonance of outdoor drama but how performances of Indianness are still seen as viable tourism endeavors.

CHAPTER FIVE

No Longer a Wooden Indian
from the History Books

Tourism, Tecumseh, and American Nationalism

Every part of this soil is sacred in the estimation of my people. Every hillside, every valley, every plain and grove, has been hallowed by some sad or happy event in days long vanished. The very dust upon which you now stand responds more lovingly to their footsteps than to yours, because it is rich with the blood of our ancestors and our bare feet are conscious of the sympathetic touch. Even the little children who lived here and rejoiced here for a brief season will love these somber solitudes and at eventide they greet shadowy returning spirits.
—Attributed to Chief Seeathl. Used on the back cover of the
1986 souvenir program for *Blue Jacket*

In the summer of 1973, playwright and journalist Jack Zierold and his wife drove from West Virginia to south central Ohio to catch a performance of a new outdoor drama. In a letter to Mark Sumner, director of the Institute of Outdoor Drama at the University of North Carolina at Chapel Hill, Zierold offered his take on the show. "The overall impression," Zierold wrote, "is— GOOD SHOW!" He thought the dialogue flowed nicely and that the playwright knew his subject well. "So far as the eye and ear are concerned," he continued, "this is probably the most beautiful outdoor drama I've seen. The score is magnificent. The departure of the tribe in Act I is moving and spectacular. (No pun intended.)"[1]

Zierold and his wife had driven all the way to Chillicothe, about an hour and a half straight south of Columbus, to see a drama based on the life and death of the Shawnee leader Tecumseh. Press releases and promotional materials had promised audience members "one of the most awesome live spectacles available to an American audience," noting that the dramatic apex of the production, the Battle of Tippecanoe, would involve more than 100 actors on seven stages on three sides of the audience, as well as three artillery pieces and simulated shell explosions.[2] The drama, simply called *Tecumseh!*, was the product of six years of intensive research and construction by members and contractors of the Scioto Society, Inc., a nonprofit organization founded in Chillicothe in 1970. The society's first goal, as a group dedicated to "cultural,

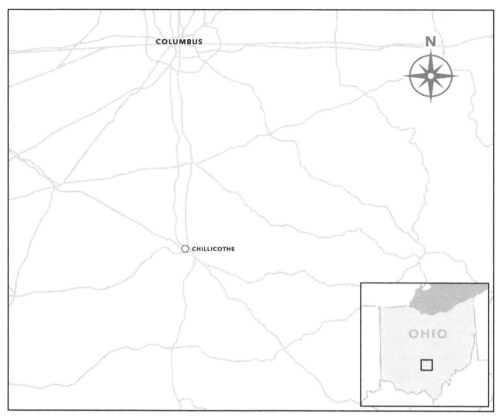

Chillicothe, Ohio. Map by Josiah Donat.

historical, educational and economic development for Chillicothe and the tri-county area along the Scioto River Valley," was to establish an outdoor drama to draw tourists to the region.[3] Members of the Scioto Society, like Al Heierman, initially thought they would do a drama about Thomas Worthington, an early nineteenth-century promoter of Ohio statehood. But another member had read Allan W. Eckert's *The Frontiersmen*, one of the books in Eckert's "Winning of America" series, and suggested asking Eckert to write the drama's script. First published in 1967, *The Frontiersmen* was a bloody, bitter epic of the battles between settlers and Indians over the lands that would become Ohio, prominently featuring Simon Kenton and, later in the book, Tecumseh. Eckert, who had never attended an outdoor drama, eventually agreed to write it. He had never heard of Worthington and suggested Tecumseh instead, using his epic novel as a starting point. According to Heierman, Eckert thought Tecumseh "was one of the three greatest men that ever lived: Jesus Christ,

Muhammad, and Tecumseh."[4] Tapped to write the script in 1971, Eckert believed that an outdoor drama "near where Tecumseh once lived would be the proper setting to retell the story of, perhaps, the greatest Indian in American history."[5]

While early reviews of the production were mostly favorable, Zierold struggled mightily with several components of the drama. He asked, perhaps rhetorically, "What makes Tecumseh so great?" He called Tecumseh "too goody-goody right off the bat. . . . He was a fine human being, but so is the local Scoutmaster." He noted that the onstage Indians proclaimed Tecumseh wise beyond his years, then rejected every piece of advice he gave them. "At everything he tries," Zierold bemoaned, "he fails." Zierold thought the drama had no resolution, noting that there was no applause when the show ended. When the house lights finally came up, signaling the end of the show, the audience "just got up and left." One section of Zierold's letter is particularly telling: "When a series of failures prepares a man for a great triumph, as in the case of Lincoln, you have drama. When a series of successes leads to a man's downfall, as in the case of Hitler, you have drama. When a series of failures only leads to catastrophe, you have only history." He liked the show, but felt cheated. "Something was missing," he mused. "As in all history, there was no resolution. Perhaps the flaw lay in Tecumseh's own life."[6]

My initial question when researching this drama was exactly that: why Tecumseh? Why, in the 1970s, would an organization dedicated to increasing tourism in the region stage a drama about an Indian who sought to overthrow the fledgling United States—especially in an era marked by radical protests by groups like the American Indian Movement (AIM)? For its fourth season in 1976, a season marked by the celebration of the American bicentennial, the Scioto Society published a press release that read, in part:

> You are no longer in the twentieth century. You are with Chiksika, the Shawnee warrior, as he leads his younger brother Tecumseh into his first battle! For the next two hours, you experience the life and death of the greatest Indian Chief ever to inhabit this continent—Tecumseh.
>
> For the first time, you fully understand the young Shawnee warrior's vision of glory. Tecumseh is no longer a wooden Indian from the history books. He lives and breathes and threatens. He threatens from strength.
>
> Tecumseh wants only what is his, but his red brothers have greater plans. Under the dire circumstances in which the Americans find themselves, if 50,000 warriors are unleashed, the whites will cave in like a house of cards.[7]

Tecumseh is, at first glance, an odd hero for an outdoor drama in Ohio. The key lies not in who Tecumseh was, but in how the drama used his life and his mission to reinterpret an important moment in American history. Happy Canyon premiered in the 1910s, an age when Pendleton sought to salvage itself as the pinnacle of the West. *Unto These Hills* opened in the 1950s, an age when the Cold War forced the nation to salvage its image as the bastion of democracy against the rise of Communism. *Tecumseh!* debuted in the 1970s, an age when the proud narrative of American nationalism had been simultaneously challenged by defeat in Vietnam and celebrated through a myriad of political, military, and culturally focused bicentennial events—and when the Cold War was far from over. Just as they had for decades, towns across the nation turned to annual performances—and, often, Indians—as a means of salvaging their economies, their histories, and even themselves. *Tecumseh!* was not alone. The Scioto Society's production was one of three outdoor dramas that opened in Ohio between 1970 and 1982, and all three centered on Native history. *Trumpet in the Land* opened in New Philadelphia, Ohio, in 1970 and tells the story of David Zeisberger and his Moravian Christian Lenape Indian followers, ninety-six of whom were massacred by a Pennsylvania militia in 1782 in what is known as the Gnadenhutten Massacre. *Tecumseh!* opened in Chillicothe in 1973. A third drama, *Blue Jacket*, which opened in Xenia, Ohio, in 1982 and closed in 2007, claimed that Blue Jacket was actually a white man named Marmaduke Van Swearingen who had been captured by the Shawnee in the 1770s. The emergence of three Native-focused outdoor dramas in one state in less than fifteen years illuminates the strength of salvage tourism and narratives of Indianness, particularly in an era marked by turbulence and violence across the country and around the globe. The oil embargo, for instance, began shortly after the metaphorical curtain closed on the first season of *Tecumseh!*.

The Institute of Outdoor Drama (IOD), now known as the Institute of Outdoor Theatre, holds the records of eighty-one productions that opened from the 1960s through the 1980s, including the three in Ohio. As a caveat, of course, these are only the records of those dramas whose organizers were in contact with the IOD. Other organizations simply contacted the IOD for advice, some even paid for feasibility studies, and others likely just had a go at creating a drama without reaching out to the IOD. The continued rise of outdoor dramas—particularly those that relied on local and regional history coupled with local and regional Indians—was a means of capitalizing on and reckoning with the past. In Ohio, this reckoning takes on a new meaning when it comes to *Trumpet in the Land*, *Tecumseh!*, and *Blue Jacket*. All three high-

A 1971 painting by W. G. Cassill of the proposed Sugarloaf Mountain Amphitheatre, Chillicothe, Ohio. Courtesy of the Ross County Historical Society, McKell Library, Chillicothe, Ohio (1995.204.01).

lighted a violent age of American history when the old Northwest was the battleground of the frontier.

From Pendleton and Cherokee to Chillicothe, Xenia, and New Philadelphia, aspirational images of Indians were co-opted and commodified through pageants and dramas. Eckert's script for *Tecumseh!*, like Hunter's script for *Unto These Hills* and Green's script for *The Lost Colony*, played fast and loose with the truth, but productions like *Tecumseh!* were not created in order to merely depict historical events. Instead, these moments in history—and the historical persons involved—were repackaged and repurposed as tourist-centered tributes to an imagined American identity. The drama in Chillicothe simultaneously has everything and nothing to do with Tecumseh. Instead, it celebrates *American* history, identity, and nationalism—even as we could argue that there is nothing more American than Indians. Tecumseh's 1813 defeat and death in the Battle of the Thames during the War of 1812 allowed the Scioto Society and its audiences to safely memorialize and commemorate Tecumseh in the context of nationalism and patriotism.

There are several reasons behind the decision to focus on *Tecumseh!* rather than either or both of the other two Ohio dramas. The likely permanent closing of *Blue Jacket* is one factor. Additionally, the content of and contestations over *Tecumseh!* more closely mirror the current productions in Cherokee and Pendleton. By examining how Tecumseh's mission becomes reimagined and reinterpreted every summer in Chillicothe, we see how this history and his life and mission become co-opted and corrupted in a very particular manner. The Scioto Society can celebrate his dream and mourn his passing *because of*—not in spite of—the fact that his mission did not succeed. Commemoration is not about the past. It's about the present, and large-scale tourism endeavors require something marketable and memorable. In a press release published in the weeks leading up to the drama's 1973 premiere, Eckert noted that two major characters shared the limelight when he wrote *The Frontiersmen*, Simon Kenton and Tecumseh: "Yet, even though what I wrote about Tecumseh was a fairly comprehensive story of his life, to me it was not quite enough, because my respect for him has become virtually boundless. I wanted very much to do more about his life. I wanted somehow to make people more aware of what a truly incredible human being he was."[8] This production simultaneously seems like the strangest drama and the one that makes the most sense. As these next two chapters will show, the Ohio dramas of the 1960s through the 1980s—but most notably *Tecumseh!*—both depend upon and disengage from one of the bloodiest and most brutal parts of American history in order to fulfill their goals.

The Old Northwest: The Epicenter of a Struggle for Empire

The Ohio backcountry was home to some of the fiercest fighting before, during, and after the American Revolution—it was, quite literally, the American frontier. Eric Hinderaker has called the Ohio Valley a "crucible of imperial experimentation" as Britain, France, the United States, and Native nations battled for control in the region.[9] Surveyors, settlers, and soldiers streamed onto Indigenous lands as Native nations and colonial forces alternately made allies and enemies of each other. The Seven Years' War and its North American component, the French and Indian War (1754–63), shattered the already shaky bonds between the British and the Native nations in the region.[10] The treaty that ended the war did not, in fact, signal the end of war. The French defeat meant that British colonists and commanders no longer felt obligated to accommodate Indians, turning instead to military force.[11]

Pontiac's Rebellion began a few months after the Treaty of Paris was signed in February 1763. Like many wars, Pontiac's was neither an isolated event nor one with a sudden impetus. Indians' anger toward increasingly restrictive British policies, particularly those implemented by British general Jeffrey Amherst, had led to a religious revival headed by a Delaware prophet named Neolin.[12] Natives in the *pays d'en haut* (an area generally considered what is now the Great Lakes region), which had formerly been claimed by France, collectively rose up against the British and their policies, laying siege to a number of forts in the region.[13] In response, a group of frontiersmen in western Pennsylvania known as the Paxton Boys massacred peaceful Susquehannock Indians at a village called Conestoga, bringing 1763 to a bloody end.[14]

Treaties were made and broken, and the violence perpetrated against Indians and settlers continued nearly unabated. The 1768 Treaty of Fort Stanwix tried to bring peace to the region by forcing the Shawnee to give up their hunting rights in Kentucky, and it is also considered the first land cession by Ohio Indians.[15] Tecumseh was born near what is now Chillicothe that same year. In the spring of 1774, Virginia frontiersmen, led by militia captain Michael Cresap, brutally murdered several Mingo Indians, including several relatives of a chief called Logan. Logan was known to be on good terms with whites in the region, but the deaths of his relatives in the Yellow Creek Massacre forever altered the Native-white relations in the area.[16] Several parties of Indians attacked settlers in the area, and these events sparked Dunmore's War of 1774. The short and somewhat obscure military campaign, named for the royal governor of Virginia who headed it, had one major engagement, the Battle of Point Pleasant.[17] The Indian confederacy, led by Shawnee chief Cornstalk, attacked the Virginia militia but was eventually forced to retreat and sign a treaty. Tecumseh's father, Puckshinwa, was killed during the battle, leaving his older brother, Chiksika, in charge of Tecumseh's military upbringing.

Dunmore's War broke out on the eve of the American Revolution, and most of the public attention has gone to the Revolution. Scholars like Hinderaker, Peter Mancall, R. Douglas Hurt, and Colin Calloway, among others, have demonstrated how critical the Ohio frontier was to the shaping of the new nation. The frontier war, as Hinderaker argues, overlapped with the Revolution but outlasted it by more than a decade.[18] The 1782 Gnadenhutten Massacre predates the end of the American Revolution, and the battles raged on the Ohio frontier long after the ink dried on the Treaty of Paris. Delegates from the Iroquois Confederacy signed a second Treaty of Fort Stanwix in 1784, much to the dismay of the tribes who were native to Ohio, including the Shawnee and the Delaware. Many refused to abide by the terms of the treaty, even as their lands were summarily lumped into the Northwest Territory under the 1787 Northwest Ordinance. Tensions still ran high in the region, as shown by the decade-long Northwest Indian War that started in 1785. The

Native forces, led by Little Turtle of the Miamis, Blue Jacket of the Shawnees, and Buckongahelas of the Delawares, landed a stunning victory in the 1791 Battle of the Wabash, a battle that author Landon Y. Jones has called "the most decisive defeat in the history of the American military."[19]

The war continued, and an American victory at the 1794 Battle of the Fallen Timbers forced the Ohio Indians to cede much of their territory. Ohio became the seventeenth state in the Union in 1803, a decade before Tecumseh would die at the Battle of the Thames. In the years after his death, the story of his life—but, more importantly, his death—would catapult Tecumseh into history as a legendary, near-mythical figure. His brother Tenskwatawa, also known as the Prophet, has been roundly condemned in both history and popular culture as a bitter, weak-hearted coward, one whose power and influence could never match that of his dead brother. However, as chapter 6 shows, the myths surrounding Tecumseh and Tenskwatawa obscure the truth behind their dreams and desires of pan-Indian unity.

This snippet of Ohio's saga, while incomplete, highlights the friction on the frontier and the hostility of the state's history. Rob Harper argues that escalating frontier conflicts, often encouraged or organized by colonial states, led to increased cycles of violence and retaliation in the region in the revolutionary era, including the massacre at Gnadenhutten.[20] In the latter half of the twentieth century and in a span of less than two decades, these historical moments became the basis for three different outdoor dramas staged in towns located within three hours of each other. From the 1960s through the 1980s, the members of the Ohio Outdoor Historical Drama Association, Inc. (*Trumpet in the Land*), the Scioto Society, Inc. (*Tecumseh!*), and First Frontier, Inc. (*Blue Jacket*), all turned toward this tumultuous period in American history for their respective tourist enterprises. And, perhaps more critically, all turned toward the Indians that helped shape this period in order to best create, market, and benefit from their productions.

Indians and Identity in the Bicentennial Moment

As in Pendleton and Cherokee, *Tecumseh!* emerged during another shift in federal Indian policy and as part of a longer history of commemoration. The biggest difference in Ohio centers on how drama organizers and civic celebrations engaged—or, perhaps more to the point, did *not* engage—with Indians and Indianness. The Shawnee were among the Native nations forced out of the lower Great Lakes throughout the first half of the nineteenth century.[21] With Indians removed from the physical environment, parades, pageants, and other civic celebrations employed what James Buss calls a narrative of "anti-conquest."[22] Chillicothe was the first capital of Ohio, and the state's centennial in 1903 was cause for celebration. Even though the city did not have the honor of hosting the Ohio Centennial Exposition, the state's General Assembly allotted $10,000 for a celebration in Chillicothe.[23] Cincinnati had hosted the Centennial Exposition of the Ohio Valley and Central States in 1888, and the celebrations continued as each state reached its centennial. In the 170-page official guide for the 1888 exposition, Indians were rarely included. There were some references to the Smithsonian's Section of Ethnology Exhibit, "Indian troubles" that had briefly stifled settlement in Cincinnati, and "specimens of work" from students at Carlisle, Haskell, and the Santee Agency, but these were overshadowed by the celebratory atmosphere.[24]

The 1916 Pageant of Indiana, staged in honor of the state's centennial, included a cast of thousands and an audience that reached the tens of thousands.[25] However, as they did in countless historical pageants throughout the medium's existence, the Indians simply faded away, nowhere to be seen in the remainder of the pageant. The onstage erasure of Indians in these early endeavors was, as Buss contends, a narrative of conquest that underplayed the very action of conquest.[26] From local celebrations and state centennials to expositions and world's fairs, the states in the region relied on writing violence and forced removal out of their celebratory scripts.[27] In 1938, a pageant in Marietta, Ohio, served as the culmination of a lengthy celebration of the 150th anniversary of the first white settlement in the Northwest Territory.[28] In 1953, the same year House Concurrent Resolution 108 enacted Termination, Paul Green's drama *The 17th Star* helped usher in the celebration of Ohio's sesquicentennial. Performed every night for nearly two weeks, the drama portrayed the state's past in what John Bodnar calls "terms that made it appear understandable, and the progressive evolution of modern Ohio and the United States was made to appear inevitable."[29]

These narratives of anti-conquest were well established by the time Ohio's trio of outdoor dramas premiered. In the latter half of the twentieth century, shifts in federal Indian policies and a continued surge of activist movements like AIM collided with local, state, and national plans for the country's bicentennial. Tammy S. Gordon has shown that planners in Philadelphia, for instance, had their sights set on the bicentennial as early as the mid-1950s. Boston, Washington, D.C., and Miami also pushed for the honor of hosting a bicentennial exposition, spending millions of dollars on feasibility studies, party planning, and promotional materials.[30] Another world's fair, akin to Philadelphia's 1876 centennial and countless others across the nation throughout the years, could showcase current accomplishments and provide a road map for the future.[31]

While the idea of a world's fair was not unique to such a momentous occasion, M. J. Rymsza-Pawlowska has argued that the degree to which the past became central to contemporary culture in the 1970s is noteworthy because, in earlier decades, "Americans had been inspired by the future, not the past."[32] This "new nostalgia" was largely due to the unrest and upheavals of the 1960s, coupled with the disappointments of Vietnam, which had left many Americans disenchanted with the present.[33] The rise of historically driven engagements in the 1970s mirrored how historical pageantry had arisen around the turn of the century amid the country's large-scale industrialization.[34] The patriotic fervor that developed as the bicentennial neared had not happened in the 1960s. There were no grand plans to celebrate the Civil War because, as Gordon contends, the Revolution was a more palatable conflict: "there were no unreformed Loyalists to be offended by the glorification of the patriot victory, and the events of the late eighteenth century were an additional hundred years in the past."[35]

The middle of the century also saw the continued development of living history museums across the country. Colonial Williamsburg had opened in the 1930s, and living history had become a major social, cultural, and economic component of how Americans sought to engage with the past by the 1970s.[36] In Ohio, a man named Erie Sauder decided to build a museum in the northwest part of the state to show how the area was settled, and he wanted future generations to "appreciate the difficult conditions early European settlers faced when they came to the area." He bought a handful of acres in early 1971, and the Sauder Farm and Craft Village opened in the summer of 1976. The Village is now the largest living history destination in the state, and it continues to expand. Its "Natives and Newcomers" addition opened in 2003—just in time for the state's bicentennial.[37]

Sauder was not alone in his nostalgia for the past. Chapter 1 described Ezra Meeker's west-to-east journeys in the early twentieth century, and the bicentennial inspired a similar stunt. The Wagon Train Pilgrimage started at five points in the West and spent a year following historical wagon trails back to Valley Forge, Pennsylvania. Rymsza-Pawlowska contends that it was one of the most heavily funded Bicentennial programs, drawing over $200,000 from the American Revolution Bicentennial Administration, and it also garnered state support and corporate sponsors. It was yet another program that celebrated American exceptionalism, invoking what Rymsza-Pawlowska calls "a triumphant history of accomplishment that was national in scope."[38] As the wagon trains rolled east, the narrative its organizers had woven about affirming "American" values and accomplishments started to unravel. Organizers tried to say that the wagoneers had "smoked a peace pipe" with Native people in Washington State, but members of the Stillaguamish tribe had actually threatened to block the wagon train's route as part of their attempt to gain recognition from the government. Another story circulated that organizers had asked other Indians in Washington to "stage an ambush" of the train as it traveled through their lands, but the tribe refused.[39] Members of the Wagon Train also professed that they were "plenty scared" when they made their way through the Dakotas, mostly because of AIM's takeover of Wounded Knee in 1973.[40]

The Wagon Train's encounters with American Indians across the country was representative of how many Natives felt about the impending bicentennial. Tammy Gordon contends that activists had had time to reflect on the "heady, direct-action days" of the civil rights movement and the subsequent movements it inspired by the mid-1970s.[41] The rise of AIM and the official end of Termination policy, enacted by the 1975 Indian Self-Determination and Education Assistance Act, brought Indians into the national consciousness and conscience. From the Indians of All Tribes' 1969–71 takeover of Alcatraz to AIM's 1972 takeover of the Bureau of Indian Affairs (BIA) in DC and the 1973 standoff at Wounded Knee in South Dakota, Indians were more visible in the public eye than they had been in years.[42]

AIM was born in Minneapolis, Minnesota, in 1968, largely in response to police treatment of Natives in the city's Franklin Avenue neighborhood.[43] Many of AIM's founders had spent time in boarding schools and prisons as federal policies kept pushing Indians off reservations and into cities.[44] By the early 1970s, AIM established itself as a radicalizing and polarizing force for Native resistance. It helped create survival schools for Native students in Minneapolis and St. Paul, but it became known for its protests and what some considered its proclivity for violence.[45] AIM members staged protests at Mount Rushmore and Plymouth Rock in 1970. After Raymond Yellow Thunder's murder in Gordon, Nebraska—just across the state line from the Pine Ridge Reservation in South Dakota—in February 1972, AIM drew almost 1,500 Indians to Gordon to protest Yellow Thunder's death and the town's treatment of local Natives.[46] Over the next few years, AIM's rise to prominence forced the government to acknowledge Native issues.

Even as AIM fanned the flames of Indigenous resistance across the nation, the idea and the ideals of Indianness could be neatly aligned with the patriotism and nationalism of the bicentennial age. Philip Deloria argues that the idea of "playing Indian" was, as Jodi Byrd notes, "endemic to the counterculture

Promotional photographs from 1975 depicting actor Mel Cobb, who spent several seasons playing Tecumseh in *Tecumseh!*. Courtesy of the Ross County Historical Society, McKell Library, Chillicothe, Ohio (1995.204.17).

movements" of the 1960s and 1970s.[47] Whenever white Americans confronted crises of identity, according to Deloria, some "inevitably turned to Indians."[48] The Round-Up and Happy Canyon had emerged in an era that called for the exclusion of Asian immigrants, and *Unto These Hills* had opened amid growing contestations over civil rights. As more and more underrepresented populations pushed for equal rights and protest movements kept gaining traction, the Scioto Society's use of Tecumseh—or, at least, Eckert's version of Tecumseh—starts to make sense. As Alfred Cave wryly notes, Tecumseh was the white man's ideal Indian: "Tecumseh is easily idealized, for he was indeed handsome, heroic, generous, and, after 1813, dead."[49] Audience members could see themselves in a man like Tecumseh. They could imagine themselves as noble and virtuous, putting a love of country above all else, and perhaps even making the greatest sacrifice. As in Pendleton and Cherokee, the productions in Ohio—and especially *Tecumseh!*—were designed to give their audiences a comfortable and reassuring respite.

Cave and other scholars have demonstrated the near-immediate mythologizing of Tecumseh in the wake of his death. By 1820, in a push to name the state's capital after him, the *Indiana Centinel* (*sic*) proclaimed that "every school boy in the Union" knew Tecumseh was "a statesman, a warrior, and a patriot."[50]

William Emmons published a play titled *Tecumseh: Or, The Battle of the Thames, A National Drama, In Five Acts* in 1836. After Tecumseh's onstage demise, another character called him "the mighty man Tecumseh! rude, [*sic*] yet great—most towering Chief that ever hatchet raised against the white man."[51] In his 1841 biography of Tecumseh, Benjamin Drake painted Tenskwatawa as "a vain, loquacious and cunning man, of indolent habits and doubtful principles," while Tecumseh's "moral and intellectual qualities" put him "above the age and the race in which his lot was cast."[52] In the two centuries since Tecumseh's demise, everyone from playwrights, painters, and politicians to scholars, sculptors, and the Scioto Society have co-opted his life, his mission, and his death. The Scioto Society combined the regional focus on commemoration, like the 1916 Indiana centennial pageant, with Tecumseh's infamy to create one of the most successful outdoor dramas in history.

"The Call to Arms for Good-against-Evil": The Genesis of *Trumpet in the Land*

Trumpet in the Land is Ohio's oldest and longest-running outdoor drama, penned by none other than Paul Green, the author of *The Lost Colony*, *The 17th Star*, and a number of other popular outdoor dramas. In the summer of 1964, a United Methodist minister named Arthur Kirk traveled to see *Unto These Hills* in Cherokee, North Carolina, and *The Stephen Foster Story* in Bardstown, Kentucky. By January of 1965, he had sent letters to both general managers asking for information on organizing and producing an outdoor historical drama. Both managers suggested he contact Mark Sumner at the Institute of Outdoor Drama, which he did. By September, Kirk had joined forces with Jack Hill, a resource development agent in the Dover, Ohio, area, to form a committee for the drama. The committee asked for an IOD feasibility study in the spring of 1966, and Sumner brought a team to town later that year. The favorable results gave rise to the Ohio Outdoor Historical Drama Association, Inc. (OOHDA), and Rachel Redinger became the president. Green agreed to write the script in 1967.[53]

As for the story line, the OOHDA turned to a dark moment in the state's past:

> Here, today, in the valley of the Tuscarawas we can visit the restored historic Schoenbrunn Mission where Ohio's first church and school were built. We can walk on the very ground of Gnadenhutten where 96 Christian Indians were brutally massacred by frontiersmen, and stand where valiant soldiers gave their lives to hold Fort Laurens.

Here in this beautiful valley, the great Chief Netawotwes and his War Chief White Eyes dreamed of an Indian commonwealth nation. David Zeisberger worked to build a world of peace for men both red and white, and Simon Girty conspired with the treacherous Mingo Indians.[54]

The OOHDA worked hard to set itself apart as a destination for tourists. An undated fund-raising brochure noted that twenty-two major outdoor dramas in the country were, "without exception, of both economic and cultural value to the areas in which they are located." The drama would be one of many tourist draws, including historic sites and the Pro Football Hall of Fame.

In the OOHDA's October 1967 newsletter, Redinger noted that tourism did not require increased taxes for building schools and other facilities that permanent residents required. Redinger and the OOHDA had to work to convince their neighbors, though.[55] Sumner was also frustrated with the Columbus-area disinterest in the drama. In an April 1970 letter to Doug McIntire, the drama's general manager, Sumner wrote, "The venal press (God, forgive, since I grew up on newspapers) has a way of ignoring or chopping to pieces projects in other areas of their states." Since newspapers were not interested in promoting the drama, Sumner suggested reaching out to travel editors and entertainment editors.[56] Amphitheater construction continued, as did Green's progress on the script, and the drama opened in the summer of 1970.

Redinger was disappointed in the first season's attendance and financials. In a letter to Sumner, she wrote, "We fell far short of what we needed, I know. . . . Our promotion fell far short. It does not pay to believe you are a success—until you are."[57] Redinger laid part of the blame on McIntire, suggesting that he was lulled into complacency by tourists who sought out the drama instead of working to pull tourists *to* the drama. She also noted that she had not had the time or the energy to do any more than she already had, and she hoped that Sumner could offer some additional advice. Sumner shared her disappointment. "You were aware of the publicity situation three months before opening," he responded. "I think the pressure of finishing the amphitheatre, hiring the company, and the illness just ate us up."[58]

Trumpet in the Land overcame its early troubles, and by 1971 the drama was in better shape. Sumner sent a letter to the governor with suggestions for state support. Even though the drama had suffered from the pressure of its opening deadline the year before, it was now competitive with similar major productions and had "every chance of long-term success provided wide range promotion of the show is accomplished."[59] Based on a 1970–95 attendance comparison for the three Ohio dramas, *Trumpet in the Land* would never enjoy the same audience numbers as *Tecumseh!*. Its attendance would hold steady from between 25,000 and 35,000 annually, while *Tecumseh!* saw much more dramatic shifts: attendance started at about 35,000 in 1973, jumped to 85,000 in 1981, fell to 50,000 in 1985, and rose to 85,000 in 1993. *Blue Jacket* would linger somewhere in between.[60]

First Frontier, Inc.: The Rise and Fall of *Blue Jacket*

In 1975, a retired Greene County, Ohio, schoolteacher named Dotty Martin, along with her husband, Don, attended an outdoor drama on a trip to North Carolina. Dotty Martin, intrigued by the drama's "fascinating display of local history" and its sheer power and scale, got in touch with Rusty Mundell, who was producing *Tecumseh!* over in Chillicothe.[61] Martin planned to have her drama focus on frontiersman Simon Kenton, but further research showed that most of Kenton's exploits occurred somewhere other than Greene County.[62] By 1978, First Frontier, Inc. became a nonprofit devoted to Martin's dream of a major outdoor historical drama "depicting the deep rooted history of Southwest Ohio."[63] The nonprofit received a study grant from the Ohio Arts Council in the summer of 1978 and planned for a feasibility study by the IOD.[64] A few days later, the *Xenia Daily Gazette* announced First Frontier's plan to buy county land at Caesar's Ford Park. The county commission was debating whether to use the land for a landfill or an outdoor drama, but an EPA study showed the area would not work well for a landfill.[65]

Opening on the heels of *Trumpet in the Land* and *Tecumseh!*, one might suggest that Ohio had enough outdoor dramas without the addition of *Blue Jacket*—and, indeed, that the country might have had its fill of dramas by the latter portion of the twentieth century. But the IOD holds the records of nearly two dozen dramas that premiered in the 1980s alone. The *Xenia Daily Gazette* noted that, despite increasing gasoline costs, attendance at outdoor dramas grew from 700,000 in 1965 to nearly two million in 1980. According to Marion Waggoner, the general manager for *Tecumseh!*, "What we have experienced here is an increase in the number of persons who wish to stay closer to home when they vacation." He continued, suggesting that, even though people were staying closer to home for vacations, they were still taking advantage of tourism enterprises like outdoor dramas.[66] Rusty Mundell, who helped bring *Tecumseh!* to life, wrote the script for *Blue Jacket*.[67] The drama depicted "the epic struggle between the Shawnee and the frontiersmen," a struggle the Shawnee were destined to lose.[68] Mundell's plot centered on the "remarkable story of a white man who was adopted into the Shawnee Nation and later became war chief of the Shawnee. The only white man ever to do so."[69] In the early twenty-first century, a team of scientists used DNA from six Blue Jacket descendants and four Van Swearingen descendants to conclude that "the popular story surrounding his relatedness to Dutch settlers is without merit."[70] Mundell and First Frontiers, Inc. soldiered on.

The drama opened in the summer of 1982 to less-than-favorable reviews. Critic Gary Gregory called the 1982 production "a bulky outdoor drama," and his 1983 report called the three-hour run time "a bit too much to ask of an audience when there is so little there to interest them."[71] Almost 50,000 people saw *Blue Jacket* in its first year, setting a record for the first-season showing of an outdoor drama, but the drama would not see attendance numbers like that again for nearly a decade.[72] In 1983, Hal Lipper wrote, "You no longer need a degree in American Indian history to follow *Blue Jacket*," although he also contended, "Clearly, *Blue Jacket* is the type of outdoor drama that only a historian could love after three viewings. Last Friday was my third visit and I can't say the production has grown enough to hold my interest."[73] Lipper struggled with the script, echoing decades-earlier concerns from *Unto These Hills* author Kermit Hunter. "Historical conflict is not necessarily stimulating drama," he noted, "and conscientious historians don't necessarily make successful playwrights." Dayton writer Richard Schwarze agreed: "The desire to react positively to the second edition of *Blue Jacket* went pretty much unrealized." One of Schwarze's biggest issues, aside from the weak characterization and ill-suited music, was that it was boring: "Good historical drama—good theater—needs energy and urgency; it needs a contagious vitality that catches us up in involvement; it needs characters with whom we can identify, 'feeling' both their elation and torment. *Blue Jacket* does not rise to either of these."[74]

Neither *Trumpet in the Land* nor *Blue Jacket* came close to *Tecumseh!* in terms of attendance or popularity. The drama's almost meteoric rise to prominence, in a sense, mirrors Tecumseh's own trajectory through history. Nostalgia for the past came to the forefront in the later part of the twentieth century alongside the continued use of Indian imagery, and contestations over the nation's upcoming bicentennial coalesced in productions like *Tecumseh!*.

Capitalizing on Chillicothe and Telling a Story of Tecumseh

The Scioto River winds its way east and south through Ohio. It passes through Kenton, named after famed frontiersman Simon Kenton. It twists and turns its way through the capital city of Columbus and continues south past Chillicothe. Chillicothe's claim to fame lies in its role as both the first (1803–10) and the third (1812–16) capital city of Ohio—and its location within the home-lands of the Shawnee until their forced removal in the wake of the War of 1812 and the rise of Andrew Jackson's Indian Removal Act. Samuel Selden, the first director of the long-standing outdoor drama *The Lost Colony* who was also involved in early decisions regarding *Unto These Hills*, first traveled to Chilli-cothe in the late 1960s. Selden was responding to a request from Chillicothe residents who hoped to replicate the success of *The Lost Colony*, which pre-miered in 1937, with an outdoor drama of their own.[75] In his trip report from September 1967, Selden suggested either Tecumseh or Mad Anthony Wayne as subject material, given that "both were appropriate to the area."[76] Local residents paid the IOD $1,000 in 1969 for a feasibility study, which would lay out the artistic and the economic potential of an outdoor historical drama in the area.[77] Sumner and two other experts traveled to Chillicothe in 1970, and the *Chillicothe Gazette* was positively giddy: "Outdoor drama has proved to be a tourist attraction, adding considerably to the local economy in other areas."[78] Later correspondence noted that there were eleven motels in the Chillicothe area, but only one hotel in Chillicothe. Nor were there any tourist homes with overnight accommodations.[79]

As noted earlier, the founding members of the Scioto Society came together in 1970 to create an outdoor drama that would serve as both a cultural and an economic development for the region. In the summer of 1970, Rusty Mun-dell, the general manager of the Scioto Society, wrote to Mark Sumner sug-gesting that "the life-study of the Shawnee chief, Tecumpseh [*sic*], with special emphasis on his mature years and his death could serve as the basis for a sym-phonic drama." Mundell also suggested including Simon Kenton, a frontiers-man for the Ohio Country and Kentucky, as a supporting character.[80] By the spring of 1971, the Scioto Society had acquired land on Sugarloaf Mountain for the amphitheater and Allan W. Eckert had agreed to write the script, using his novel *The Frontiersmen* as inspiration. In a letter to Mark Sumner, Mundell said he was pleased with the work they had done so far. "We are finally begin-ning to move quite rapidly," Mundell wrote. "As you have warned, I shall en-deavor to ensure it is not *too* rapidly!"[81]

On the surface, there were few bumps in the road as production moved along. According to Brandon Smith, the drama's CEO during my 2015 visit to Chillicothe, the Ohio National Guard "came in and did a lot of work here." They cleared the land, built parking bays, and brought in helicopters for the water tower, among other things. "The theater would never have been built without government support," Smith said. "I'm not even sure that you could get by with that kinda stuff now, bringing the National Guard to build," he

Construction on what would become the Sugarloaf Mountain Amphitheatre in Chillicothe, Ohio. Courtesy of the Ross County Historical Society, McKell Library, Chillicothe, Ohio (2004.105.05).

continued. "But they [meaning Governor James Rhodes, and state representative and eventual Lieutenant Governor Mryl Shoemaker, among others] were very powerful, and they believed in Southern Ohio. And Southern Ohio, at that time, late '60s, early '70s, was, and in many ways still is, Appalachia. And so these guys were open and willing to listen to anybody's idea to create jobs and economic opportunity in the area."[82] Shoemaker and state senator Henry Armstrong had pushed a $125,000 grant through the Ohio House in 1973.[83] In the end, the National Guard contributed $500,000 in labor and services, as well as the use of construction equipment.[84] According to Scioto Society volunteer Stuart Withers, reminiscing about the construction during the drama's twenty-fifth anniversary season, the National Guard took on the project as a training exercise since they had initially been an infantry unit.[85]

One of the biggest issues in Chillicothe, as it was in Cherokee, was the script. In May of 1972, Sumner and Mundell sent each other a series of letters outlining their problems with the draft. Mundell had passed along the comments of George Mallonee, who had worked on both *The Lost Colony* in North Carolina and *Wilderness Road* in Kentucky. "The playwright has let us down," Mundell and Mallonee wrote. "The dialogue is very stilted. You can see John Wayne standing by a horse saying these things, and the camera man switching to the sunset." Still, Mundell thought the script was salvageable: "I am sure worse scripts for outdoor dramas have been written, and that the plays for which they were written have eventually made it."[86]

In response, Sumner sent Mundell a four-page, single-spaced letter outlining his own concerns. *The Frontiersmen* weighed in at nearly 700 pages, and there were some issues trying to translate the book for the stage. "The script, as you sense, is not ready in my opinion," Sumner wrote. "I will try and explain why. Lord knows, these dramas are ten times as complicated as a movie script."[87] Many of Sumner's notes were minor yet crucial, the suggestions of a man who had spent years helping shape outdoor dramas across the country. However, some of his points underscored what he hoped would be the dramatic crux of the production:

> Perhaps as Tecumseh approaches the meeting with his brother he is met by several followers who protest the actions of the Prophet, or at least question the sincerity of Tenskwatawa's leadership of the village. If Tecumseh's loyalty causes him to brush aside these complaints and defend his brother to them, it would set up both his motivation to question the Prophet as he does in Scene 5, and to not kill Tenskwatawa after the disaster of the battle. In any case, the sense of tragedy will be enhanced by having some of the emotional responsibility fall to Tecumseh because he did not act on the complaints. The tradegy [*sic*] is Tecumseh's first, then one for all the Indian nations.[88]

Sumner's suggestions highlight a key component of outdoor historical dramas—the focus on the dramatic, if not the downright tragic, elements rather than the historical ones. He suggested Eckert look to Shakespeare, offering snippets spoken by Othello and Macbeth as each character's tragedy nears its self-destructive end. "The real tragedy is the loss of Tecumseh's dream as a practical possibility," Sumner continued. "There must be considerable self-realization for Tecumseh here."[89]

Sumner also sent the script to Samuel Selden, who had some concerns of his own. While it was a promising start and a professional script by an experienced writer who knew and respected his material, Selden commented that, in general, there was "too much talking about things and not much of doing things." He thought its time range was too expansive, causing it to lose its dramatic drive and suspense. His biggest qualm, though, was not with how Eckert painted the Indians. "Shouldn't just a little more be done for our ancestors, the White Revolutionists?" Selden asked. "They are generally presented as such skunks in this script." Instead, he suggested adding a moment either at or near the end of the drama where William Henry Harrison would "acknowledge his respect for an able, admirable adversary whom he wished he could have known under other circumstances."[90]

In order to be successful in Ohio in the 1970s, a drama focused on the rise of a pan-Indian movement aimed at eliminating colonial imposition would have to be just that—tragic. In this historical moment during the rise of AIM, itself a pan-Indian movement, the creation of *Tecumseh!* seems at once relevant and awkwardly ill-informed. During the Vietnam War era, which also saw the rise of revisionist films like *Little Big Man*, Indians were used to tell an American story of anticolonialism. In an age of national commemoration and on the cusp of the American bicentennial, the romance of Indian resistance was a marketable and malleable construct. In Ohio, where a governor sent the National Guard to Kent State in 1970 and a governor sent the National Guard to build the infrastructure for the drama in Chillicothe, Tecumseh was the safest Indian to salvage. As chapter 6 demonstrates, the almost Frankenstein-like deconstruction and re-creation of Tecumseh has brought millions of dollars and millions of visitors to Chillicothe. As in Pendleton and Cherokee, the question, as always, remains: at what cost?

In the weeks and months leading up to the drama's premiere, the city, the region, and the state were abuzz with promotional materials. An undated news release trumpeted that the drama was scheduled to open on June 30, 1973. It was praised by the program director of the New York State Council for the Performing Arts as "a powerful theatrical statement, reaching a large, important audience."[91] Another noted that "'TECUMSEH!' tells the story of the troubled Ohio country frontier circa 1812. Dramatizing the life of one of the most powerful figures in American history, the great Shawnee chief Tecumseh, the production reenacts the crucial Battle of Tippecanoe."[92] Governor John J. Gilligan proclaimed that the drama's opening day would be named "*Tecumseh!* Day" in honor of the drama, hoping that it would provide "the nucleus" for a tourist trade in south-central Ohio. The state's director of economic development, David Sweet, proudly noted that the production "is of historical, entertainment and cultural significance, and economic benefit, to all Ohioans. . . . We feel that this undertaking by the Scioto Society will give impetus to economic betterment of the (south-central Ohio) region and will provide a unique attraction for all Ohioans." Like the governor, Sweet also said that the drama would contribute to the state's efforts to establish the region as a major vacation and tourist center. He also remarked that the state hoped to establish a new state park in the region.[93]

In the summer of 1973, a mere six years after Selden came to town, more than 81,000 people traveled to Chillicothe to see this new outdoor drama.[94] A Louisville critic groused that long exposure to and association with outdoor drama had made him a bit cynical. They were usually "imitative, simple-minded and regionally chauvinistic," Dudley Saunders wrote, and mostly "piddling melodramas that neither arouse nor intrigue us, and their comic relief is traditionally provided by actors playing old drunks." But the drama in Chillicothe, although it was far from a finished work, was "potentially one of the best outdoor dramas I've seen." The amphitheater was ruggedly beautiful, and the show was "frequently exciting, often provocative, original in approach, authentic in décor, generally interesting and even quite moving on a couple of occasions."[95]

Others were not as enthused. Jill Wiltberger argued that "the play's the thing, and therein lies the emphasis—and the problem." The actors were competent, but they struggled under the weight of a cumbersome script. The script was so expansive that "no other character is allowed time to develop, let alone to offset or complement the character of Tecumseh." If the drama was to be an educational experience as well as entertainment, it had to be comprehensible, and it had to be understood in order to be appreciated. "A man of Tecumseh's stature," Wiltberger concluded, "deserves this much, at least."[96] Wiltberger's critiques hit the heart of the outdoor historical drama conundrum—how to condense history into less than three hours (including intermission), and how to make that history exciting enough that people would drive several hours and hundreds of miles to see the show. Like Green and Hunter, Eckert had "no qualms about the 'adjustments' of history which are sometimes required by the tricky mechanics of drama."[97] That September, theater professor Christian Moe sent a letter to Sumner with his take on the production. "This one is going to be a winner," he declared. Moe had some reservations about the opening scenes and what he called the "scant comedy in the script," but he found the script and production to be "a fine start for a first year."[98] In the decade that followed, the Scioto Society sold over 852,000 tickets to the drama.[99] *Tecumseh!* was undoubtedly a financial success, and it became the benchmark for measuring the relative success or failure of other outdoor dramas in Ohio and across the country.

Salvaging Tourism in Ohio

Even as *Blue Jacket* maintained higher attendance numbers than *Trumpet in the Land*, neither one ever came close to *Tecumseh!*. In 1985, *Unto These Hills* was the most-attended drama, *Tecumseh!* was fifth, *Blue Jacket* was seventh, and *Trumpet in the Land* was ninth. Despite this status, *Blue Jacket* still showed a deficit of $129,000 heading into the 1986 season. Marion Waggoner, hired as the new producer, quickly cut the drama's operating budget by $87,000. He cut six cast members, eliminated the marketing director, cut travel, meeting, and telephone expenses, cut staff salaries, and made technical staff cuts. He wanted to change the opening scenes, the dialogue, and the structures in the amphitheater.[100] In a memo to Sumner, Waggoner wrote, "This is a *tough situation* here in Xenia!"[101]

As with many tourism endeavors, *Blue Jacket*'s success ebbed and flowed over the years. But First Frontier, Inc. was in trouble by the early 2000s. An article in the *Cincinnati Enquirer* referenced the dispute over Blue Jacket's heritage, but the show's assistant director argued that that was not the focus of the drama. "We're based on history, but we know the story is not 100 percent accurate," Scott Galbraith said. "What's most important is the meaning of who the Shawnee were, how they lived and why they fought for their way of life."[102] Attendance kept declining, and First Frontier struggled to stay afloat and to stay relevant. The organization's "2003 Marketing & PR Plan" suggested that the decline was partly due to a nationwide trend "influenced by the economy, 9/11, the West Nile Virus and the upcoming war."[103]

The IOD did a performance audit of *Blue Jacket* in 2003. Scott Parker, the director of the IOD, sent a lengthy report to the executive director of the Greene County Convention & Visitors Bureau who had requested the study. Parker noted that *Blue Jacket* was among a number of dramas struggling with attendance but that there were other significant issues as well, including inappropriate actions by the management in response to the loss of earned income and the First Frontier board's failure to note them.[104] First Frontier continued to ignore the contestations over the drama's story line and stubbornly stuck to its Van Swearingen story. Tracy Leake, the chief of operations for First Frontier, also admitted that financial difficulties might be the death knell for the drama. "I feel it is important to mention that audience numbers are down in all outdoor drama," Leake said. "Families are choosing to stay in their living rooms instead of venturing out for entertainment. It is very important to keep all outdoor dramas alive, in order to keep the history of our country alive."[105]

Despite First Frontier's best efforts, *Blue Jacket* only survived one more year. First Frontier estimated that only 12,000 people saw the production in 2007, a far cry from the 30,000 to 50,000 annual visitors the drama had come to expect.[106] The *Dayton Daily News* opened its 2007 review of the drama by writing, "That's our story and we're sticking to it." The reviewer, Terry Morris, pointedly brought up the DNA study, noting, "In other words, *Blue Jacket* is the same *Blue Jacket* it's been for 26 years: a theatrical presentation."[107] The Ohio Department of Development awarded First Frontier a $40,000 grant from its Division of Travel and Tourism and its Economic Development Division in the fall of 2007 in hopes of sustaining the drama.[108] Unlike the other dramas in Ohio and around the country, First Frontier had built a drama on a narrative that could not withstand the brunt of history. Even as Green, Hunter, and Eckert built their scripts on shaky history, the feeble foundation of *Blue Jacket* came crumbling down when the drama went dark in 2008.[109] Mundell sued First Frontier in 2008 for nonpayment of royalties dating back to 2002, and Greene County sued First Frontier in 2010 for breaking a long-standing lease and failure to repay a $250,000 loan.[110]

In 2009, the Greene County Convention & Visitors Bureau estimated that the drama's closing had a negative impact of up to $750,000 on the local economy, and the amphitheater came down in 2017.[111] The failure of *Blue Jacket* stands in stark contrast to the continued success of *Trumpet in the Land* and *Tecumseh!*. *Blue Jacket* is not alone in its collapse, just as the other two are not alone in their continued production, but *Blue Jacket* shows us the ramifications of salvage tourism. The Gnadenhutten Massacre and the reconstruction of Shawnee resistance effectively draw their audiences into their amphitheaters by centering on the emotional, the nostalgic, and the romantic. Would *Blue Jacket* have survived if the character were not portrayed as a white-man-turned Indian? Maybe. Perhaps not.

In a 1991 press release, the Scioto Society announced that actor Jamieson K. Price would take the lead role in that summer's production of *Tecumseh!*. The press release proudly noted that Price enjoyed performing "'living history'; bringing the past alive for the present to see." Price had spent the last two summers playing the lead role in the *Blue Jacket* drama an hour northwest of Chillicothe. The author asked Price how he felt about playing "such a legendary historical figure," to which Price replied, "I think Tecumseh was the epitome of the American Indian, he came so close to changing the history of the United States. I often wonder what might have happened if Tecumseh would have won? What would the world be like today?"[112]

A photograph by Jon Heierman depicting actor Mel Cobb, who played Tecumseh, in 1973. Courtesy of the Ross County Historical Society, McKell Library, Chillicothe, Ohio (1995.204.12).

Author and playwright Allen Eckert echoed Price's sentiments more than a decade later: "Had Tenskwatawa not interfered and had the plan succeeded, would the Indian then have retained their own lands in perpetuity? Most likely not, despite Tecumseh's dream that they would. For a time the whites could probably have been held at bay, but eventually the encroachment would have begun again and the taking of the land would have resumed and increased by whatever means possible." In this book's final chapter, I examine the state of *Tecumseh!* in the twenty-first century. The production, like the failed *Blue Jacket*, centers on a handful of disputed and disproven narratives but, unlike *Blue Jacket*, is still economically viable. "So why, then," Eckert asked rhetorically in 2003, "in the face of such monumental failure, do we remember Tecumseh?" He was not just a fine man or a powerful warrior or a memorable Indian leader, Eckert mused. Tecumseh became, he argued, one of the most remarkable human beings in the history of the world. "Why do we remember Tecumseh?" Eckert wrote. "How could we forget?"[113]

CHAPTER SIX

The Great Pretenders

Playing Indian in Tecumseh!

Tecumseh was one of the early sightseers of the Adena region. Follow the lead of
this Shawnee chief and discover a land rich in Indian lore and scenes of yesteryear.
—The Ohio Department of Economic and Community Development

Chillicothe sits in south central Ohio, nearly equidistant from Kentucky and
West Virginia and about an hour's drive south of Columbus. Out of the three
locations in this book, it is the closest to a moderately large airport. As you
travel from Columbus, the urban capital's industrial feel quickly gives way to
farmlands and small towns, which continues until you get to Chillicothe. With
a population around 21,000, the town straddles the Scioto River that twists
and turns its way through a good portion of the state. The amphitheater itself
sits on the northern part of Chillicothe off a dirt road that's just barely wide
enough for a car heading north and a car heading south to comfortably meet
each other. While the Happy Canyon arena sits in the busiest part of Pendleton, the Sugarloaf Mountain Amphitheatre, like Cherokee's Mountainside
Theatre, is far enough away from the main part of town to feel as though
nothing else exists.[1]

   When I arrived, Brandon Smith, the 2015 producer and CEO for *Tecumseh!*,
was waiting for me. We hopped in his truck (which handles the terrain much
better than my little rental car), and he gave me a tour of the property. We drove
past a series of cabins that house the performers over the show's summer run,
cabins that seem cute and quaint but likely lose their appeal by the end of the
season. Once we got back to the amphitheater, he introduced me to Albert Heierman, one of the people who were instrumental in bringing *Tecumseh!* to life
in Chillicothe. As we sat on a bench between the ticket windows and the gift
shop, Heierman proudly relayed stories about the early years of the drama.
He told me that he sees the drama about ten times each summer, so by then
he'd seen it well over 400 times.[2] Heierman is known as one of the people who
traveled to Oklahoma to meet with the Absentee Shawnee and get their bless-
ing in the years before the drama's premiere. "You're really going to love this
show," he said as I handed my ticket to the usher. "It's the best outdoor drama
in the country."[3]

I settled into my seat at the back of the amphitheater. I aimed to play the tourist at *Tecumseh!*, and I wanted to see the show how the majority of visitors—not a historian—would see it. I'd taken the behind-the-scenes tour, which mostly centered on revealing the secrets behind the fake blood packets that nearly every character required. I'd eaten at the Terrace Buffet, which feeds an average of 180 visitors a night. It's slower during the week—maybe sixty to seventy people—but on a Saturday it can have up to 600 diners.[4] I'd strolled through the Mountain Gallery Gift Shop, stuffed to the brim with all the plastic bow and arrow sets and wolf-adorned shirts you'd expect to find. Smith had told me earlier that the gift shop turns anywhere from $50,000 to $70,000 in profits each year, so it's a significant source of income for the organization. "We've tried a whole number of different things," he said, "including buying hand-crafted, all hand-crafted toys from Native American tribes. And nobody bought them." They sell thousands of little feathered spears with a "Made in China" tag, and they'll sell a few pieces of Native-crafted jewelry and other items each year.[5]

I'd visited the on-site mini-museum, where I learned that everything in the cases was considered pre-historic—for Ohio, meaning anything before 1550. Anything made after 1550, the period after contact, was considered historic. Ken Factor, the person in charge of the museum, pointed out artifacts from mound-builders, items that had been found in local farmers' fields, and objects from the Hopewell tradition.[6] I found it interesting that, by focusing on the prehistoric, they could avoid any mention of the Shawnee removal in the wake of Tecumseh's defeat. As the audience filled the seats, it was time for the show to start.

Six nights a week from June to September, an actor playing the famed Shawnee chief Tecumseh strides to the top of a faux-rock cliff at the Sugar-loaf Mountain Amphitheatre in Chillicothe, Ohio. He looks down on his eager followers. "They will not be Shawnee or Chippewa or Sioux or Chero-kee," he proclaims. "They will be *Indians!*" The scene ends triumphantly with warriors yelling, Indian women dancing, and a spotlight on Tecumseh. But the actors portraying Tecumseh and his confederation of warriors are not Indians. Instead, actors painted with the same shade of Disney-fied copper-colored makeup with impossibly black wigs atop their heads fill the stage, and Tecumseh's political vision for a strategic, pan-Indian alliance is reduced to sheer spectacle, the actors' voices echoing hollowly throughout the amphitheater. I spent several nights in August sitting in the outdoor theater watching people who are paid to play Indian, their artificially deepened voices reciting dialogue that film and performance scholar Jacquelyn Kilpatrick would call the "pronoun-challenged . . . all-purpose Indian speech."[7] *Tecumseh!* seems determined to show its audience the story of what could have been but would not be, leaving Tecumseh's dream in the dust when the lights go down.

This production, simply called *Tecumseh!*, has been staged in southern Ohio since 1973. A local civic group, the Scioto Society, produces the drama, which has become a regional economic mainstay. *Tecumseh!* is not the only outdoor drama that focuses on Native history, although it is somewhat unique in the sense that its casting remains so predominantly white. Happy Canyon has a century-long history of a Native cast for the Indian pageant part of the show. The makeup of *Unto These Hills* has slowly shifted from using the Carolina Playmakers in lead roles to a more diverse cast composed of members of the Eastern Band and other Native actors. *Tecumseh!* has rarely cast Natives in leading roles. During my last trip to Pendleton, Jason Hill, the president of Happy Canyon, told me a story about a trip he took to Chillicothe. He could barely conceal his amusement as he imitated his Chillicothe contact: "Your show uses REAL Indians?" What are the ramifications of these casting decisions, and how do actors in redface—in the twenty-first century, no less— become enveloped in the discourses surrounding these performances of indigeneity and Native history? This is not to say, of course, that Happy Canyon and *Unto These Hills* are above reproach, but the historical implications of playing Indian in *Tecumseh!* provide a critical window into the power of performance and its literal role in creating a public historical narrative. The purposeful manipulation of Tecumseh's life and mission through the mechanisms of outdoor drama are a powerful example of salvage tourism.

While chapter 5 centered on the creation of the production, this chapter follows the drama from its inception into the twenty-first century in order to understand why—and how—the drama functions within a contemporary tourist environment. Unlike Happy Canyon, which added narration in the early 2000s, and *Unto These Hills*, which returned to its original script in 2017 after more than a decade of attempted interventions, current productions of *Tecumseh!* are fairly similar to the one that premiered in 1973. Even in the wake of historical research that undercuts the drama's plotline, nothing has changed. The Scioto Society clings to the Tecumseh they invented. They have no choice, no other option. To recognize, acknowledge, and reconcile the Tecumseh of history with the Tecumseh of *Tecumseh!* would require a complete reframing of how to comfortably celebrate and mourn the man they mythologize, and this reframing would likely have a devastating effect on the production and the local economy it supports.

Re-creating Tecumseh

The popular narrative and legacy of Tecumseh have grown and shifted since his death at the Battle of the Thames in 1813 during the War of 1812. R. David Edmunds has argued that if white men could have designed an "ideal Indian," they would have designed Tecumseh, who defines the Euro-American concept of the "noble savage."[8] Tecumseh's nemesis, William Henry Harrison, famously wrote that Tecumseh was the kind of man who "would perhaps be the founder of an Empire that would rival in glory that of Mexico or Peru" if he had been born in a different era. Harrison reportedly called Tecumseh "one of those uncommon geniuses, which spring up occasionally to produce revolutions and overturn the established order of things."[9] The drama encourages tourists to "witness the epic life story of the legendary Shawnee leader as he struggles to defend his sacred homelands in the Ohio country." It paints Tecumseh as a patriot defending his homelands against foreign invasion—even though this foreign entity was the United States.[10] A promotional brochure for the inaugural season pits Tecumseh against future president Harrison, noting, "In the heart of one burned a deep and abiding love for his people, his land, and his way of life. In the soul of the other was the dream of power: the presidency of the United States . . . and you are an eye witness as the flames and fury of the Battle of Tippecanoe explodes around you, shattering the dreams of one man, fulfilling the desires of the other and determining the fate of a nation."[11]

The romanticization and memorialization of Tecumseh in Chillicothe initially appears, quite simply, misplaced. His carefully constructed confederation of Indigenous leaders and nations, who subsequently allied with the British in order to stop American expansion, seems an odd birthplace of an American hero. But, as Richard White suggests, the remaking of Tecumseh and his "assimilation into the mythology of Anglo-American society," culminating in the "American adulation of Tecumseh," shapes Tecumseh as "a miracle, a figure of genius who arose among savages."[12] A 1997 special edition of the *Chillicothe Gazette*, which celebrated the drama's twenty-fifth anniversary, called Tecumseh "one of the most important and powerful Native American leaders of history" while noting that he was "almost successful," having "never achieved the goal he died trying to reach."[13] His death, for White, is a merciful one, as he did not live to see the "years of exile and the legacy of defeat and domination."[14]

The drama takes the phrase "artistic license" to a new level, favoring romantic plot twists over a faithful historical interpretation. In the style of a Paul Green or Kermit Hunter script for an outdoor drama, the focus is on the drama, not the history. The drama paints his brother, the prophet Tenskwa-tawa, as a sniveling, conniving reprobate, the antagonistic opposite of the righteous Tecumseh. The audience is given no reason to root for Tenskwatawa, and his apparent lack of political aptitude and self-control in the face of Harrison's military advance is portrayed as the downfall of Tecumseh's dream of an Indian confederacy. Edmunds and Adam Jortner are among the scholars who argue that Tenskwatawa, not Tecumseh, was the backbone of the movement. Tecumseh's diplomatic and military prowess, coupled with his reputation, made him the logical choice to travel in search of Indigenous political allies, even as Tenskwatawa's visions galvanized the push for an Indian alliance against the encroaching United States.[15]

This history, though, does not a popular drama make. By inviting tourists into forcibly ceded Shawnee territory to see a theatrical retelling of a critical point in Shawnee history, the drama includes a parallel story line of Tecumseh's supposedly star-crossed love for Rebecca Galloway, the daughter of a Scottish immigrant. This story, as Edmunds argues, is "so patently fictitious that it taxes the credulity of all but the most gullible adherents of nineteenth-century romanticism."[16] In 1992, several newspaper articles proclaimed that, nearly twenty years after the drama premiered, Eckert had unearthed information that showed that Tecumseh had not fallen in love with a white woman named Rebecca Galloway. This story line is threaded throughout the drama, and one of the emotional cruxes of the drama occurs when Tecumseh asks Rebecca to marry him. She agrees, but only on one condition: that he give up his people and his ways and live as a white man. "This is all fabrication," Eckert was quoted as saying.[17] The Shawnee had been saying that from the start. A 1973 article about twenty Shawnee who came to the drama's premiere quoted Sallie Tyner, an older Shawnee woman, who questioned the drama's use of that plotline. "There are several different versions of that," the article read, before moving on to less controversial subjects.[18]

Like First Frontier, Inc., the producers of *Blue Jacket*, the Scioto Society refused to alter the script. "We don't feel it's appropriate to change it," producer and artistic director Marion Waggoner said in the early 1990s. "I think one thing we have to remember is that outdoor dramas are not supposed to be a pure history lesson." He continued, noting, "We have a proven product. We don't feel Rebecca and Tecumseh is an issue. The play is still fairly accurate."[19] The Romeo-and-Juliet bent to *Tecumseh!* was part of what helped make the drama successful. The fact that the story, which had been challenged since it first emerged, was inaccurate was not as important as driving tourists and their dollars to Chillicothe.

Waggoner was not alone in his refusal to accept historical facts. An opinion piece in a local paper praised Waggoner's decision: "We do *not* particularly like having our romantic bubble punctured. Eckert could have skipped that bit of research—next thing you know somebody's going to insist that Abraham Lincoln's first love wasn't Ann Rutledge." The author continued, happily remarking that "Becky and Tecumseh will continue their doomed circumspect relationship, possibly to the disgust of historians, but to the delight of audiences who we hope will flock to the Sugarloaf Mountain Amphitheatre in the summer of '92."[20]

One of the constant struggles throughout this book is the tug-of-war between the dramatic and the historical. Some might scoff at this, wondering why it matters that the dramatists take such liberties with their subject matter. It's just a performance, they might say, it's not a research paper. But the subject matter does, in fact, matter. Not all of the members of the Confederated Tribes of the Umatilla Indian Reservation appreciate the story line in Rawley's Happy Canyon. Members of the Eastern Band weren't thrilled with the way their histories and their ancestors were portrayed in Hunter's script for *Unto These Hills* for the first fifty years of the drama. Mundell's script for *Blue Jacket* came under attack for perpetuating the notion that Blue Jacket wasn't a Shawnee by birth but was instead a Dutchman named Marmaduke Van Swearingen. Eckert's script for *Tecumseh!* takes similarly large leaps into the fantasy realm, and yet the drama continues to succeed.

Eckert's script relegates Tecumseh's resistance against the United States to a secondary story line. Tecumseh looms large in many facets of American mythology and the American imagination, and his life—and perhaps more so his death—occupies a complicated space in the narrative of early American history. If his mission had been successful, the trajectory of American history would have been drastically different. Since 1973, tourists have come to Chillicothe to relive a story whose ending they already know. Tecumseh does not, cannot succeed and, six nights a week, the audience settles comfortably in their seats to watch Tecumseh's dream die with him in an outdoor amphitheater in southern Ohio.

The qualities that Europeans and Americans admired in Tecumseh were the qualities they hoped to see in themselves. By playing Indian—literally—in *Tecumseh!*, the audience and the Scioto Society have co-opted his life, his mission, and his death as their own origin story. The man and the myth become one: Tecumseh's legacy is that of the "bravest of the brave," and his defeat at the hands of the still-young American nation assured Americans and the nation alike of their superiority.[21] Philip Deloria has argued that Indianness

An actor explains some of the stunts used in *Tecumseh!*. This was part of a backstage tour at the Sugarloaf Mountain Amphitheatre. Photograph by author.

provides not only the impetus but the precondition for what he calls "the creative assembling of an ultimately unassemblable American identity," noting that Indians have moved in and out of the most important stories various Americans have told about themselves since the colonial era.[22] Performing "Indian Americanness," then, establishes the groundwork for a singular national identity.[23] This identity is one wherein Tecumseh himself is an ancestor of America and, by extension, Americans. The drama commemorates Tecumseh's dream but celebrates his failure, inviting its audience to participate in a collective moment of mourning and triumph.

By unraveling the threads that hold this narrative together, this chapter demonstrates how Tecumseh is deconstructed and resurrected as *Tecumseh!*. The script, which has remained relatively unchanged since the show premiered, highlights the salvaging of historical scraps that make up the drama. The Scioto Society's dogged insistence on adhering to a romanticized, mythologized, and historically inaccurate narrative is a telling example of how Indians have been commodified in outdoor dramas and consumed by millions of tourists. The model of the tourist, with what Marita Sturken calls "its innocent pose and distanced position," participates "uncritically in a culture in which notions of good and evil are used to define complex conflicts and tensions."[24] The audience unquestioningly accepts Tecumseh and Simon Kenton as good and Tenskwatawa, coupled with the men Kenton leads, as evil, with no room in between.

Remembering and Reinventing Tecumseh

As the Scioto Society worked to raise support and funds and build an outdoor amphitheater in the late 1960s and early 1970s, they also needed someone who could write a play worthy of their subject. While Kermit Hunter had written a few plays before the Cherokee Historical Association offered him the chance to write the script for *Unto These Hills*, the Scioto Society turned to a man known more for his books: Allan W. Eckert. Eckert was a prolific and popular writer known primarily for his "Winning of America" series. With titles like *The Conquerors* (1970) and *Gateway to Empire* (1982), the six-book series demonstrates that Eckert was firmly entrenched in the ideological enchantment that celebrated American expansion and exceptionalism. He also published books about frontiersman Simon Kenton and the Shawnee chief Blue Jacket during his long career. Other books centered on Tecumseh's nephew Spemica Lawba (renamed Johnny Logan by the U.S. general who kidnapped him) and, of course, on Tecumseh himself.

Eckert's script for the drama was based on his 1967 book *The Frontiersmen*, the first book in the "Winning of America" series. His author's note in *The Frontiersmen* roundly proclaimed, "This book is fact, not fiction," noting that he had done seven years of extensive research before publishing the book. While it was the result of "a close study of a multitude of documents written in the period 1700 to 1900," he also admitted that "certain techniques normally associated with the novel have been utilized, but in no case has this been at the expense of historical accuracy."[25] In a likely attempt to capitalize on the popularity of the series and the drama, Eckert released *A Sorrow in Our Heart: The Life of Tecumseh* in 1992, which drew rather heavily on *The Frontiersmen*, in some instances lifting passages of text directly from one book to the other. Critics were not easily convinced by Eckert's claims to historical accuracy. One reviewer called it "a biography that succeeds better as fiction," wryly contending that its euphemistic "interpretative zeal" strayed from, or at least embellished, the historical record "to the point of being suspect."[26]

This embellishment is key to understanding the legacy the drama creates and perpetuates. *The Frontiersmen* weighs in at nearly 700 pages, most of which is devoted to the story of Simon Kenton. Tecumseh eventually becomes a parallel character, but Eckert's saga is bookended by Kenton's birth in 1755 and his death in 1836. When Eckert turns his attention to the Shawnee and the other Native nations in the surrounding areas, the characters become caricatures. He delights in regaling his reader with tales of torture, often spending pages and pages outlining what happened to the hapless settlers and soldiers who had the misfortune of falling into the Indians' clutches, and the book's body count begins to resemble Shakespeare's *Titus Andronicus*. As gratuitous as it may be, the bloody and brutal scenes are a critical element of the text: according to Eckert, a young Tecumseh, disgusted at the Shawnee torture and ritualistic killing of a prisoner captured in battle, vows to end the practice. The older warriors deride him, only to be convinced by Tecumseh's passionate oratory. "Tecumseh," Eckert wrote, "was destined to become the greatest leader the Shawnee tribe had ever known."[27]

Tecumseh! played to about 35,000 people in its opening season.[28] Its summer run, while in line with the vast majority of outdoor dramas, was a lucky break for the Scioto Society with the onset of the oil embargo in the fall of 1973. In a letter to Rusty Mundell at the end of November, Mark Sumner, the director of the Institute of Outdoor Drama, admitted that it was too soon to have many facts on the gasoline shortage situation, which could have devastating effects on the nation's tourism industry in the subsequent summer. Sumner noted that the travel industry contributed more than $28 billion to the nation's total income and directly employed more than three million people. "If the travel industry is depressed or destroyed," Sumner wrote, "so will the rest of the economy, I expect. Present Washington, D.C. thoughts are not reassuring ones, but it is very hard to see through the mass media hysteria."[29]

As with innumerable outdoor dramas staged on an annual basis, those involved with the production kept tweaking the script between the first and the second season. They introduced new characters, cut some others, and added some new scenes.[30] The character of the Tribal Historian, who served as a narrator of sorts akin to those seen in the older historical pageants, was cut, as "its liabilities outweighed its assets as an integral part of the drama."[31] A new character was Tecumapese, sister to Tecumseh, Tenskwatawa, and Chiksika. The character had appeared in an early draft of the script but was cut for 1973, and then added back in in 1974.[32] Eckert admitted that her role was not the one to cut. "Now reinstituted, her role adds a vitality of great importance," he wrote; "she acts as a catalyst between these characters and helps immensely in adding dimension to their roles as well as her own."[33] He'd also added a new scene showing a confrontation between Tecumseh and William Henry Harrison, one that clearly revealed "the unbridgeability [*sic*] of the gap which has developed between the Indians and the young government of the United States."[34]

While attendance in Chillicothe rose to about 46,000 in the 1974 season, organizers also had to reckon with a number of rainouts, and the Scioto Society was feeling the financial pinch.[35] Sumner went to Chillicothe in August, in between trips to dramas in Harrodsburg, Kentucky, and Dover, Ohio.[36] He was impressed with what he saw and, upon his return to Chapel Hill, he sent a letter addressed to "the Nameless Indians and Settlers of TECUMSEH!" While he enjoyed the entire show, he particularly wanted to thank the actors who "made the most of the opportunities to take the audience back to the realities of the days portrayed in the production" through pantomime and action "where the only fact is your character's presence."[37] It was the first time Sumner had been able to see the show from beginning to end. He had tried twice during the previous season, only to get rained out both times. His note to the ensemble, with its focus on taking the audience "back to the realities" of the historical moments on the stage, was the culmination of years of reworking the production. He also wrote to Eckert, praising the rewrites as "a first class outdoor drama" that would continue to grow.[38]

Tecumseh! would maintain its status as the top drama in the state—and one of the top dramas in the country—for decades. After an article ran in the *Dayton Journal Herald* in the summer of 1975, the IOD was inundated with forty different requests from Ohioans for information on the currently running outdoor dramas. A Mrs. Standsbury wrote to the IOD in late July, confessing, "Having just seen 'Tecumseh,' my enthusiasm is rampant."[39] Attendance in Chillicothe rebounded from the previous year, and nearly 60,000 people saw the drama in 1975.[40] The drama's fourth season would be a turning point for the Scioto Society. The nation celebrated its bicentennial in 1976, and *Tecumseh!* became one of Ohio's touchstones for the celebrations. More than 70,000 people saw the drama that year, and the total economic impact in that year alone was more than $12 million.[41] The decision to place the drama in the midst of the bicentennial seems, like the creation of the drama itself, incongruous. As the following section shows, the use of Tecumseh in the bicentennial showcases how Indianness became the genesis of Americanness, and how Indians became the forebears of Americans.

Tecumseh and the Bicentennial: Unpacking 1976

In early April of 1976, President Gerald Ford sent a letter to the Scioto Society. "For two centuries our Nation has grown, changed, and flourished," he wrote. "A diverse people, drawn from all corners of the earth, have joined together to fulfill the promise of democracy." He boasted that the bicentennial was "rich in history and in the promise and potential of the years that lie ahead," a chance to reflect on America's past, achievements, traditions, diversity, freedoms, government, and "our continuing commitment to a better life for all Americans." He commended the Scioto Society on its bicentennial production of the drama, and ended his letter by contending that "efforts such as this are helping to make our great national celebration a memorable and meaningful one for all."[42] On the surface, Ford's letter is a remarkable invocation of the promise of America. On the other hand, there is a hefty dose of irony in a letter calling on citizens to "join together as races, nationalities, and individuals" when the premise of the drama centers on a man who sought to bring Native nations together in opposition to the United States.

That same year, the Scioto Society created a number of press releases to promote the fourth season of *Tecumseh!*. The press releases focused on everything from Simon Kenton to Rebecca Galloway, with occasional mentions of the Shawnee leader but rarely anything about the Shawnee as a whole. The democratic undertones of the press releases were less overt than the calls for peace and understanding in the early souvenir programs of *Unto These Hills*, but they do underscore how Tecumseh, the Shawnee, and Indians in general were co-opted and swept into the hullabaloo around the bicentennial. One asked its readers to name America's greatest frontiersman. Even though Daniel Boone or Davy Crockett might come to mind, the greatest "musket shooting, indian fighting, bear hunting frontiersman of them all" was none other than Simon Kenton. Most important was his almost twenty-year relationship and rivalry with Tecumseh. "When Tecumseh lay dead at the battle of Thames in Ontario," the press release continued, "afrontiersman was asked to identify the body, so it's scalp could be taken. According to the indians he identified the wrong man purposely because of hes great respect for Tecumseh"[43] (all errors appear in original text.) Here, Tecumseh becomes a supporting character in his own life. By celebrating Kenton in all his musket-shooting and bear-hunting glory, with only thinly veiled references to the frontier violence that characterized the era, Kenton's actions—and those of American soldiers, settlers, squatters, vigilantes, frontiersmen, missionaries, and government officials—can be redeemed, remembered, and reimagined on stage. Tecumseh is merely a vehicle for a nostalgic return to the early years of America.

As shown in chapter 5, another press release, simply called "Description of the Drama," went straight toward potential audience members' senses of adventure and read, in part,

> You are no longer in the twentieth century. You are with Chiksika, the Shawnee warrior, as he leads his younger brother Tecumseh into his first battle!
>
> For the next two hours, you experience the life and death of the greatest Indian Chief ever to inhabit this continent—Tecumseh. . . .
>
> For the first time, you fully understand the young Shawnee warrior's vision of glory. Tecumseh is no longer a wooden Indian from the history books. He lives and breathes and threatens. He threatens from strength. . . .
>
> It is not merely a drama, but a pilgrimage into the past . . . when these brave warriors, courageous chiefs, fighting frontiersmen, and stolid soldiers actually walk again, the very ground they tred [*sic*] so long ago.[44]

Tecumseh, again, plays a supporting role here. The sentimental justification for finally understanding his "vision of glory" is couched in terms of bringing the past to life, of turning a boring historical narrative into a thrilling drama. Actor Mel Cobb, who originated the role, came back to Chillicothe for the bicentennial. "I feel closer to this role than to any other work I have ever done," read another press release, this one quoting the actor himself. "Perhaps that is because I feel so close to the man. . . . Tecumseh is not a figment of an author's futile imagination. He was a living breathing human being."[45]

"The bicentennial belongs to everybody," proclaimed a press release on Rebecca Galloway, the teenager who supposedly captured Tecumseh's heart.[46] Published several years before the rise in research proved this narrative false, it says that, after she refused to accept his offer of marriage because he refused to acquiesce to her demand that he live as a white man, she asked Tecumseh for one final promise. She asked that he never allow his men to torture a white prisoner—and that he kept that promise until he died. The character of Rebecca is a combination of Juliet, Belle, and Pocahontas: a star-crossed lover, the girl who tames and teaches the beast, and the girl who keeps the peace between the warring Indians and whites. This story is, in Edmunds's words, "patently fictitious," but Galloway becomes another means through which Tecumseh's mission becomes whitewashed and palatable for non-Native tourists.

The promotional materials tried to cover every major player in the drama, from Kenton and Galloway to, in a sense, Tecumseh and Tenskwatawa. One titled "The Shawnee Prophet," ostensibly about Tenskwatawa, blithely called the fighting in the Ohio Territory a "deadly struggle between the Americans, the British, and the Indians. All three sides claimed a right to the land. The Indian said it was his to begin with, the British claimed it for King George III, and the Americans made a seventeenth state of the Union out of it eventually."[47] By attempting to appeal to as many audience emotions as possible, the drama purposely repackaged itself to capitalize on the national sentiments of the bicentennial.

The late 1970s also saw the inclusion, on souvenir programs, audition information packets, and promotional materials, of a quote from a Native leader named Seeathl,[48] the namesake of the city of Seattle:

> When the last red man shall have perished, and the memory of my tribe shall have become a myth among the white men, these shores will swarm with the invisible dead of my tribe. . . . At night when the streets of your cities and villages are silent and you think them deserted, they will throng with the returning hosts that once filled and still love this beautiful land. The white man will never be alone. Let him be just and deal kindly with my people, for the dead are not powerless. Dead, did I say? There is no death, only a change of worlds.[49]

I stared at this program for a long time when I found it in the archives. Why, I wondered, was a speech from a Duwamish/Suquamish chief used to promote an outdoor drama about a Shawnee who took up arms against the United States? And then I found another excerpt from the speech—but this time it was in a 1986 program for *Blue Jacket*:

> Every part of this soil is sacred in the estimation of my people. Every hillside, every valley, every plain and grove, has been hallowed by some sad or happy event in days long vanished. The very dust upon which you now stand responds more lovingly to their footsteps than to yours, because it is rich with the blood of our ancestors and our bare feet are conscious of the sympathetic touch. Even the little children who lived here and rejoiced here for a brief season will love these somber solitudes and at eventide they greet shadowy returning spirits.[50]

Historian Coll Thrush has suggested that the speech, said to have been given during treaty discussions in the 1850s, might be what the Tecumseh of *Tecumseh!* became—a figment of the collective imagination. The speech did not appear in print for more than thirty years after the Treaty of Point Elliott, and it falls in line with what Thrush calls the "Victorian prose lamenting the passing of the 'red man.'" Stories like these, Thrush contends, are not necessarily about their Indian subjects. Instead, they often have far more to do "with the people telling them."[51]

Seeathl, like countless images of other Indians, had a "symbolic resuscitation" in the 1970s, thanks to the environmental undertones in the heavily edited and republished speech.[52] Philip Deloria argues that the speech's authorship and its history did not necessarily matter to those who encountered it. Instead, it was "the words themselves and the people who encountered them, interpreted them, and derived meaning and import from their emotionally charged cadences."[53] For white Americans in the 1970s, an Indian was an Indian, and the supposedly salvaged words of a western Washington Indian were, for the Scioto Society, First Frontier, and their intended audiences, easily interchangeable with their stories of once-Western-but-now-Midwestern-Indians who hoped to save their lands from the clutches of a growing colonial force.

The meaning of Tecumseh changed over the years. An undated tourism brochure from the 1970s or 1980s called Tecumseh "one of the early sightseers" of the region, while previous materials had centered on his fierce fight to save his homelands.[54] In the decades following its premiere, the Scioto Society would remake and remarket Tecumseh, shifting slightly in order to accommodate the changing nature of the American tourism industry—and to appease the mercurial temperament of the American tourist.

Following *Tecumseh!* into the Twenty-First Century

While other organizations grew complacent in their marketing and promotional efforts, the Scioto Society kept working to attract audiences over the years. Some efforts were successful, while others, as we might expect, were not. In the late 1970s, the Scioto Society proposed creating a historically themed "recreation-entertainment attraction" on five acres adjacent to the amphitheater. "Wilderness Ohio" would stimulate summer tourism and extend the tourism season from spring to fall, immersing visitors in the lifestyles of eighteenth- and early nineteenth-century settlers and Indians in the area.[55] The three-part attraction would include "Prairie Station," a prototype of an early Ohio settlement; "Fort Bull," an authentic reproduction of the forts built in the area; and "Chalahgawtha," a re-creation of an Indian village in the era of Simon Kenton. The amusement park never materialized, since the society was unable to raise the nearly $10 million needed for its construction.[56] The thought of a themed amusement park in southern Ohio seems an unconventional pairing with an outdoor drama, but the Scioto Society was not alone in its plans to broaden its tourist attractions and lengthen its tourist season. Amusement parks like Cherokee's Frontier Land and the proposed "Wilderness Ohio" could pull in the people who enjoyed going to places like Six Flags, Disney World, and Dollywood, potentially increasing attendance at the drama and having a larger economic impact on the region.

Little changed in the way of promotional materials and newspaper articles on the drama. A 1988 article noted, "It's hard not to get tied up in the action, and it's hard not to feel anything but sad at the end. Tecumseh fails to unite the tribes, but most people already know that." The author continued: "After all, had he succeeded, we might all be sweating out these drought-filled summer days in our air-conditioned wig-wams. The Indians might well have stopped the white-man's advance, instead of being practically pushed off the planet."[57] The biggest questions continually focused on the rhetorical—the what if. A 1994 article in *Country Living* magazine plaintively outlined that "all Tecumseh wanted was the Shawnee land west of the Ohio River returned to his people. The Shawnee, however, were too few in number to stem the ever-increasing tide of white settlers. But what if all the tribes of the Ohio Country banded together?"[58] The key was that the drama never sought to excoriate or indict the audience members for the things that happened in the past. In the same *Country Living* piece, producer and artistic director Marion Waggoner firmly said that the drama was not "a guilt trip for white people, nor is it an over-glorification of Native Americans." The director, Brent Gibbs, agreed. "There are no cardboard-cutout villains or heroes here," Gibbs said, "just two opposing forces that fought to the death for the land upon which we all now live."[59]

By the 1990s, *Tecumseh!* showed no signs of slowing down. In 1991, outdoor dramas posted an attendance gain for the second year in a row as other national tourist and entertainment industries continued to slump. Summer movie grosses dropped by 10 percent, and outdoor musical concerts saw a 25 percent decline in ticket sales. Even Disney World posted a 10 to 15 percent drop in attendance. *Tecumseh!* was the third-most-attended drama in the nation, and outdoor dramas were a $30 million industry that generated a $500 million economic impact on the national travel and tourism industry.[60] Attendance at *Tecumseh!* hit 86,000 in 1993. By 1997, it had an annual economic impact of more than $8 million and was one of the top three dramas in the nation.[61] This was all because, as the *Chillicothe Gazette* so succinctly said, "Tecumseh never achieved the goal he died trying to reach."[62] The drama did not hire a Native actor as Tecumseh until 1990 when Jose Andrews, a Wampanoag, was cast in the title role, and a press release proudly noted, "This is the first time in eighteen seasons that a Native American has starred in the title role."[63] The Scioto Society occasionally cast other Natives as Tecumseh, as it did in 1996 with Jack Kohler, who played the role for several years, but it has never seemed key to the drama.[64]

By 1997, there were ninety-one outdoor dramas in thirty-one states and the District of Columbia. Forty-three were historical dramas like *Unto These Hills* and *Tecumseh!*, while thirty-eight were Shakespeare companies and ten were religious dramas or passion plays.[65] The outdoor drama industry has ebbed and flowed over its nearly 100-year lifespan, with dramas opening and closing or opening, closing, and reopening over the decades. Like other dramas, *Tecumseh!* has had to reckon with and adapt to changes in the tourism industry. Its organizers have revamped the box office, which did not have computers until the mid-2010s. Until then, they used a ticket company that printed a paper ticket for every seat for every show. The box office was crammed with racks and racks of tickets, and when people called to order tickets the box office workers would put the tickets in little envelopes until the day of the show. While it worked for a long time, Brandon Smith realized that "people are used to being able to go online and buy a ticket. They want to know exactly where they're sitting."[66]

I nodded, because I'd done exactly that when I'd gone online to buy my tickets. The updated system, which cost the Scioto Society about $40,000, also meant increased fees that were then reflected in the ticket prices, but it was a risk the organization had to take in order to stay relevant. Attendance has fluctuated in recent years, and the seasons of selling 80,000 to 90,000 tickets are long gone. By the mid-2010s, annual attendance hovered around 40,000 to 50,000. The Scioto Society has started to diversify its offerings, adding concerts and seasonal attractions like "The Sleepy Hollow Experience at Haunted Mountain," which has turned the amphitheater into a terrifying Halloween event for the month of October since the early 2010s. "I don't think there will ever be a day when a hundred thousand people are going to see an outdoor drama in this country ever again," Smith said. "Any of them. People will go outdoors and see a symphony for an evening . . . but tastes have changed a little bit. People generally like to be in air conditioning in the summer."[67] He'd been working on different ways to market a drama that was more than forty years old, from billboards, radio, and television ads to Facebook, online, and movie theater ads.[68]

I asked him what Tecumseh—and *Tecumseh!*—meant. "I guess there's a couple answers to that," he said. "There's the economic answer and then there's the kind of spiritual answer."[69] There is, of course, the immediate economic impact, such as where the company spends more than a million dollars a year in the community from salaries to the actors going to coffee shops and putting gas in their cars, along with the additional income local businesses derive from tourists. There is the additional support from local and state governments because of the economic impact. "It means full hotel rooms, it means glitzy restaurants, it means gift shops selling items to people."

He continued. "In a more spiritual sense, I think the story of Tecumseh speaks to a large group of people in a way that a lot of outdoor dramas don't. Just because of the story and the nature of the story. The story is one of coming together as a community to try and achieve something greater than what you could achieve on your own." He struggled to remember the quote verbatim, but he turned to a phrase attributed to the Shawnee leader: "A simple twig breaks, but the bundle of twigs is strong." "I think people identify with that," Smith said. "It's a very American kind of story."[70] For Al Heierman and his wife, the story of Tecumseh has taken on a new meaning for them. "It's one of the few stories," Heierman said, "where the Indian turns out to be the hero. Like my wife says—she gets choked up all the time, we get so involved with it that it's hard on us, I guess—why couldn't he win, you know? And then she thinks, well, maybe I wouldn't be here if he did."[71] Tecumseh's life has been couched in the meaning of his death. It comes as no surprise to anyone sitting in the Sugarloaf Mountain Amphitheatre that Tecumseh dies, and that

A photograph from a scene toward the end of *Tecumseh!* when the character of Simon Kenton discovers the body of Tecumseh. In this scene, Kenton purposely misidentifies the body in order to preserve Tecumseh's dignity. Mel Cobb played Tecumseh and D. Wade McClain played Simon Kenton in this 1973 inaugural season. Courtesy of the Ross County Historical Society, McKell Library, Chillicothe, Ohio (1995.204.09).

his dream of an Indian confederacy dies with him. And if the drama is going to remain economically viable, it needs to stay that way. The comfort of his defeat cushions the final blow. Deloria maintains that Native resistance "came to be defined through the ascendant ideology of the vanishing Indian, which held its contradictions in suspension with ferocious power. Indians had a pre-destined doom, and that knowledge helped erase or justify the later military campaigns against them." This inevitable disappearance becomes "bitter-sweet and lamentable, with the disingenuous air of sadness."[72] The drama reflects contested notions of Native resistance, removal, and remembrance, at once tragic and unfortunate, preordained and unavoidable. These strategies of remaking and reenacting, as Marita Sturken argues, recode and renarrate history within new frameworks.[73]

"That's Tecumseh, Ain't It?": When Tecumseh Comes to Life

As I did in Pendleton and as I did in Cherokee, I found my seat for another production of *Tecumseh!* The drama, like the other two, begins while it's still somewhat light outside. It begins in 1784 when Tecumseh was a teenager. A group of Shawnee, led by Tecumseh's older brother Chiksika, lay in wait for a group of frontiersmen led by Simon Kenton. The Shawnee capture one of the frontiersmen after the battle, and the man is systematically tortured. The Shawnee take turns slashing his chest, burning him, and, finally, scalping him, and the warrior wielding the knife triumphantly claims that his brother's death has been avenged at last. Tecumseh tries in vain to save the man, much to the disgust of the older Shawnee. Chiksika, who became a leader among the Shawnee after the death of their father in the 1774 Battle of Point Pleasant, orders the men to let Tecumseh speak. In an eloquent speech, Tecumseh shames the warriors into rejecting these "traditional" rituals, vowing to fight nobly instead.[74]

Tecumseh is quickly set apart from his countrymen, who are painted as ruthless and resentful. He is beyond reproach, with his brother, Tenskwatawa, and future president William Henry Harrison framed as his antagonists. He is perpetually portrayed as a matchless man, almost superhuman in his patience, persistence, and political acumen. By creating a category occupied solely by Tecumseh, the drama continually reminds us, as Richard White argues, that Tecumseh becomes a symbol of the alternative, the paradoxical nativist who had resisted the Americans.[75] In the next scene, a dying Shawnee captured by Kenton boasts that Tecumseh will be greater than both Chiksika and their father, Pucksinwah, who had died many years earlier.

Eckert's script quickly moves forward a few years to a split among the Shawnee. Some have reluctantly agreed to move farther west in hopes of stopping further white expansion, but Tecumseh and his siblings are among those who refuse to leave. The script barrels along, and Blue Jacket appears at the end of the first wedding at the settlement at Kenton's Station. Blue Jacket asks to arrange a prisoner exchange, and Simon Kenton warily agrees before upping the ante to include a peace treaty talk. We finally meet Tenskwatawa in scene 5 when he excitedly tells their sister, Tecumapese, that he'll sit in his first council that night. She warns him to be quiet and listen, but his excitement turns to anger at her suggestion.

During the council's discussion of the upcoming treaty talks, Tenskwatawa's howling assertion that the Shawnee should kill all the whites overshadows Tecumseh's carefully measured deliberation. The rest of the men reluctantly agree to discuss peace, even though they show no trust in Kenton and the other frontiersmen. Tensions are high as the scene shifts to the prisoner exchange, and two of the frontiersmen—who have, since the first scene, shown themselves to be less honorable and virtuous than Kenton—sneak off and steal the Shawnee horses. A battle soon begins, and the final shot kills Chiksika.

Here, as in *Unto These Hills* and countless other outdoor dramas, the play-wright's focus is not necessarily on historical accuracy. Chiksika did not die due to a nefarious horse-stealing-gone-awry-during-a-prisoner-exchange. But Eckert uses this moment of white treachery to show how the character of Tecumseh became, in the words of Eckert's narrator, "a great avenger."[76] In the next scene, Tecumseh makes his way across the stage as the narrator explains the Shawnee triumph of St. Clair's defeat at the Battle of the Wabash and the subsequent American victory at the Battle of Fallen Timbers. The Galloway family enters, delighted at finding an empty piece of land. James Galloway, the patriarch of the little family, tells his wife and daughter that this once was Indian land, but a military officer had ordered it burned in the wake of war. The conversation between Tecumseh and the Galloways paint James as a man who respects the former Shawnee lands. James listens as Tecumseh tells him what areas not to disturb because they served as burial grounds, and James promises not to split up and sell off the land.

In the eighth scene—the last before intermission—Tecumseh plans his first journey outside the Shawnee lands in hopes of finding other nations who want to join his cause. Tecumseh tells Tenskwatawa that he will need to be in charge while Tecumseh is gone. Tenskwatawa questions Tecumseh's decision, arguing, "They won't obey me as they obey you!" But Tecumseh has a plan, one worth quoting here:

> TECUMSEH (*confidently*): They will! . . . and this is why: although, unlike me, you lack the gift of prophecy, nevertheless you will now become a great prophet to our followers.
> TENSKWATAWA (*incredulously*): I? How? I cannot even predict if the sun will shine tomorrow!
> TECUMSEH (*laughs shortly*): Before I leave here—and during each time I return—I will give to you alone the prophecies which you will pass on to our people as if they were your own. When these come true—as they will!—you will become known and respected as a great prophet and they will do your bidding.[77]

In their last moment together before Tecumseh's departure, he warns his brother not to give William Henry Harrison any reason to attack. Before Tecumseh leaves, he explains to his followers why he's leaving and why his brother will be in charge. Here, the audience is privy to Tecumseh's famous oratory skills, which give way to what the audience reads as a war dance—in Eckert's words, the "Indians are yelling, wildly leaping, yipping, gyrating."[78]

We meet Harrison in the first scene of act 2. He demands to know what his men have discovered about Tecumseh's plan, but none of his men have any proof except "the vaguest of innuendo."[79] But Kenton arrives with the news Harrison both desires and fears: Kenton has heard from other Indians about Tecumseh's plan and admits to Harrison, "I'm skeered o' only one Indian, an' he's Tecumseh. . . . Tecumseh aims t' take this whole country back, an', by God, 't wouldn't surprise me 'twere it too late already t' stop 'im."[80] In the next scene, Tecumseh tries in vain to get more of his fellow Shawnee—including Blue Jacket—to join his movement, but he does not succeed.

Eckert moves back to the Galloway farm for the first time since we met the family in the first act. James asks Tecumseh about the councils he's been holding, and the audience is led to believe this is the first time there has been tension between the two men in their long friendship. Tecumseh deflects the question, asking to take James's daughter, Rebecca, for the late-night canoe ride she has always asked for. James and his wife agree and Tecumseh and Rebecca exit, leaving her parents behind. We see Tecumseh and Rebecca cross the pond in the canoe before alighting on shore. It is clear they care for each other—perhaps even love each other—but neither can bring themselves to admit it.

The action moves back to the village, and Tenskwatawa has transformed himself into the epitome of a despot. Eckert's description of his luxurious clothes, coupled with the stage direction for a number of "attractive young maidens in simple, rather revealing pullover shifts" attending to him, paint a picture of a man who's let fame and power go to his head.[81] Tecumseh returns, both baffled and angry at how his brother has ruled in his absence. Tecumseh wonders aloud if he should have their sister's husband lead while he's away, but Tenskwatawa's plea forces Tecumseh to relent—but only if Tenskwatawa will once again heed his instructions. Tecumseh leaves, satisfied that his brother will listen. But Tenskwatawa calls *his* right-hand man, ordering him to take warriors to a nearby settlement and kill the cattle.

Tecumseh has gone back to see Rebecca. He kisses her and professes his love for her, and she does the same for him. He asks her to marry him, but she fears she cannot adapt to his way of life. He suggests an "agreeable combination" of tribal life and the life she knows, but she asks him what will happen when war arises between the Indians and the whites, and she asks how they will raise their children. Finally, Rebecca agrees to marry him—but only if he will agree to abandon his way of life and live with her people the way they do. Tecumseh kisses her one last time, but says he cannot do that and will not visit her again.

Tecumseh and Harrison meet face-to-face for the first time in the drama toward the end of act 2. Tecumseh has come to protest the government's acquisition of Indian lands, and he demands Harrison return the land and leave. Their discussion quickly turns to near-violence when Tecumseh confronts the Indian who arranged the sale but had no right to do so. One of Tecumseh's allies slips up, alluding to Tecumseh's upcoming trip to see tribes in the South. Harrison correctly infers that Tenskwatawa will be in charge in Tecumseh's absence and plans to march toward Prophetstown since he knows Tenskwatawa will attack first.

In the next scene, Tenskwatawa orders the attack. He meets resistance from several people, including his sister, Tecumapese, and threatens to have her killed if she speaks again. As the stage directions note, "The power of TENSKWATAWA seems supreme at this time."[82] He commands the warriors to fight, and the battle begins. After a lengthy and sufficiently theatrically bloody battle, it is clear the Indians have lost. In Eckert's notes, he suggested leaving a five-second pause before beginning the next scene since "experience has shown that audience will be applauding during this interval."[83]

Tecumapese enters with her husband, Wasegoboah. The defeat has crushed Tecumseh's movement, but Tecumseh has not yet returned. Wasegoboah tells his wife they have found Tenskwatawa and bound him to a tree, awaiting Tecumseh's judgment. When Tecumseh returns, it seems plausible that he will kill his brother. But, shortly after his return, Tecumseh announces he will let his brother live—but that his fate will be worse than death:

> In one day you have destroyed what I have taken over ten summers to build, and which now can never be rebuilt. In one day you have destroyed the hopes of *all* Indians. You are a liar, a cheat, a fool filled with the lust for power. You are no longer "The Prophet." You are no longer my brother. You are no longer a Shawnee, nor even an Indian. . . . I will not kill you, but your death begins this day, and it will be years in coming, for each day you will die a little more. From this time forward you will live with scorn and disgust, with the hatred and distrust of all men. You will be without family or friends. You will be without a people and you will live the rest of your miserable life outside the villages of those you sought to rule, and who now despise you. From this day forward you will be all alone, and when at last death becomes final for you, no living creature will mourn.[84]

Tecumseh realizes that their only hope now rests in an alliance with the British. We meet them in the final scene, and Eckert draws them as fearful and foppish, ready to retreat without putting up even the smallest of fights.

Here, as in chapter 4, I do not painstakingly demonstrate all the places where the script loosely plays with history. But the final scene of *Tecumseh!*, perhaps more than the others, is necessary for understanding the crux and contradictions of the drama. The entire drama is enveloped in an ominous layer, and the audience is continually haunted by the specter of dramatic irony. The audience clearly understands the significance of Tecumseh's scripted words and actions, and yet the meaning is, of course, lost on the character itself. But there we sit, in near-breathless anticipation, as the climactic final battle begins. We know, deep in our hearts, that Tecumseh will not succeed. His decade of strategic and shrewd diplomatic and political maneuvers is all for naught. His carefully crafted alliance is seemingly destroyed by his brother's betrayal. Even with the understanding that Tecumseh's moments are numbered, we are riveted to the scene before us. Tecumseh has told his warriors that there will be no glory, only defeat. He tells his warriors that he will die in the battle. He gives away every weapon he owns except his war club. He gives one warrior a small ramrod, ordering him that, if Tecumseh falls, the warrior is to strike Tecumseh four times with the ramrod. If he does this, Tecumseh will rise—but if he does not fulfill this deed, Tecumseh will not rise, and the audience does not need to be told that the confederation will die with Tecumseh.

Despite the premonitions, the omens, and the historical hindsight, the audience collectively inches closer to the edges of their seats as the frenetic pace of the battle builds. Tecumseh is shot, as we know he will be, and he falls to the ground. The battle continues, and finally there is but one warrior left—the one with the ramrod. Ducking gunfire that comes at him from all sides, he makes his way to the body of his fallen leader. Three times he raises the ramrod, and three times he strikes Tecumseh's body. As the warrior lifts his arm for the fourth and final time, a bullet cuts him down. He falls, as Tecumseh did, and the audience holds its collective breath. We wait for the warrior to rise again, but we know he will not. Tecumseh's prophecy rings true, and the Shawnee leader lies prostrate on the ground, never to rise again.[85]

But this is why the drama continues to celebrate Tecumseh's failure. As the audience members sit on ceded Shawnee lands, *Tecumseh!* invites its audience to participate in a collective moment of mourning. The sun has already set, leaving the stage lights and the stars as the only source of illumination. An aura of solemnity hangs in the air as a handful of men make their way toward one of the bodies on the dusty ground. They gently lift the body over their heads, stopping only to let the dead man's sister tenderly kiss the motionless figure before they slowly walk up the slight hill stage left. His sister takes his war club and leads an impromptu processional of mourners holding torches

In this 1973 photograph taken by Jon Heierman, actors playing Shawnee Indians carry the body of Tecumseh, played by Mel Cobb, offstage. Courtesy of the Ross County Historical Society, McKell Library, Chillicothe, Ohio (1995.204.13).

offstage into the woods. As they slowly move offstage, the voice-over narrator reminds the audience that no white man knows, or will ever know, where the Shawnee put the body of their beloved Tecumseh. Two actors, one standing on each side of the pond, throw their torches into the water. Their flame, like the flame of Tecumseh's dream, disappears, and the stage goes black.[86] But once the stage is empty, the house lights suddenly flicker back on, and the audience members gather their things and make their way toward the exits, excitedly discussing the production they've just witnessed.[87] It was, after all, just a performance. It doesn't matter that there's no historical evidence supporting this romanticized idealization of Tecumseh's death.

Seeing *Tecumseh!* is different from seeing Happy Canyon or *Unto These Hills*. Unlike in Pendleton, where the Happy Canyon arena is just a few miles from the CTUIR, or Cherokee, where the amphitheater sits on the Qualla Boundary, the Shawnee whose history is transformed on stage now have reservations thousands of miles away from the amphitheater. The Shawnee, forced out of what is now Ohio, are now three distinct nations: the Absentee Shawnee Tribe, the Shawnee Tribe, and the Eastern Shawnee Tribe of Oklahoma. The Eastern Shawnee, like the Confederated Tribes of the Umatilla Indian Reservation and the Eastern Band of Cherokee Indians, built a casino on their reservation. The Indigo Sky Casino in Wyandotte, Oklahoma, has helped the Eastern Shawnee build and diversify its economy, and the casino revenue has increased tribal social services and educational opportunities.[88] The Shawnee Tribe recently opened the Golden Mesa Casino in Guymon, Oklahoma, with the hopes of having nearly a $34 million impact on the region.[89] The Absentee Shawnee operate two branches of the Thunderbird Casino: one in Norman, Oklahoma, and one in Shawnee, Oklahoma.

Despite the Scioto Society's description of the early relationship between the tribe and the organization, it does not appear as though any of the Shawnee nations feel the same today. Benjamin J. Barnes, the Second Chief of the Shawnee Tribe, has written that it seems as if the Shawnee have been "brought in to fill the public's appetite to celebrate the conquest of the Indian" since the early twentieth century.[90] He argues that the story of Tecumseh and Rebecca Galloway plays well in their former homeland, even though this "fictional portrayal of Tecumseh and Native Americans dressed in garish outfits does not represent Shawnee material cultural traditions, or any of the peoples in the Ohio valley." Barnes writes that a group of Absentee Shawnee saw the drama as recently as 2014, but he hoped that "someday Shawnees will be able to visit with the cast and crew of *Tecumseh!* as advisors rather than ticket holders."[91] Laura Peers contends that "representations always have multiple interpretations; nor are they ever finalized, either in their creation or in their reception. These sites are always works in progress, continually revised through contestation, negotiation, and compromise."[92] In Chillicothe, the narrative salvaged in the drama is one that centers on Indigenous disappearance and American innocence.

None of these productions, regardless of their economic impact, is without fault. But it is striking to see how these three productions have wrestled with history both on and off the stage since their respective inceptions. Throughout the years I've spent working on this book, I've tried to understand what elements of history make for a good historical pageant or outdoor drama. As *Tecumseh!* draws a picture of Tecumseh that the Shawnee do not recognize or support, it remains to be seen if the Shawnee will ever have a larger part to play.

Should You Ask Me, Whence These Stories?
The Power of Salvage Tourism

In 1972, Mark Sumner, the director of the Institute of Outdoor Drama (IOD), responded to an inquiry from Mr. Bernard Atz of Uniontown, Pennsylvania. Atz had called the IOD to gather information about the locations of failed dramas and reasons for the failures. "They are 'thinking of building an amphitheatre,'" the memo read, "and want to avoid those errors of past companies."[1] In his response, Sumner warned Atz, "Dramas have failed for a combination of reasons generally rooted in the lack of understanding of both personnel and sponsors as to the magnitude of the effort required for the artistic part of the production, coupled with being locked in to script and production date too late for corrections and changes."[2]

Sumner continued. "At the same time," he wrote, "at least two productions were 'changed to death' over a period of the first three years and failed to generate new audiences." He was glad to answer specific questions as much as he could, but he asked Atz to remember that "dramatic production is so complex, and so many managers and artists combine to present the product, that the room for error is ALWAYS great."[3] Sumner included a list of nearly thirty defunct dramas in eight states, including Gatlinburg, Tennessee's *Chucky Jack*, the drama that had pulled some audience members away from *Unto These Hills* during its brief run. Even dramas on Daniel Boone and Davy Crockett weren't immune to the whims of the tourism industry. Some were later revived, but most of the dramas on Sumner's list had closed for good.[4]

Another 1972 document from the IOD offered tips on producing a successful outdoor drama. "Haste is the biggest single reason for outdoor drama failure," the document began. For many years, dramas had been built on "a last minute crash basis" that forced management to focus on construction instead of promotion, left directors without completed scripts, left casts rehearsing elsewhere, and left promotion, "which should have a tremendous outreach, as a hasty makeshift aimed at audiences only in the immediate area." Unsurprisingly, "fully fifty percent of the earlier outdoor dramas failed to be artistically and financially profitable."[5] Aside from the more technical aspects, like an "unimaginative director" or a quickly written script without much historical research, the notes also highlighted the need for a historically relevant location in order to capitalize on the historical entertainment audience's sense of pilgrimage. "Each of these plays must have a reason for being," the notes continued, "which will motivate people at home to get in the car and visit the amphitheatre." Proximity to historical ground was also key.[6]

It's unclear if Atz's dream ever became reality.[7] But even in the mid-to-late twentieth century, the combination of history and the potential for tourism and economic windfalls kept drawing people and organizations to outdoor drama. An undated IOD document titled "Ten Points that Should Be Considered by Everyone Planning to Produce an Outdoor Play" warned potential producers to make sure the script was strong and that actors and staff could put on "a shining performance." Was the theater in a good location, and was there community support? Was there "a sizeable body of transients, such as tourists," who would come to the drama, and was there audience potential in nearby metropolitan areas? Were there additional tourist attractions, and were there adequate dining and housing accommodations?[8]

Even the most well-intentioned and best-laid plans could—and often did—go awry. The capricious nature of the tourism industry claimed as many productions as there were moderate and runaway successes. Unlike historical pageants, the vast majority of which ran out of steam in the early to mid-twentieth century, outdoor dramas continue to draw audiences year after year. In 2018, the IOT (the IOD became the Institute of Outdoor Theatre in 2014 to reflect the broader focus on outdoor performances) published information on outdoor historical dramas, religious or passion plays, and Shakespeare productions in forty-five states (all but Alaska, Hawaii, Louisiana, Mississippi, and Wyoming). Outdoor historical dramas have been staged in nearly every state since the early twentieth century, and residents in all but one state—Wyoming—have contacted the IOD/IOT.

This is more than a phenomenon or a passing fad. In the 1960s, residents in Dover–New Philadelphia, Ohio, asked the IOD to do a feasibility study for what would become *Trumpet in the Land*.[9] The Robeson Historical Drama Association staged *Strike at the Wind*, centered on an "Indian Robin Hood" character, from the mid-1970s to the mid-1990s, and tried to revive the show at the end of the decade.[10] In the 1980s, Battle Ground, Indiana, hoped to stage a drama around the town's most famous event, the Battle of Tippecanoe.[11] Despite the shifting trends in tourism, many outdoor dramas still go on every year. The IOD received requests for feasibility studies well into the 2000s. Residents of Greenville, Ohio, requested one in 2002 because they wanted to add a drama to the town's annual Annie Oakley Days festivities.[12]

These successes, of course, are offset by the dramas that didn't make it. In 2007, the Hiawatha Club of Pipestone, Minnesota, about 200 miles southwest of Minneapolis and St. Paul, announced that its *Song of Hiawatha* pageant would live for just one more season. Organizers of the pageant, which had opened in 1948, cited declining attendance as the reason for closing.[13] Several years earlier, the National Park Service called the pageant "an important link between Pipestone National Monument, the town of Pipestone, the surrounding region, and a public interested in history and culture." It was a boon for the local economy, bringing "visitors, media attention, and a sense of vitality to the Pipestone area" and contributing to "an enlivened cultural and economic environment."[14] But Mick Myers, head of the Pipestone Chamber of Commerce and a member of the Hiawatha Club that produced the pageant, cited increased competition in the region from casinos and a nearby pageant about Laura Ingalls Wilder. Jay Gabler called the pageant "a living time capsule," having survived the heyday of pageantry and "the time when it would occur to anyone that it would be a great idea to dress several dozen European-Americans in headdresses and enact a Native American legend as told by a white New Englander."[15]

According to Sally J. Southwick, the town of Pipestone clung to the legacy of Longfellow's poem. By the 1940s and 1950s, civic and community leaders began to "reassert themselves as cultural custodians of local Indian heritage" as part of Pipestone's identity development, "particularly in the communal sense of custodianship over carefully defined local heritage and identity based on generalized images of American Indians."[16] The pageant capitalized on Indian history and gave its non-Native organizers the ability to tell a particular version of Indigenous history. Like countless other organizers and producers across the country, Pipestone and the Hiawatha club positioned themselves as the purveyors of regional Native history that drew on ideas of Indianness and identity to create a tourist-centered production.

Like many pageants and dramas, *Song of Hiawatha* relied on the beauty of the region and its historical connections and connotations.[17] The rise and fall of Pipestone's pageant mirrors the fate of countless other pageants and dramas throughout the twentieth and twenty-first centuries. The vast majority of these productions began as regional enterprises bent on creating or enhancing the tourist environments and economies of their respective locations. Happy Canyon, *Unto These Hills*, and *Tecumseh!* were created by and performed for non-Native tourists seeking an escape from the havoc of modern life. The use of American Indian history as the basis for these productions demonstrates the widespread power of the potential economic windfalls to be gained by commodifying indigeneity. From Wild West shows and world's fairs to local celebrations, Indigenous peoples and their images became fodder for commercial enterprises.

From the dusty ranges of Oregon to the mountains of North Carolina to the pastoral feel of southern Ohio, images of Indians permeated the regional tourist environments. Boosters and businesses pounced on the possibility of turning their towns into havens for city folks who had grown weary of the hustle and bustle of modern American life. Scholars John Troutman and Philip Deloria have respectively suggested that "popular fantasies of Indianness" and the simultaneous "romanticization of Indianness" played pivotal roles in the growing antimodern movement at the turn of the twentieth century.[18] Pageants and dramas were just one of the ways countless small, often remote towns jostled for the upper hand in the tourist economy.

There were many potential benefits for towns like Pendleton, Cherokee, and Chillicothe. In Pendleton, the changing nature of Pendleton's economy that drove city leaders to host a round-up and an Indian pageant and Wild West show stemmed from what they considered to be the destruction of their identity as Westerners. The economy in Pendleton was shifting toward a more staid wheat and wool environment, not the "wild and wooly" lifestyle that had defined Pendleton in its early years. By producing the Round-Up and Happy Canyon, non-Natives in Pendleton were able to convince themselves that, despite the changing landscape of the economy, they were still the Wild Westerners they had always considered themselves to be. By incorporating local Indian history into the production and incorporating local Indians into the Round-Up, Pendletonians portrayed the town's history as one embedded in the fabric of the West.

In Cherokee, the Eastern Band and its history had been fodder for commercial enterprises for decades by the time the drama premiered. The Cherokee Historical Association (CHA) commandeered this history by the end of World War II, turning it into a melodramatic production that was so keen on depicting its notions of authentic Indians that it completely marginalized and excluded the Eastern Band. By the early twentieth century, *Unto These Hills* was no longer commercially viable. The CHA, desperately seeking a way to salvage the drama, struggled to stay relevant as the Eastern Band and regional tourism industries keep diversifying. Success in Chillicothe far outpaced its regional counterparts in Xenia and New Philadelphia. The different fates of the three outdoor dramas in Ohio, all of which focused on a similar era in American and American Indian history, highlight the capricious nature of tourism, an industry where the consequences are often as important as the benefits.

At first glance, the three productions at the core of this book are seemingly incompatible, and their differences seem to far outweigh their similarities. But despite the differences among them, these three productions are manifestations of a critical component of the history of Indigenous performance and performances of indigeneity. None came to life as a means of preserving Indian history for the local and regional Indians whose histories formed the basis of each production. Rather, as shown throughout this book, the concept of salvage tourism is the thread that binds these three together. Salvage tourism functioned in unique ways in each production, each region, and each time period examined herein. In all three instances, Indianness became the most promising and potentially profitable factor.

Did salvage tourism function in 1970s Chillicothe the same way it did in turn-of-the-century Pendleton or midcentury Cherokee? Not necessarily, and we should not expect it to look the same in each town and each production. Salvage tourism is not meant as a static interpretation. *Tecumseh!* did not emerge in the same historical moment as Happy Canyon or *Unto These Hills*, and each production maintains a different relationship with the concept of salvage tourism. But salvage tourism allows us to see how and why each production emerged when it did. Amid changes in federal Indian policy and contestations over citizenship and identity, salvage tourism's use of the imagined, ideal Indian allowed tourist audiences to envision themselves not as tourists but as part of a romanticized past, a past driven by the dream of innocence and what Marita Sturken calls the "culture of comfort."[19]

The evolution of the practice from Pendleton in the 1910s, Cherokee in the 1950s, and Chillicothe in the 1970s into the twenty-first century highlights how salvage tourism served as an escape from reality as economic, cultural, and political conditions changed throughout the twentieth century. In Pendleton, the late nineteenth- and early twentieth-century policies of allotment and assimilation that sought to turn Indians into Americans collided with questions of immigration and citizenship. Cold War contestations led to calls for the termination of the relationship between Native nations and the federal government, and the Eastern Band's tourism industry helped save the nation from the fate that befell numerous other Native nations. In the age of the American Indian Movement and rising Indigenous resistance, the Scioto Society turned to its most famous Indian, Tecumseh, in order to reckon with contemporary anxieties over identity and belonging.

The importance of salvage tourism lies in its ability to serve as a framework for a wide range of interpretations of Indianness. In 2010, nearly a century after Happy Canyon opened in Pendleton, a new outdoor drama—a retelling of James Fenimore Cooper's *Last of the Mohicans*—premiered in Lake George, New York. While this drama seems to have suffered the same fate as hundreds of dramas across the country that have gone dark, its creation and production highlight the ways in which salvage tourism continues to manifest itself. Unlike contemporary heritage tourism, which seeks to authentically represent the past, these pageants and dramas continue to rely on dramatic interpretations of history or the "spirit" of history. Unlike the Confederated Tribes of the Umatilla Indian Reservation, whose cultural institute essentially refutes the final ⸻ of Happy Canyon, salvage tourism requires the suspension of ⸻ Cherokee, the Eastern Band's mere presence and rise as a⸻ ⸻er contradict Hunter's dramatic telling of their history. ⸻construction of Tecumseh's life, mission, and death ⸻quences of salvage tourism's insistence on twisting his-

⸻ed how these three productions, individually and col-
⸻ within distinct regional tourist economies in dis-
⸻ted the motivations of organizers, promoters, local
⸻tions. Existing scholarship has mainly dealt with
⸻ld West shows, Indian fairs, and powwows and
⸻onstrate the importance of American In-
⸻ dramas because they sought—and con-
⸻ and Indianness in a distinctly regional
⸻me of these pageants and dramas still
⸻dly successful forces the discussion to
⸻espite their many differences, one con-
⸻a lens for the past and the present, the
⸻ll, these three productions encapsulate
⸻with ideas of identity, nationhood, and

n interchangeably throughout this book as broad terms
of what is now known as the United States. I also use
angeably, particularly in reference to the qualities and
ed on and incorporated into these tourist-centered per-
pecific affiliations (such as Ojibwe, Eastern Band, and
le and applicable.

Bayfield: Bayfield Chamber of Commerce and Visitor

i.
Karen Wilber, September 25, 2013.
ge.
t Workers Here.
lished by the Bayfield Civic League (Bayfield, Wiscon-
as part of Bayfield's Sesquicentennial celebrations, and
bookshelf at Erickson's.
s Indian Pageant, *Bayfield Progress*, August 26, 1924."
d, WI: Bayfield Progress Print), 1923.
l Patriotism," 90–92.
rical Society, *Minnesota History Bulletin*, 470.
rical Society, 470.
nsas, 255–57. The Medicine Lodge Indian Peace Treaty
t was staged every five years from 1941 to 1961, and then
5. It was staged again in 2011 to celebrate Kansas's sesqui-

position in Oklahoma," 159, 161.

ha Pageant," and Gabler, "Pipestone's Hiawatha Pageant."
Performance over Policy." Other scholars have also dis-
onsin tourism endeavors, such as Larry Nesper, Steven
Grant Arndt.
ids Indian Pageant"; Bayfield Heritage Association, "Sec-
h Pageant" souvenir program. There is a dearth of sources
pecially compared with the 1924 and even the 1925 produc-
ld County Journal, Lars Larson explained that the pageants
h an Indian opera in 1926. People were more interested in a

log-rolling tournament, so the opera was not restaged until 1929 for the Washburn-Bayfield homecoming. Lars Larson, "The Indian historical pageant of '20s had short run," *Bayfield County Journal*, January 10, 2013.

18. "Ramona" Outdoor Play, Ramona Bowl Amphitheatre.

19. Letter from Helen Hunt Jackson to Thomas Bailey Aldrich, May 4, 1883, as cited in Hochman, *"Uncle Tom's Cabin,"* 160.

20. Moylan, "Materiality as Performance," 226.

21. Rothman, *Devil's Bargain*, 10.

22. Gassan, *Birth of American Tourism*, 2–4; Sears, *Sacred Places*, 4.

23. Nash, *Wilderness and the American Mind*, xiv.

24. Aron, *Working at Play*, 132.

25. McNally, "Indian Passion Play," 108.

26. See, for instance, Aron, *Working at Play*; Brown, *Inventing New England*; Desmond, *Staging Tourism*; Gassan, *Birth of American Tourism*; Löfgren, *On Holiday*; Shaffer, *See America First*; and Werry, *Tourist State*, among others.

27. Trachtenberg, *Shades of Hiawatha*, xviii.

28. Trachtenberg, xxii.

29. See Glassberg, *American Historical Pageantry*.

30. Glassberg, 1.

31. Glassberg, 140.

32. Troutman, *Indian Blues*, 154.

33. "The Show," *Tecumseh!*.

34. P. Deloria, *Indians in Unexpected Places*, 191.

35. "Department of Anthropology," *Smithsonian Institution*.

36. Archabal, Introduction to *Chippewa Customs*, 4.

37. Troutman, *Indian Blues*, 159.

38. See Gruber, "Ethnographic Salvage," 1294; Troutman, *Indian Blues*; Raibmon, *Authentic Indians*; Kramer, *Blood of Government*; Gross, *What Blood Won't Tell*; Bernardin, MacFarlane, Tonkovich, and Graulich, *Trading Gazes*.

39. Desmond, *Staging Tourism*, 39.

40. Sears, *Sacred Places*, 4; Bederman, *Manliness and Civilization*, 173; Nash, *Wilderness and the American Mind*, 143.

41. Gruber, "Ethnographic Salvage," 1297.

42. Sturken, *Tourists of History*, 3–4.

43. Many thanks to my colleague Joseph Whitson for framing—quite literally—this analogy.

44. Shaffer, *See America First*, 309.

45. Shaffer, 4.

46. Shaffer, 4.

47. Sturken, *Tourists of History*, 9.

48. "Cherokee Drama on List of Nation's Top Shows," *Waynesville Mountaineer*, July 6, 1950.

49. "Drama," *Time* (July 10, 1939), 48.

50. Avery, "Introduction: At *The Lost Colony*," in Green, *Lost Colony*, 1.

51. Green, "Preface," v–viii.

52. Koch, *Raleigh*; Free and Lower, *History into Drama*, 111.

53. Avery, "Introduction: At *The Lost Colony*," 2.

54. Avery, "Introduction: At *The Lost Colony*," 2–3.

55. Avery, "Introduction: At *The Lost Colony*," 3; "A Note on the Text" in Green, *Lost Colony*, 21.

56. Koch, "Drama of Roanoke Island," 13.

57. Selden, "American Drama in the Open Air," 8.

58. Free and Lower, *History into Drama*, 94.

59. *Encyclopedia Americana* 21:97; see Avery, *Paul Green Reader*, and Glassberg, *American Historical Pageantry*.

60. Avery, *Paul Green Reader*, 11.

61. Avery, 11. Avery has also argued that these historical pageants have been of little interest to those who study theater or culture other than the social aim of devising and maintaining a sense of the past.

62. Free and Lower, *History into Drama*, 100.

63. Green, "Preface," xiv.

64. Green, "Author's Note," vii.

65. Green, "Playmaker's Progress," 86.

66. Hunter, "Theatre Meets the People," 128.

67. Glassberg, *American Historical Pageantry*, 242–43.

68. Glassberg, 254.

69. Glassberg, 275.

70. Kenny, *Paul Green*, 148–49.

71. Glassberg, *American Historical Pageantry*, 275.

72. "Former Lost Colony Producer Dies in Chapel Hill," *Outer Banks Sentinel*, June 27, 2017.

73. "Former Lost Colony Producer"; "Mark Reese Sumner," Institute of Outdoor Theatre, June 20, 2017.

74. Mark Reese Sumner, "An Investigation of Existing Outdoor Drama Techniques and a Determination of Methods to Improve Training," Institute of Outdoor Drama (1967), 2. IOD/IOT archives, box 133, folder a.

75. Sumner, "Investigation of Existing Outdoor Drama Techniques," 3.

76. H. Davis, "Theatre of the People," 39.

77. Green, "Preface," xv–xvi.

78. H. Davis, "Theatre of the People," 39.

79. Trotman, "Does *The Lost Colony* 'Work'?," 147.

80. OOHDA fund-raising brochure. IOD/IOT archives, box 149, folder b.

81. Finger, *Cherokee Americans*, 117.

82. Lindsey, "Outdoor Historical Dramas."

83. Smithers, "Cherokee Epic," 3.

84. William Shakespeare, *As You Like It*, act 2, scene 7.

Chapter One

1. The title of this chapter comes from "Days of Old West Are Lived Again at Happy Canyon," *Daily East Oregonian*, September 20, 1917. The story of the first Round-Up is based on a Katrina Phillips interview with Randy Thomas, Round-Up Publicity Director,

September 10, 2014, Pendleton, OR; Willingham, "First 100
tion in the epigraphs can be found here: Furlong, "Epic Dr
ton Is All Ready to Let 'Er Buck at Roundup," *Sunday Orego*

2. Laegreid, "Rodeo Queens at the Pendleton Round-Up

3. Furlong, "Epic Drama of the West," 376.

4. *Brigadoon*, a 1947 musical by Alan Jay Lerner and Fred
town in the Scottish highlands that appeared only once eve
did appear, the town and its citizens were charmingly anach

5. "'Happy Canyon' Will Be Open to Public Wednesday
September 21, 1914.

6. "'Happy Canyon' Promises to Visitors Big Time This
tember 11, 1914.

7. "'Happy Canyon' Promises to Visitors"; "'Happy Car
Fair Pavilion," *Daily East Oregonian*, September 2, 1914.

8. "An Advertised Indian," *East Oregonian*, Pendleton, 1 1

9. The title for this epigraph comes from the Happy Car

10. Grafe, "Lee Moorhouse," 429.

11. Grafe, 430.

12. Conner, "Round-Up Reminiscences," 47.

13. Grafe, "Lee Moorhouse," 430.

14. Conner, "Round-Up Reminiscences," 47.

15. See Conner, "Round-Up Reminiscences," and "From   Generation."

16. "Company History," Pendleton Woolen Mills.

17. "How the Round-Up Grew from Modest Beginning to Show of World Proportions," *East Oregonian Round-Up Souvenir Edition*, September 11, 1913; Willingham, "First
100 Years," 17.

18. Willingham, "First 100 Years," 16–17.

19. Willingham, 17.

20. Willingham, 16.

21. Allison, "Annual Event Comes Long Way," 7.

22. Grafe, "Lee Moorhouse," 441.

23. Grafe, 441–47.

24. Cronon, "Foreword," xi. Scholars like William G. Robbins and Tom Marsh, among
others, demonstrate how early emigrants to Oregon fully believed that this land was, in fact,
promised to them. David Peterson del Mar writes that Oregon was formed "in strife's crucible" as several European nations and, later, the United States, jostled for power and control over the region's abundant natural resources, something they could only accomplish by
removing the Native peoples from what became the state of Oregon. See Peterson del Mar,
Oregon's Promise, 39.

25. In the early nineteenth century, both the United States and Great Britain occupied
what's now the Pacific Northwest (see Marsh, *To the Promised Land*, 3). Lewis and Clark's
overland expedition through Native lands spurred the publication of countless pamphlets,
books, and articles on the topic, turning Oregon into what Marsh calls "a mythical vision
before there were any Oregonians at all" (Marsh, *To the Promised Land*, 4). American settlers
established provisional governments in 1841, 1843, and 1845, and an 1846 treaty between the

United States and Britain settled the boundary issue between the two parties. Oregon became a territory in 1848, and statehood followed in 1859. See Marsh, *To the Promised Land*,
and Corning, *Dictionary of Oregon History*.

26. Marsh, *To the Promised Land*, 12. Oregon's provisional government, created in 1843,
outlawed slavery in June of 1844, giving slave owners in the region three years to free en-
slaved people. However, the same government ordered free blacks out of the territory by 1846.
See Pierce, *Making the White Man's West*, 131. While the 1848 creation of Oregon Territory also
outlawed slavery, the Oregon legislature passed a bill in 1849 that prohibited free Blacks and
those of mixed heritage from settling in Oregon. According to Jason Pierce, some legisla-
tors feared that the presence of African Americans in Oregon would lead to alliances with
Native populations in the region, thereby "instilling into their mind feelings of hostility
toward the white race." See Pierce, 132. The territory would continue to ban both slavery
and African Americans throughout the 1850s. See Pierce, 131, 134. Early Oregonians, for
Marsh, "chose not to confront the dilemma of defining and maintaining race relations between white and black." See Marsh, *To the Promised Land*, 13. Oregon was not alone in its
restrictive legislation—Peter Burnett, the first governor of California, had started calling for
excluding Chinese immigrants and African Americans as early as 1849. See Pierce, *Making
the White Man's West*, 129.

27. Marsh, *To the Promised Land*, 22. Unlike its successor, the 1862 Homestead Act, wherein
European immigrants, Hispanics, and African Americans were able to file claims, the Oregon Donation Land Law explicitly excluded nonwhites from claiming land in Oregon.
Pierce notes that more than 2.4 million people, including many African Americans, filed
claims under the Homestead Act. While Marsh notes that the act was notable in allowing
women—even those who were married—to hold property in their own name, the codifica-
tion of race-based exclusion highlights the goal of keeping Oregon as white as possible.

28. Limerick, *Legacy of Conquest*, 45. According to Section 4 of the Oregon Donation
Land Law, eligibility was "granted to every white settler or occupant of the public lands,
American half-breed Indians included, above the age of 18 years, being a citizen of the United
States, or having made a declaration according to law of his intention to become a citizen."
See McDougall, Philips, and Boxberger, *Before and After the State*, 280n40.

29. Marsh, *To the Promised Land*, 23.

30. See, for instance, Trafzer, "Legacy of the Walla Walla Council, 1855," 398.

31. See "Notice," *Oregon Arbus*, issues from July 7, 1855; July 14, 1855; July 21, 1855; August 11,
1855; August 25, 1855; October 6, 1855; and October 13, 1855.

32. Settlers in the territory voted overwhelmingly for statehood (7,200 to 3,200) and against
slavery (7,700 to 2,600). See Marsh, *To the Promised Land*, 44. However, they also voted to
exclude free Blacks from settling in the state by an even greater margin (8,640 to 1,081). See
Pierce, *Making the White Man's West*, 135–37. White Oregonians, according to David Peterson del Mar, "wanted a white state." Peterson del Mar, *Oregon's Promise*, 82.

33. Peterson del Mar, *Oregon's Promise*, 83, 108.

34. *Oregonian*, November 2, 1866 via *The Oregon History Project* (https://oregonhistory
project.org/articles/historical-records/act-to-prohibit-the-intermarriage-of-races-1866/#
.XRpMXOhKjMX). Chinese immigrants were the largest minority population in Oregon
from the 1860s to the 1880s, even accounting for errors in the census. See Peterson del Mar,
Oregon's Promise, 111. Oregon, of course, was not the only state to call for legislation barring

Chinese immigration. Even though California "catalyzed and spearheaded the movement for exclusion," to quote Stuart Miller, Patricia Limerick and others have shown that the 1882 Chinese Exclusion Act had national support and met little opposition. See S. C. Miller, *Unwelcome Immigrant*, 191; Limerick, *Legacy of Conquest*, 264. The legislation, which had a ten-year duration, was renewed in 1892. It became permanent in 1902 and was not repealed until 1943. See Limerick, 269.

35. "Are Forninst the Chinese: Pendleton People Sign Chinese Exclusion Petition," *East Oregonian*, Pendleton, November 30, 1901, 5.

36. "No Chinese Wanted," *East Oregonian*, Pendleton, February 22, 1902, 4. The paper admitted that "there are fields of labor in our country in which Chinese could render service," mostly in industries "where white persons are unwilling to undertake for the wages which employers can afford to pay." However, the editorial continued, the "working people would feel injured," which carried the potential threat of violence and retaliation against those willing to work for those wages. By December 1903, the paper noted that more than 100 Chinese men had been living in the city the previous year but that many had "departed in the past few months." Most of those who remained were employed as cooks, although others worked as janitors and in laundries. See "Pendleton's Chinese," *East Oregonian*, Pendleton, December 22, 1903, 7.

37. The paper claimed that "many who have known them in the west" considered them "as destructive to American wages standards and American Ideals as are the Chinese." The paper also cited a recent interview with San Francisco mayor Eugene Schmitz, who declared, "I would sooner see the bars let down to the Chinese than to witness unrestricted Japanese immigration." "The Chinese are dangerous enough," Schmitz warned, "but the Japanese, with their education, American manners and cheap labor, would soon drive all competition out of business." See "Coolies May Come," *East Oregonian*, Pendleton, June 17, 1905, 5. Five years later, with the inaugural Round-Up on the horizon, there were about 500 Chinese living in Pendleton. As Keith May admits, however, these official census numbers are likely incorrect and lower than the actual number of residents. Still, these numbers were more than six times the number recorded in 1900. See May, *Pendleton*, 26.

38. See Robbins, *Landscapes of Promise*.

39. Robbins, 102.

40. Marsh, *To the Promised Land*, 62.

41. Marsh, 63.

42. Robbins, *Landscapes of Promise*, 146, 163. John Minto, writing in 1902, argued that the interests of cattle breeders preceded sheep keeping and opposed the extension of sheep because cattle could be left "free to range at will," because cattle would not stay on rangelands "soiled by the presence of sheep grazing," and that adding sheep to a cattle range meant an increased risk for losing cattle during a hard winter. See Minto, "Sheep Husbandry in Oregon," 237.

43. Laegreid, "Rodeo Queens at the Pendleton Round-Up," 9; May, *Pendleton*, 59; Willingham, "Pendleton Woolen Mills."

44. Robbins, *Landscapes of Promise*, 147.

45. May, *Pendleton*, 27.

46. Robbins, *Landscapes of Promise*, 150; May, *Pendleton*, 60; Grafe, "Lee Moorhouse," 437.

47. E. Jones, *Oregonian's Handbook*, 275–76. Over the last five years, Jones proclaimed in 1894, Pendleton had "enjoyed a growth that has been surpassed by no inland point of the state." Over the next five years, he added, the opportunities for advancement, "which will be taken advantage of by a wealthy and progressive class of people, promise even greater things for the city in the future than has accrued to the place in the past." Jones boasted that stock raising, wool growing, and farming were the leading industries in Umatilla County, "owing to the unexcelled opportunities afforded" in the region.

48. E. Jones, *Oregonian's Handbook*, 278–79.

49. E. Jones, 279.

50. "Grading Up Cattle," *East Oregonian*, March 14, 1904.

51. "Cunningham's Rise to the Position of Sheep King," *East Oregonian*, December 5, 1905. Known as the "sheep king of Oregon," Cunningham's company eventually became "the largest and most profitable in the entire Pacific Coast region." He sold the company in 1905 and retired from the industry he'd helped shape over the last several decades.

52. "Charles Cunningham Discusses Sheep and Wild Animals," *East Oregonian*, September 14, 1907. He blamed the cutting of the open range, the threat of lower tariffs on wool and hides, and wild animals, and he insisted that wild animals killed half of Oregon's domestic animals. "Every family in Portland," he thundered, "is keeping a coyote and feeding it on the highest priced meat to be had."

53. See Blee, "Completing Lewis and Clark's Westward March," 232–53.

54. Advertisement in *East Oregonian*, August 16, 1902, 6.

55. "Buffalo Bill's Work," *East Oregonian*, August 16, 1902, 6; advertisement in *East Oregonian*, August 16, 1902, 6.

56. Interview with Randy Thomas, Round-Up publicity director, September 10, 2014.

57. "Wild West in West: This Is the Land of the Strenuous Life," *East Oregonian*, August 21, 1902, 2.

58. Laegreid, "Rodeo Queens at the Pendleton Round-Up," 9.

59. The May 22, 1903 issue of the *Morning Oregonian* was filled with details about the president's visit, gushing, "The spirit of the people was stirred as never before in this city." See "Guest of a Day," *Morning Oregonian*, May 22, 1903, 1. Organizers sealed a copper box filled with mementos in the cornerstone, including, among other items, photographs, documents from the state historical society, the imprint of the Jefferson Medal, paintings and signatures of Lewis and Clark, and bits of wood, rocks, and leaves from significant locations and ships. See "Cornerstone Is Laid for Great Lewis and Clark Monument at City Park," *Morning Oregonian*, May 22, 1903, 9.

60. Like previous world's fairs and expositions, such as the 1893 Columbian Exposition in Chicago and the 1904 Louisiana Purchase Exposition in St. Louis, Portland's world's fair simultaneously celebrated American progress and expansion. See Blee, "Completing Lewis and Clark's Westward March," 233 and 236. Dan McAllen, a dry-goods merchant, had seen the success of San Francisco's 1894 Midwinter Fair. The fair, itself modeled after the 1893 Columbian Exposition, hoped to draw international attention to San Francisco. Also see Rydell, *All The World's a Fair*.

61. A commemorative booklet from the 1905 Lewis and Clark Exposition boasted that the "broadening of intelligence, the advancement of discovery, inventions, science, agriculture

and all the useful arts and industries which has taken place, within the last hundred years, has placed our country in a position which is rapidly becoming the most commanding among the nations of the earth." See Reid, *Lewis and Clark Centennial Exposition Illustrated*, 3. Visitors would be privy to, among other things, agricultural, forestry, and technological displays; an "Oriental Exhibits Palace"; the "Foreign Exhibits Building"; and various state buildings representing states of the Pacific Northwest.

62. Abbott, *Great Extravaganza*, 54; Blee, "Completing Lewis and Clark's Westward March," 251.

63. Miller and Portland Rose Festival Foundation, *Portland Rose Festival*, 7; Donahue, *Portland Rose Festival*, 11.

64. Miller and Portland Rose Festival Foundation, *Portland Rose Festival*, 7–8.

65. Larsen, *Missing Chapters*, 6.

66. Larsen, 15.

67. "Camping along the Old Trail: Ezra Meeker Is Backtracking the Route He Followed 54 Years Ago," *East Oregonian*, Pendleton, March 28, 1906, 1. The paper also explained that there would be a small admission fee to attend since Meeker was "voluntarily making this extraordinary journey," and the fee would help defray the expenses of the trip. "Ezra Meeker Will Speak," *East Oregonian*, Pendleton, March 28, 1906, 1. Meeker finished the 2,600-mile trek in late January of 1907. More than twenty towns along the trail had already built monuments, and others planned to do the same. Meeker was satisfied with the results, proudly noting, "The work is going on and it won't be long before the old way will be marked with shafts suitably inscribed. It was a long journey for an old man to make, but I feel repaid." See "At Journey's End: Ezra Meeker Is Now at Indianapolis," *East Oregonian*, Pendleton, January 30, 1907, 2. In 1910, the year of the first Pendleton Round-Up, eighty-year-old Ezra Meeker made his third ox-team trip along the Oregon Trail. See "Trail Taken Again, Ezra Meeker at 80 to Recross Continent behind Oxen," *Morning Oregonian*, March 15, 1910, 12.

68. "Is Badly Tied Up: Federal Judge Needed in the Oregon District," *East Oregonian*, Pendleton, September 19, 1905, 11. While the *East Oregonian* confidently pointed to Arnold's ability as a salesman and the orders coming in from places like Montana, Sheuerman & Son did not move to buy the mill after their one-year lease. See "Woolen Mills in Operation," *East Oregonian*, Pendleton, June 16, 1906, 11.

69. "Will Save the Woolen Mill: Active Committee Now at Work on Plans for Retaining Industry," *East Oregonian*, Pendleton, October 10, 1908, 1. Rice referenced Sheuerman's $10,000 profit from a few years earlier, and explained why Sheuerman decided not to buy the mill. The article, though, does not share Sheuerman's decision with the readers. After an impassioned speech by G. M. Rice, cashier at the First National Bank, at the 1908 meeting, the association agreed to try to save the mill. The association chose six men for the committee and ended the meeting more optimistically than they had begun it.

70. "Importance of the Move," *East Oregonian*, Pendleton, December 3, 1908, 5.

71. "Cost of Labor Is Prohibitive: Why Oregon Cannot Compete in the Textile Industry," *Morning Oregonian*, Portland, September 14, 1907, 11. The article featured Oregon's infamous Charles Cunningham and R. S. Rhodes, an East Coast wool manufacturer. Rhodes bemoaned the decline in the quality of Oregon wool, calling it a "mystery" as to why the people of Oregon had not done more to promote the establishment of more woolen mills. Among other potential culprits, Cunningham raised the issue of the cost of labor in the

West and the East, noting that the women and children who worked in East Coast mills earned only 40 or 50 cents per day. In Oregon, according to Cunningham, "even hobo labor costs over $2.25 to $2.50 a day," and that did not even take into account "the labor good enough for mill work" that would cost over $3.00 a day.

72. See "Pendleton's Roots Began Nearly 140 Years Ago," *Textile World*, September 1, 2001, 42; "History of Bishop Clothing and Woolen Mill Store," *Statesman Journal*, Salem, Oregon, September 28, 2014, E9; Lomax, "Thomas Kay Woolen Mill," 102–39.

73. "Pendleton Fabric Expertise—A Story of Generations," *Pendleton Woolen Mills*.

74. "Mass Meeting for Monday: Woolen Mill Proposition Will Be Settled Then," *East Oregonian*, Pendleton, December 30, 1908, 8.

75. "Bishop Brothers Preparing to Begin Constructing Woolen Mill," *East Oregonian*, Pendleton, February 20, 1909, 1. See also Willingham, "Pendleton Woolen Mills"; May, *Pendleton*, 60.

76. "Newsy Notes of Pendleton: Moorhouse Returns Home," *East Oregonian*, Pendleton, June 9, 1910, 8; "Relics Go to Astoria: Moorhouse Exhibit Includes Many Indian Weapons," *Sunday Oregonian*, Portland, August 6, 1911, 38.

77. "Pendleton Woolen Mills a Community Affair; History of Industry Here," *East Oregonian Round-Up Souvenir Edition*, August 27, 1912, 8.

78. "Men Who Manage Round-Up Get No Pay for Services; They Are Amateurs and They Work for Pendleton," *East Oregonian*, Souvenir Round-Up Edition, September 12, 1913, 6; Willingham, "Pendleton Woolen Mills."

79. Allison, "Annual Event Comes Long Way," 3.

80. Willingham, "Pendleton Woolen Mills," 17.

81. Willingham, 17.

82. "A Frontier Exhibition" advertisement, *Daily East Oregonian*, September 29, 1910; "Why Is the Round-Up [*sic*]?," *East Oregonian*, September 14, 1911.

83. "Great Northwest Round-up Ushered In—Let 'Er Buck; Carnival of Cowboys On" and "The Round-Up," *Daily East Oregonian*, September 29, 1910.

84. Furlong, *Let 'Er Buck*, xxxi.

85. "Why Is the Round-Up [*sic*]?" *East Oregonian*, September 11, 1914.

86. "How the Round-Up Grew from Modest Beginning to Show of World Proportions," *East Oregonian Round-Up Souvenir Edition*, September 11, 1913.

87. Happy Canyon souvenir program, 1967, 7.

88. "Fair History," Umatilla County Fair; Ron Ingle, "A Tale of Two Centennials," Northwest Opinions, *East Oregonian*, August 4, 2014, http://www.northwestopinions.com/East -oregonian/letter-a-tale-of-two-centennials/.

89. "Happy Canyon Night Show," souvenir program, 2012, 15.

90. "Commercial Association Is Working to Boost Round-Up," *Daily East Oregonian*, September 9, 1914.

91. "'Happy Canyon' Will Be Name of Town in Fair Pavilion," *Daily East Oregonian*, September 2, 1914.

92. "Crowd of 15,000 Cheers Round-Up Events," "Immense Crowd Here for 1st Day," *East Oregonian*, September 24, 1914.

93. "Noted Traveler-Author Arrives for the Round-Up," *Daily East Oregonian*, September 21, 1914.

94. "Crowds Begin to Arrive Here for Round-Up; Ideal Weather Greets Vanguard of Visitors," *Daily East Oregonian*, September 21, 1914.

95. Furlong, "Epic Drama of the West," 368.

96. "Noted Traveler-Author Arrives for the Round-Up," *Daily East Oregonian*, September 21, 1914.

97. Furlong, "Epic Drama of the West," 369.

98. "'Happy Canyon' Promises to Visitors Big Time This Year," *Daily East Oregonian*, September 11, 1914.

99. "'Happy Canyon' Promises to Visitors Big Time This Year."

100. "Annual Seat Sale for the Round-Up Biggest on Record"; "Walla Walla, Waitsburg and Dayton People Coming"; "Look Out for Crooks Is Warning Given Visitors," *East Oregonian*, September 22, 1914.

101. "All Businesses Will Close Afternoons of Round-Up," *Daily East Oregonian*, September 21, 1914.

102. "Round-Up Crowd Will Be Just as Large as in 1913," *Daily East Oregonian*, September 21, 1914.

103. "Society Pages," *Daily East Oregonian*, September 21, 1914.

104. "Frontier Stunts Will Please the Visitors to Happy Canyon," *Daily East Oregonian*, September 22, 1914.

105. "'Happy Canyon' Has Historical Ancestor," *Daily East Oregonian*, September 14, 1914.

106. "'Happy Canyon' Promises to Visitors Big Time This Year."

107. "'Happy Canyon' Has Historical Ancestor."

108. "Immense Crowd Here for 1st Day," "Crowd of 15,000 Cheers Round-Up Events," "3000 People Enjoy Wild Days of '49," *Daily East Oregonian*, September 24, 1914.

109. "3000 People Enjoy Wild Days of '49."

110. "3000 People Enjoy Wild Days of '49."

111. "Happy Canyon Opens Tonight," *Daily East Oregonian*, September 23, 1914; "'Happy Canyon' Promises to Visitors Big Time This Year."

112. "3000 People Enjoy Wild Days of '49."

113. "Carefree Crowd Enjoys the Fun of Happy Canyon," *Daily East Oregonian*, September 25, 1914.

114. "Happy Canyon Again Scene of Big Crowd," *Daily East Oregonian*, September 26, 1914.

115. "The Round-Up the Biggest Spectacle of Its Kind," *Daily East Oregonian*, September 26, 1914.

116. "Round-Up the Biggest Spectacle of Its Kind."

117. "Frontier Village Closes to Regret of Large Throng," *Daily East Oregonian*, September 28, 1914; "'Happy Canyon' a Success with Net Balance of $875," *Daily East Oregonian*, October 2, 1914.

118. "Pendleton Back to Normal after City's Guests Depart," *Daily East Oregonian*, September 28, 1914.

119. "'Happy Canyon' a Success with Net Balance of $875."

120. "Old Timer Recalls Many Incidents of Early Western Days," *Daily East Oregonian*, December 5, 1914.

121. "Happy Canyon Will Be Made 1915 Feature," *Daily East Oregonian*, August 4, 1915; "Happy Canyon," *Daily East Oregonian*, August 5, 1915.

122. "Old Days to Be Lived Again in Frontier Style," *Daily East Oregonian*, September 22, 1915.

123. "Roulette Draws Throngs to Bet Round-Up Bucks," *Daily East Oregonian*, September 23, 1915. The paper effusively wrote, "Cowboys and cowgirls put on a horseback quadrille, bucking horses, steers and burros were mounted, 'Spender's Bank' was held up by desperadoes, Indians whooped and yelled as they pursued a fleeing white man full of arrows and then gave way before shooting cowboys. The village fire department rescued whole families from the burning 'Stagger Inn' and the village band rendered selections. . . . It was some little old show when taken all together and not until after midnight did the fun cease, and even then the streets were crowded by people loth to take to their beds."

124. Conner, "Round-Up Reminiscences: 'You Can't Eat Lound-Up!,'" 47; Allison, "Annual Event Comes Long Way," 3; Happy Canyon souvenir program 2012, 3; Happy Canyon souvenir program 2012, 15; "Anna Minthorn Arrives," *Daily East Oregonian*, April 7, 1906.

125. Conner, "From Generation to Generation," 264.

126. "Mountain Forest Changes into Frontier Town; Transformation Takes Place at Happy Canyon," *Daily East Oregonian*, August 29, 1917.

127. Happy Canyon souvenir program 1967, 3; Happy Canyon souvenir program 2012, 10.

128. "Senate Concurrent Resolution 2," March 8, 2011, in Happy Canyon souvenir program 2012, 31.

129. "Centennial Plan Is a Unique Affair," *Sunday Oregonian*, Portland, August 6, 1911, 10.

130. "Centennial Plan Is a Unique Affair," 10.

131. Shaffer, *See America First*, 3.

132. "Festival Association Out for Share of $500,000," *Sunday Oregonian*, Portland, May 18, 1913, 2.

133. "Open River Fete Event of Gayety," *Morning Oregonian*, Portland, May 4, 1915, 3.

134. "Schooner Mobile No More Comfortable than Ox-Wagon, Says Ezra Meeker," *Sunday Oregonian*, Portland, September 17, 1916, 7.

135. "Willamette University Stages Story of Oregon: Past Is Vividly Recalled," *Morning Oregonian*, Portland, June 9, 1919, 5.

136. "Giant Historical Pageant Thrills Several Thousand," *Willamette Collegian*, Salem, June 14, 1919, 1, 4.

137. "Community Service Planning Beautiful Historic Event," *Dalles Daily Chronicle*, April 26, 1921, 1.

138. "Historical Pageant," *Dalles Daily Chronicle*, April 29, 1921, 6.

139. "Real Indians in Pageant," 378.

140. "A Trail Blazer Crosses Divide: Ezra Meeker of Oregon Trail Fame Succumbs at Age 97 Years," *Athena Press*, Athena, December 30, 1928, 9. The year before his death, as the president of the Oregon Trail Memorial Association (OTMA), he successfully lobbied Congress to mint a half-dollar coin commemorating the Oregon Trail. Nearly 100 markers and monuments had been built along the trail in the twenty-odd years since Meeker's first expedition eastward, and the OTMA hoped that sales of the commemorative coins would spur the development of even more markers and monuments, including one in the nation's capital. See *Oregon Trail*, 3.

141. *Oregon Trail*, 5.

Chapter Two

1. Brock, *Money Trees*, 11.
2. The title of this chapter comes from an interview with Chief Carl Sampson and family conducted by Katrina Phillips in Pendleton, Oregon on September 11, 2014. The quoted information in the epigraphs can be found here: Furlong, "Epic Drama of the West," 374; Smith, "Foreword," 7.
3. Conner, "Round-Up Reminiscences," 46.
4. Peers, *Playing Ourselves*, 65.
5. Interview with Clay Briscoe, Happy Canyon court director, and Jory Spencer and Marisa Baumgartner, 2014 Happy Canyon princesses, conducted by Katrina Phillips in Pendleton, Oregon, on September 11, 2014. The Happy Canyon princesses, like other rodeo and festival royalty, travel to participate in other events throughout the region. Court directors like Briscoe can serve as chaperones and publicity directors, among other things.
6. "History and Culture," Confederated Tribes of the Umatilla Indian Reservation.
7. Hill, "Happy Canyon," 230.
8. Schneider, "Pendleton"; "History: City of Pendleton," City of Pendleton.
9. Interview with Randy Thomas, Round-Up publicity director, conducted by Katrina Phillips in Pendleton, Oregon, on September 10, 2014.
10. Sinks, "Drive Down Eastern Oregon."
11. Imada, *Aloha America*, 32.
12. Senate Concurrent Resolution 2, March 8, 2011 in Happy Canyon souvenir program, 2012, 31.
13. Allison, "Annual Event Comes Long Way"; Conner, "Round-Up Reminiscences," 59.
14. Interview with Clay Briscoe, Happy Canyon royalty and Indian director, and Jory Spencer and Marisa Baumgartner, 2014 Happy Canyon princesses, September 11, 2014.
15. The title for this epigraph comes from "Tradition, Tradition!," music and lyrics by Jerry Bock and Sheldon Harnick, *Fiddler on the Roof*, 1964.
16. Interactions, performances, and announcements witnessed by the author during the 2014 Pendleton Round-Up and Happy Canyon Indian Pageant and Wild West Show.
17. Peers, *Playing Ourselves*, xix.
18. Peers, 36.
19. Furlong, "Epic Drama of the West," 374.
20. P. Deloria, *Indians in Unexpected Places*, 60.
21. Collins was the 2014 Pendleton Round-Up Indians director (interview with Rob Collins, conducted by Katrina Phillips in Pendleton, Oregon, on September 10, 2014). Randy Thomas, Pendleton Round-Up publicity director, also called the Pendleton Round-Up the "largest single economic impact in Umatilla County" (interview with Randy Thomas, September 10, 2014).
22. O'Neill, "Rethinking Modernity," 11.
23. Cattelino, "Casino Roots," 67.
24. P. Deloria, *Indians in Unexpected Places*, 3.
25. Arnold, "Work and Culture in Southeastern Alaska," 162–63.
26. Interview with Sophia Bearchum Enos and David Wolf, conducted by Katrina Phillips in Pendleton, Oregon, on September 11, 2014.

27. Interview with Corey Neistadt, Happy Canyon properties and publicity director, conducted by Katrina Phillips in Pendleton, Oregon, on September 11, 2014.

28. Ellis, "Five Dollars a Week," 194.

29. Ellis, 195.

30. Rosenthal, "Dawn of a New Day?," 93.

31. Antonio Sierra, "Round-Up Financial Report Shows Expanding Enterprise," *East Oregonian*, March 8, 2018; Kathy Aney, "Round-Up Stockholders Raise Voices over Director Qualifications," *East Oregonian*, November 21, 2018.

32. Whelan and Rollier, "Contributions of Indian Gaming," 4.

33. "Tenth Annual Indian Land Consolidation Symposium Set for October 16–19," *Spilyay tymoo* (Warm Springs, OR), October 5, 2000, 8; Antonio Sierra, "Economic Jackpot," *East Oregonian*, November 3, 2014.

34. See Cattelino, *High Stakes*.

35. Richard Cockle, "Wildhorse Casino Expands, Fuels Reservation Resurgence, Economy in Eastern Oregon," *Oregonian*, February 28, 2011.

36. "Foundation History," Wildhorse Foundation.

37. Confederated Tribes of the Umatilla Indian Reservation, *2016 Annual Report*, 1.

38. "Video Presentation," Tamástslikt Cultural Institute.

39. Conner, "Round-Up Reminiscences," 47.

40. Tammy Malgesini, "Wildhorse Pow Wow Keeps Beat for 25 Years," *East Oregonian*, July 3, 2019.

41. Research notes, Happy Canyon Indian Pageant and Wild West Show, 2012 and 2014.

42. Happy Canyon souvenir program, 1967, 7. The title for this epigraph comes from research notes, Happy Canyon Indian Pageant and Wild West Show, September 10, 2014.

43. Jade McDowell, "Happy Canyon Memorializes Original Home," *East Oregonian*, May 10, 2016.

44. Jonathan Bach, "$1.5M Mezzanine Project Complete," *East Oregonian*, August 28, 2015.

45. Jonathan Bach, "Repainting a Classic," *East Oregonian*, August 28, 2015.

46. Research notes, Happy Canyon Indian Pageant and Wild West Show, September 10, 2014.

47. Happy Canyon souvenir programs, 2012 and 2014, 7.

48. For more on how white Americans in the Progressive Era used constructions of Indian captivity to "prove that their violent national development had been just," see Varley, *Americans Recaptured*.

49. Research notes, Happy Canyon Indian Pageant and Wild West Show, 2014.

50. Happy Canyon souvenir program, 2012, 7.

51. Interview with Corey Neistadt, Happy Canyon properties and publicity director, September 11, 2014.

52. Interview with Neistadt, September 11, 2014.

53. Interview with Neistadt, September 11, 2014.

54. Interview with Neistadt, September 11, 2014.

55. White, *"It's Your Misfortune,"* 4.

56. P. Deloria, *Indians in Unexpected Places*, 60.

57. Sturken, *Tourists of History*, 15.

58. See Suzanne Kennedy, "Happy Canyon Marks a Century of Family Tradition," *East Oregonian*, September 1, 2016; "Happy Canyon Joins Elite List as Oregon Heritage Tradition," *East Oregonian*, September 10, 2016.

59. "Let's Get Ready to Round-Up," *East Oregonian*, September 13, 2016. The title for this epigraph comes from a conversation with Bobby Spencer. Interview with Bobby Spencer and Rayne Spencer, conducted by Katrina Phillips in Pendleton, Oregon, on September 12, 2014.

60. Interview with Sophia Beachum Enos and David Wolf, September 11, 2014.

61. Conner, "Round-Up Reminiscences," 47.

62. Interview with Jason Hill, Happy Canyon president, conducted by Katrina Phillips in Pendleton, Oregon, on September 11, 2014.

63. Interview with Randy Thomas, Pendleton Round-Up publicity director, September 10, 2014.

64. Imada, *Aloha America*, 17.

65. Imada, 18.

66. Conner, "Round-Up Reminiscences," 52.

67. Interview with Bobby Spencer and Rayne Spencer, September 12, 2014.

68. Interview with Viola Minthorn, conducted by Katrina Phillips in Pendleton, Oregon, on September 11, 2014.

69. Interview with Tessie Williams, conducted by Katrina Phillips in Pendleton, Oregon, on September 11, 2014. Information regarding her induction into the Hall of Fame from "Pendleton Round-Up & Happy Canyon Hall of Fame." Information regarding her role in the tribal community from "Heroic at 80," Tamástslikt Cultural Institute.

70. Interview with Chief Carl Sampson and family, September 11, 2014.

71. Interview with Chief Carl Sampson and family, September 11, 2014. A similar version of the death of Pio-Pio (also called Pio-Pio-Mox-Mox) appears in an essay titled "Pio-Pio-Mox-Mox" by J. F. Santee in the *Oregon Historical Quarterly* (1933), 164–76.

72. Happy Canyon Indian Pageant and Wild West Show, September 14, 2012.

73. Conner, "Round-Up Reminiscences," 54.

74. Happy Canyon souvenir program, 1967, 4.

Chapter Three

1. "Please, Please Change That Title," *Waynesville Mountaineer*, October 20, 1949.

2. The title of this chapter comes from Hunter, *Unto These Hills*. The quoted information in the epigraph can be found here: "The Cherokee Historical Association presents *Unto These Hills*," 1951, Institute of Outdoor Theatre archives, box 133, folder g. Hereafter abbreviated as IOD/IOT.

3. "Please, Please Change That Title."

4. Connor, *History*, 22.

5. In January 1950, Harry Buchanan sent a letter to Joe Jennings, the Indian agent on the Qualla Boundary and the treasurer of the Cherokee Historical Association. He had written to the president of Paramount Theatres asking whether there was a song called "The Cherokee Trail" and, if so, if it was copyrighted. Buchanan learned there was no song, book, or motion picture called "The Cherokee Trail," but it seems as if the CHA had committed to

the title *Unto These Hills* by that point. See Letter from Harry Buchanan to Joe Jennings, January 16, 1950, IOD/IOT archives, box 139, folder c.

6. Connor, *History*, 18; citing Umberger, "History of *Unto These Hills*," 41.

7. Connor, *History*, 20; Umberger, "History of *Unto These Hills*," 51.

8. Kermit Hunter, "Letters to Editor," *Waynesville Mountaineer*, November 3, 1949.

9. "It Looks Like 'Unto These Hills,' Whether Right or Wrong," *Waynesville Mountaineer*, November 3, 1949.

10. W. C. Medford, "Don't Like Title 'Unto These Hills,'" *Waynesville Mountaineer*, November 21, 1949.

11. These dramas are included in the archives of the Institute of Outdoor Theatre, formerly the Institute of Outdoor Drama (IOD). There are certainly other productions that were not in contact with the IOD, but even without those notes the popularity of outdoor dramas—regardless of their relative success or failure—is a key component of the burgeoning postwar tourism era.

12. "Unto These Hills—A Drama of the Cherokee," *Waynesville Mountaineer*, February 2, 1950.

13. *Unto These Hills* was one of several outdoor dramas to open in the area in the twentieth century.

14. Thompson, "Staging 'the Drama,'" 13.

15. Taylor, "Brief History of the Outdoor Drama," 1.

16. Borstelmann, *Cold War and the Color Line*, 268.

17. Borstelmann, 46.

18. Finger, *Eastern Band of Cherokees*, 21.

19. Perdue and Green, *Cherokee Removal*, 1; Finger, *Eastern Band of Cherokees*, 4.

20. Perdue and Green, *Cherokee Removal*, 17.

21. Miles, *Ties That Bind*, 113.

22. Prucha, *Great Father*, 52.

23. Numerous scholars have examined the Marshall Trilogy, its effects on the Cherokee, and its effects on federal Indian law more broadly. See, for instance, Miles, *Ties That Bind*; Perdue and Green, *Cherokee Removal*; Wilkins and Lomawaima, *Uneven Ground*, among others. The title for this epigraph comes from "Arts, Craft School to Be Part of the Cherokee Drama," *Waynesville Mountaineer*, April 20, 1950.

24. Perdue and Green, *Cherokee Removal*, 21.

25. Perdue and Green, 110–11.

26. Perdue and Green, 113.

27. Resources regarding events preceding and including Cherokee removal include Perdue and Green, *Cherokee Removal*; Miles, *Ties That Bind*; Finger, *Eastern Band of Cherokees*; Perdue, *Cherokee Women*; and Heape, *Trail of Tears*, among others.

28. Stephens, "Beginnings," 213.

29. "Arts, Crafts School to Be Part of the Cherokee Drama," *Waynesville Mountaineer*, April 20, 1950.

30. Finger, *Eastern Band of Cherokees*, 17.

31. Finger, 19.

32. Finger, 20–21.

33. Mooney, *Myths of the Cherokee*, 131.

34. Finger, *Eastern Band of Cherokees*, 28.

35. King, "Origin of the Eastern Cherokees," 166, cited in Beard-Moose, *Public Indians, Private Cherokees*, 31.

36. Smithers, "Cherokee Epic," 5 and 17.

37. Kutsche, "Tsali Legend," 329–30.

38. Beard-Moose, *Public Indians, Private Cherokees*, 32–33.

39. The history of the Cherokee Nation, the Eastern Band, and Cherokee removal has been well documented by numerous scholars, but there may be more unpublished works on *Unto These Hills* than published ones. Costume designer Suzanne Davis wrote "Indian Costumes for *Unto These Hills*" as her master's thesis in 1954, while Wallace Umberger Jr.'s 1970 dissertation examined the production from 1941 to 1968. In 1982, the Cherokee Historical Association published a short book titled *History of Cherokee Historical Association, 1946–1982*, tracing the organization from its inception through its then almost-four-decade existence. More recent work includes Christina Taylor Beard-Moose's 2009 *Public Indians, Private Cherokees: Tourism and Tradition on Tribal Ground*, which examines the nature of tourism on the Qualla Boundary, the home of the Eastern Band. Similarly, Michael Thompson's 2009 dissertation, "Staging 'the Drama': The Continuing Importance of Cultural Tourism in the Gaming Era," includes a firsthand account of the 2006 production of *Unto These Hills . . . a Retelling*, the first year Hunter's script was not produced. Thompson's work is significant because it "explores the social conflicts, negotiations, creative processes and performances surrounding this change as the tribe steered its most public representation of the past from a narrative of accommodation to one of Cherokee nationalism." Thompson places *Unto These Hills* in the context of the growing gaming industry, noting that social changes on the Boundary are due in large part to the tourist shift away from *Unto These Hills* and toward the Boundary's casino. These works help illuminate the history and motivations behind the original *Unto These Hills* as a drama that was so eager to create a wildly successful tourist endeavor that its organizers continually ignored the Indians whose history was staged every summer in the mountains. Annette Bird Saunooke's "Cherokee Royalties: The Impact of Indian Tourism on the Eastern Band of Cherokee Identity" and Heidi L. Nees's "'Indian' Summers: Querying Representations of Native American Cultures in Outdoor Historical Dramas" are among the theses and dissertations that have examined components of the drama. Additionally, Andrew Denson examines the drama in *Monuments to Absence: Cherokee Removal and the Contest over Southern Memory*, as does Gregory D. Smithers in "A Cherokee Epic: Kermit Hunter's *Unto These Hills* and the Mythologizing of Cherokee History," 1–30.

40. Finger, *Cherokee Americans*, 98; Denson, *Monuments to Absence*, 56; citing French and Hornbuckle, *Cherokee Perspective*, 35.

41. Duncan and Riggs, *Cherokee Heritage Trails Guidebook*, 33.

42. Saunooke, "Cherokee Royalties," 5.

43. Saunooke, 11–12.

44. Saunooke, 29; Finger, *Cherokee Americans*, 32; Lewis, *Sovereign Entrepreneurs*, 50.

45. Chiltoskey, *Cherokee Fair and Festival*, 5, as cited in Beard-Moose, *Public Indians, Private Cherokees*, 86; Finger, *Cherokee Americans*, 32.

46. Chiltoskey, *Cherokee Fair and Festival*, as cited in Beard-Moose, *Public Indians, Private Cherokees*, 86.

47. "Cherokee Indian Fair October 6–9," *Jackson County Journal*, Jackson County, September 30, 1925, 1.

48. "Cherokee Indian Fair," *Concord Daily Tribune*, Concord, September 21, 1925, 4.

49. Denson, *Monuments to Absence*, 59.

50. Bruyneel, *Third Space of Sovereignty*, 97.

51. Bruyneel, 100–101.

52. Denson, *Monuments to Absence*, 3.

53. Denson, 5–6, 8.

54. Kelly, "Indian Reorganization Act," 292–93.

55. Finger, "Termination," 153.

56. Finger, *Cherokee Americans*, 118–19; Lewis, *Sovereign Entrepreneurs*, 85.

57. Lewis, *Sovereign Entrepreneurs*, 61.

58. See, for instance, Troutman, *Indian Blues*, and Raibmon, *Authentic Indians*.

59. Beard-Moose, *Public Indians, Private Cherokees*, 77–86.

60. See Saunooke, "Cherokee Royalties," 11, 58–59; Nees, "'Indian' Summers," 174; Lewis, *Sovereign Entrepreneurs*, 55.

61. Lewis, 55; Finger, *Cherokee Americans*, 163.

62. Thompson, "Staging 'the Drama,'" 4.

63. Frome, *Strangers in High Places*, as cited in Beard-Moose, *Public Indians, Private Cherokees*, 24.

64. French and Hornbuckle, *Cherokee Perspective*, 26–27, as cited in Beard-Moose, *Public Indians, Private Cherokees*, 24.

65. Saunooke, "Cherokee Royalties," 18.

66. Finger, *Cherokee Americans*, 99.

67. Finger, 99.

68. Raibmon, *Authentic Indians*, 146.

69. "The Spirit of the Great Smokies: A Pageant Commemorating the One-hundredth Anniversary of the Great Removal, 1835–1935" (Cherokee, NC: Cherokee Indian Reservation, 1935), Museum of the Cherokee Indian archives, 1.

70. Thompson, "Staging 'the Drama,'" 42.

71. Cherokee Indian Fair and Folk Festival souvenir program, Cherokee Indian Fair Association, "Motoring through the Mountains."

72. See Cothran, "Working the Indian Field Days"; Raibmon, *Authentic Indians*.

73. Denson, *Monuments to Absence*, 73–74.

74. Cherokee Indian Fair and Folk Festival souvenir program, Cherokee Indian Fair Association, "Motoring through the Mountains."

75. Denson, *Monuments to Absence*, 75.

76. "Indian Festival May Be Held In Tourist Season," *The Ruralite* (Sylva, NC), October 8, 1935. Courtesy of "Motoring through the Mountains—1930s: Cherokee," Travel Western North Carolina, Hunter Library Digital Programs and Special Collections at Western Carolina University, http://www.wcu.edu/library/digitalcollections/travelwnc/1930s/1930 cherokee.html.

77. Finger, *Cherokee Americans*, 100.

78. Denson, *Monuments to Absence*, 76; Finger, *Cherokee Americans*, 100.

79. Ellis, "Five Dollars a Week," 192.

80. Connor, *History*, 8–9.

81. Connor, 8–9; *Unto These Hills: A Drama of the Cherokee, 1540–1950* souvenir program, 17, IOD/IOT, box 139, folder d.

82. Denson, *Monuments to Absence*, 7.

83. Connor, *History*, 7.

84. John Parris, "Delegation of Cherokee Indians Will Retrace 'The Trail of Tears,'" *Carteret County News-Times*, Carteret County, May 4, 1951, 10; Denson, *Monuments to Absence*, 148.

85. Smithers, "Cherokee Epic," 2.

86. Beard-Moose, *Public Indians, Private Cherokees*, 26; Connor, *History*, 1.

87. Connor, 7.

88. Connor, 8.

89. Finger, *Cherokee Americans*, 98.

90. Finger, 98.

91. *Unto These Hills* souvenir program, 17; Connor, *History*, 8–9.

92. Connor, 9.

93. Finger, *Cherokee Americans*, 115; Connor, *History*, 10.

94. Connor, 10; Letter from Sam Selden to Albert Bell, January 27, 1948, IOD/IOT, box 133, folder b.

95. Connor, *History*, 14–15.

96. Letter from Harry Davis to Al Bell, March 11, 1948, IOD/IOT, box 133, folder b.

97. Letter from Harry Davis to Al Bell, April 9, 1948, IOD/IOT, box 133, folder b.

98. "Number of Cherokees in Drama, 'Unto These Hills,'" *Waynesville Mountaineer*, August 3, 1950; Connor, *History*, 17.

99. Connor, 17.

100. Umberger, "History of *Unto These Hills*," 41.

101. Kilpatrick, *Celluloid Indians*, 51.

102. "Ready To Open Cherokee Drama," *Waynesville Mountaineer*, June 29, 1950.

103. In 1940, John Collier, commissioner of Indian affairs, suggested that famed anthropologist Ella Deloria should write a pageant for the Indians of Robeson County, now known as the Lumbee. While Deloria structured the pageant around their traditional agriculture and social institutions and included song-and-dance scenes, she also "capitalized on the general public's lack of knowledge about specific Indian cultures and rituals by adding cultural symbols and regalia that were from the Plains and not the Southeast." See Lowery, *Lumbee Indians*, 221–23.

104. Stephens, "Beginnings," 215.

105. Connor, *History*, 17.

106. Letter from Harry Davis to Harry Buchanan, August 19, 1949, IOD/IOT, box 134, folder b.

107. Smithers, "Cherokee Epic," 10–11.

108. Letter from Samuel Selden to Harry Buchanan, August 2, 1949, IOD/IOT, box 139, folder c.

109. Thompson, "Staging 'the Drama,'" 9.

110. Umberger, "History of *Unto These Hills*,"45.

111. Denson, *Monuments to Absence*, 141.

112. Hunter, "History or Drama?," *South Atlantic Bulletin*, May 1953, 3, as cited in Hayes, "Study of Hero-Building and Mythmaking," 61, in Thompson, "Staging 'the Drama,'" 114.

113. Finger, *Cherokee Americans*, 117.

114. *Unto These Hills: A Drama of the Cherokee, 1540–1950* souvenir program.

115. Dudziak, *Cold War Civil Rights*, 250.

116. Dudziak, 49.

117. Dudziak, 13.

118. Denson, "Native Americans," 13.

119. Denson, *Monuments to Absence*, 9.

120. Roland, *Improbable Era*, 39.

121. See Denson, "Native Americans."

122. Denson, 14.

123. Dudziak, *Cold War Civil Rights*, 49.

124. Dudziak, 49.

125. Philp, *Termination Revisited*, 68.

126. See Philp, *Termination Revisited*, 71–74.

127. V. Deloria, *Custer Died for Your Sins*, 72 and 76.

128. Philp, *Termination Revisited*, 71 and 75; Finger, "Termination," 155.

129. Finger, 161. It is also noteworthy that Jennings put the Menominee of Wisconsin in category four, but the Menominee were among the first tribes to be terminated under HCR 108.

130. E. Carl Sink, "Efforts Being Made to Raise $8,000 in Next Three Weeks for Pageant," *Waynesville Mountaineer*, May 15, 1950.

131. "White to Manage Cherokee Drama; Sink the Publicity," *Waynesville Mountaineer*, February 13, 1950.

132. "Veteran Showman to Direct Cherokee Drama," *Duplin Times*, Kenansville, NC, March 12, 1950.

133. "Arts, Craft School to Be Part of the Cherokee Drama," *Waynesville Mountaineer*, April 20, 1950.

134. "Harry Buchanan Cites Value of Cherokee Drama to This Entire Area," *Waynesville Mountaineer*, April 24, 1950.

135. "Manager Is on Job for Cherokee Drama," *Waynesville Mountaineer*, May 11, 1950.

136. Connor, *History*, 31.

137. "Harry Buchanan Cites Value of Cherokee Drama to This Entire Area," *Waynesville Mountaineer*, April 24, 1950.

138. "Business Manager Is on Job for Cherokee Drama," *Waynesville Mountaineer*, May 11, 1950.

139. "Haywood Library to Sponsor Essay Contest," *Waynesville Mountaineer*, May 15, 1950.

140. E. Carl Sink, "Efforts Being Made to Raise $8,000 in Next Three Weeks for Pageant," *Waynesville Mountaineer*, May 15, 1950.

141. "Bishop Gives $300 to Indian Drama," *Waynesville Mountaineer*, June 12, 1950.

142. "Unto These Hills a Cherokee Drama," *Waynesville Mountaineer*, May 19, 1950.

143. "Cherokee Drama Being Rehearsed 'Round the Clock," *Waynesville Mountaineer*, June 12, 1950.

144. "Cherokee Drama Ready for Public Says the Director," *Waynesville Mountaineer*, June 23, 1950.

145. "Cherokee Drama to Open for Season on Saturday," *Waynesville Mountaineer*, June 29, 1950.

146. "Every Indian in North America Invited to Drama," *Waynesville Mountaineer*, June 12, 1950. "Eskimo" is widely considered to be a derogatory term. The preferred terms are Inuit or Yupik.

147. Hunter, "Story of the Cherokee," 20–21.

148. Stephens, "Beginnings," 217.

149. Interview with John Tissue, August 2, 2012.

150. *Unto These Hills* souvenir program, 13–15.

151. The 1950 souvenir program only includes biographies of named characters, excluding, for instance, those portraying Indian Maidens, Indian Youths, Other Villagers, Spanish Soldiers, U.S. Soldiers, Loiterers, and Square Dancers.

152. P. Deloria, *Indians in Unexpected Places*, 6.

153. "Indians Use Make-Up—To Look Like Indians," *Waynesville Mountaineer*, August 7, 1950.

154. "Number of Cherokees in Drama, 'Unto These Hills,'" *Waynesville Mountaineer*, August 3, 1950; "Cherokee Indians on the Stage," *Waynesville Mountaineer*, July 20, 1950.

155. "18,000 Have Seen Drama to Date," *Waynesville Mountaineer*, July 12, 1950.

156. W. Curtis Ross, "'Unto These Hills' Is Far Better Than Expectations," *Waynesville Mountaineer*, July 3, 1950.

157. Ross, "'Unto These Hills' Is Far Better Than Expectations," *Waynesville Mountaineer*, July 3, 1950. The title for this epigraph comes from the same article.

158. Tom Outlaw, "Capital Letters," *Waynesville Mountaineer*, July 20, 1950.

159. "Special Bus Will Make Trips to the Cherokee Drama," *Waynesville Mountaineer*, July 6, 1950.

160. "Junaluska Tours from Lake Junaluska," *Waynesville Mountaineer*, July 20, 1950.

161. "Overflow Crowd Delays Curtain Time of Drama," *Waynesville Mountaineer*, August 3, 1950.

162. "Number of Cherokees in Drama, 'Unto These Hills,'" *Waynesville Mountaineer*, August 3, 1950.

163. "Cherokee Drama Will Close on Labor Day Night," *Waynesville Mountaineer*, August 21, 1950.

164. "Last Performance of Indian Drama on Monday," *Waynesville Mountaineer*, August 31, 1950.

165. "Drama Proves Profitable to Cherokees," *Waynesville Mountaineer*, October 30, 1950.

166. "Still a Drawing Card," *Waynesville Mountaineer*, October 26, 1950.

167. Gassner, "Broadway in Review," 349.

168. Finger, *Cherokee Americans*, 116; Hunter, "Theatre Meets the People," 134; Stephens, "Beginnings," 217.

169. Stephens, 216.

170. Caison, "'We're Still Here,'" 47.

171. Hunter, "Theatre Meets the People," 128.

172. Connor, *History*, 13.

173. Lewis, *Sovereign Entrepreneurs*, 54.

174. "Visit Cherokee," Visit Cherokee NC.

Chapter Four

1. "Fire Claims Pageant Inn in Heart of Cherokee," *Asheville Citizen-Times*, February 28, 2014; "Pageant Inn Badly Damaged by Fire," *Cherokee One Feather*, March 1, 2014.

2. The title for this chapter comes from an interview with Eddie Swimmer, July 31, 2012.

3. "Park Statistics," National Park Service, Great Smoky Mountains National Park.

4. Beard-Moose, *Public Indians, Private Cherokees*, 116.

5. Interview with John Tissue, conducted by Katrina Phillips in Cherokee, North Carolina, on August 2, 2012.

6. Other scholars, such as Annette Bird Saunooke and Heidi L. Nees, have written master's theses and doctoral dissertations that discuss tourism in Cherokee, including *Unto These Hills*. Again, scholars could not have foreseen the recent nature of the return to the Hunter script.

7. See Beard-Moose, *Public Indians, Private Cherokees*; Thompson, "Staging 'the Drama.'"

8. Thompson, "Staging 'the Drama,'" 47.

9. Borstelmann, *Cold War*, 11.

10. Letter from Harry Buchanan to Carol White, May 12, 1952, IOD/IOT, box 134, folder b.

11. Letter from Harry Buchanan to Samuel Selden, October 23, 1951, IOD/IOT, box 134, folder b; Beard-Moose, *Public Indians, Private Cherokees*, 62.

12. Certificate of Incorporation, Tsali Institute of Cherokee Research, 1951, as cited in Beard-Moose, *Public Indians, Private Cherokees*, 62.

13. "A Statement of the Projects of The Cherokee Historical Association, Inc., Cherokee, North Carolina" (Cherokee, NC: Cherokee Historical Association, n.d.), IOD/IOT, box 133, folder c.

14. "Cherokee Community Life," *Asheville Citizen-Times*, June 6, 1954, IOD/IOT, box 136, folder f; "Pride Runs Deep in Oconaluftee Indian Village, Cherokee, North Carolina, Celebrating 50th Anniversary Season," Oconaluftee Indian Village press release, 2002, IOD/IOT, box 138, folder f. Living-history villages became popular in places like Colonial Williamsburg in the 1920s and 1930s, and national parks across the country began adopting the practice shortly thereafter. See Lewis, *Sovereign Entrepreneurs*, 63.

15. Connor, *History*, 32.

16. See Denson, *Monuments to Absence*, 135–58; Finger, "Termination," 162, 166.

17. Finger, "Termination," 163.

18. See, for instance, "Copy of a Voluntary Statement, Made by W. P. McCoy, Member of the Tribal Council of the Eastern Band of Cherokee in 1953," September 10, 1953; "Statement from F. Wilbur Allison, Chief Police, Cherokee, N.C. Concerning Alleged Disorderly Conduct in Government Dormitories," February 10, 1954; "Copy of Voluntary Statement, Made by Henry Bradley, Former Chief of the Eastern Band of Cherokee Indians, and a Member of the Tribal Council in 1953," n.d.; and "Copy of Voluntary Statement, Made by John A. Crowe, Chairman of the Community Club of Wright's Creek, and a Member of the Tribal Council in 1954," n.d., IOD/IOT, box 133, folder c.

19. Letter from Robert J. Ballantyne, United States Department of the Interior Bureau of Indian Affairs, to Mr. Joe Jennings, May 31, 1950, IOD/IOT, box 136, folder b. General information letters sent to cast members in 1955 and 1962 also reference staying in the agency dormitories—see "Excerpt from 'General Information Letter,' Third Season, *Unto These*

Hills," IOD/IOT, box 133, folder c; and "General Information to the Members of the 1962 Company," IOD/IOT, box 137, folder e.

20. "Copy of Voluntary Statement, Made by John A. Crowe, Chairman of the Community Club of Wright's Creek, and a Member of the Tribal Council in 1954" in "A Statement of the Projects of The Cherokee Historical Association, Inc., Cherokee, North Carolina" (Cherokee, NC: Cherokee Historical Association, n.d.), IOD/IOT, box 133, folder c.

21. Finger, "Termination," 163.

22. Letter from Bill Sharpe to Senator W. Kerr Scott, November 17, 1954, as cited in Finger, "Termination," 163–64.

23. Finger, "Termination," 164–65.

24. "National Attendance Record Set by 'Unto These Hills,'" *Asheville Citizen*, September 9, 1954, IOD/IOT, box 136, folder f.

25. *Unto These Hills: A Drama of the Cherokee* souvenir program, 1950, IOD/IOT, box 139, folder d. See also 1954–57 programs, IOD/IOT, box 139, folder e.

26. *Unto These Hills: A Drama of the Cherokee* souvenir program, 1958, IOD/IOT, box 140, folder a.

27. Memorandum from "A Group of Concerned Americans Who Have Recently Witnessed the Cherokee Indian Play, 'Unto These Hills,'" 1962, IOD/IOT, box 134, folder c.

28. "New Attraction in Western N.C. Is 'Frontierland,'" *Durham Morning Herald*, October 25, 1963. I have seen references to the theme park as both Frontierland and Frontier Land.

29. Beard-Moose, *Public Indians, Private Cherokees*, 102–3.

30. Letter from Harry Davis to Mark Sumner, August 25, 1965, IOD/IOT, box 134, folder c.

31. Letter from Mark Sumner to Margie Douthit, May 5, 1966, IOD/IOT, box 134, folder c.

32. Letter from Anne Mallard Davis to Mrs. Thelma Foley, May 30, 1967, IOD/IOT, box 134, folder c.

33. *Unto These Hills* souvenir program, 1971, IOD/IOT, box 140, folder c.

34. Saunooke, "Cherokee Royalties," 46.

35. Letter from Margie Douthit to Mark Sumner, April 22, 1974, IOD/IOT, box 134, folder d.

36. Cherokee Historical Association Press Release, June 1976, IOD/IOT, box 137, folder c.

37. Letter from Carol White to Judy Barringer, Mark Sumner, and North Carolina Theatre Arts, October 12, 1979, IOD/IOT, box 136, folder a.

38. Saunooke, "Cherokee Royalties," 46–47.

39. Letter from Scott J. Parker to The Honorable Marc Basnight, Senator, February 28, 1995, IOD/IOT, box 134, folder d.

40. Notes on the 1996 Olympics from Cherokee Historical Association, *1997 Annual Report*, IOD/IOT, box 135, folder e.

41. Letter from Scott J. Parker to Ed Benson, Barry Hipps, and Bill Hardy, December 10, 1997, IOD/IOT, box 134, folder f.

42. Letter from Scott J. Parker to Mrs. Marsha Cameron, July 14, 1998, IOD/IOT, box 134, folder f.

43. Beard-Moose, *Public Indians, Private Cherokees*, 115–16.

44. Letter from Scott J. Parker to Barry Hipps, August 3, 2000, IOD/IOT, box 134, folder f.

45. Letter from Scott J. Parker to Barry Hipps, July 17, 2001, IOD/IOT, box 134, folder f.

46. Thompson, "Staging the Drama," iii.

47. Letter from Peter Hardy to Scott Parker, January 14, 2005, IOD/IOT, box 134, folder f.

48. See "Casino's Popularity Could Hurt Theater," *News & Observer*, Raleigh, NC, June 24, 2003; "A Drama Threatened," *Charlotte Observer*, June 22, 2003; "Casino's Success Endangers Outdoor Drama," *News-Topic*, Lenoir, NC, June 24, 2003, among others. IOD/IOT, box 137, folder a.

49. UNC News Release, "'Unto These Hills' Rewritten, Staged by Cherokee from Tribe's Viewpoint," University of North Carolina at Chapel Hill News Service.

50. UNC News Release, "'Unto These Hills' Rewritten, Staged by Cherokee from Tribe's Viewpoint," University of North Carolina at Chapel Hill News Service.

51. Thompson, "Staging the Drama," iv.

52. See Beard-Moose, *Public Indians, Private Cherokees* and Denson, *Monuments to Absence*.

53. Thompson, "Staging the Drama," 11.

54. "*Unto These Hills*," Cherokee Smokies, http://www.cherokeesmokies.com/unto_these _hills.html.

55. "Welcome to 'Unto These Hills,'" Cherokee, North Carolina.

56. Thompson, "Staging the Drama," 49.

57. Beard-Moose, *Public Indians, Private Cherokees*, 103, 144. Beard-Moose continually refers to the peak of mass tourism from 1960 to 1980, although it is important to note the timeline given by one of her sources, Henry Lambert—an Eastern Band member who made a living by "chiefing," the practice wherein a Native man would dress up as a stereotypical American Indian (usually garbed as one would expect to see a Plains Indian) and talk to tourists and pose for photographs within the Eastern Band's lands (Beard-Moose, *Public Indians, Private Cherokees*, 80–86). According to Beard-Moose's 2006 interview with Lambert, the high point of the tourist industry among the Eastern Band was from the 1950s to the 1970s (Beard-Moose, *Public Indians, Private Cherokees*, 144).

58. Beard-Moose, *Public Indians, Private Cherokees*, 33.

59. Thompson, "Staging the Drama," 329.

60. Thompson, 15.

61. Thompson, 19.

62. Beard-Moose, *Public Indians, Private Cherokees*, 139.

63. Thompson, "Staging the Drama," 2.

64. Thompson, 79.

65. Thompson, 24. The title for this epigraph comes from "Betrayed," *The Producers*, directed by Susan Stroman, written by Mel Brooks, (DVD) 2005.

66. Beard-Moose, *Public Indians, Private Cherokees*, 138.

67. Beard-Moose, 139.

68. Beard-Moose, 140.

69. Murphy, *People Have Never Stopped Dancing*, 263; UNC News Release, "'Unto These Hills' Rewritten, Staged by Cherokee from Tribe's Viewpoint," University of North Carolina at Chapel Hill News Service.

70. Norma Wilson called his *New Native American Drama: Three Plays* "distinctive, both in being the first substantial collection of Native American Drama and in their unique organic structures." See Wilson, "New Native American Drama," 84.

71. John J. O'Connor, "TV Weekend; American Indian Dancers and Sammy Davis Tribute," *New York Times*, February 2, 1990, http://www.nytimes.com/1990/02/02/arts/tv -weekend-american-indian-dancers-and-sammy-davis-tribute.html.

72. "'Unto These Hills' Is Far Better Than Expectations," *Waynesville Mountaineer*, July 3, 1950; Perdue, *Cherokee Women*, 13–15.

73. UNC News Release—"'Unto These Hills' Rewritten, Staged by Cherokee from Tribe's Viewpoint," University of North Carolina at Chapel Hill News Service.

74. Beard-Moose, *Public Indians, Private Cherokees*, 141.

75. According to Thompson, a preteen boy refused to sing in Cherokee, eventually admitting that he only wanted to be in the show in order to make money. A tribal elder who had been in thirty-three previous productions was taken aback when Geiogamah asked her to sing or read lines for a potential speaking role—it was the first time she had been offered the chance to audition for a role outside the crowd scenes. See Thompson, "Staging the Drama," 221–25.

76. The ambivalence that had long characterized the Eastern Band's relationship to *Unto These Hills* extended to the rehearsals, where writer/director Geiogamah and choreographer Marla Bingham, a Mashpee dancer and choreographer, often struggled to keep participants focused. See Murphy, *People Have Never Stopped Dancing*, 211.

77. Thompson, "Staging the Drama," 259–66.

78. Interview with John Tissue, conducted by Katrina Phillips in Cherokee, North Carolina, August 2, 2012.

79. Thompson, "Staging the Drama," 29.

80. Geiogamah, "American Indian Theater 2013: Not Running on Empty Yet," 332.

81. During a rehearsal for the new Eagle Dance sequence, Geiogamah and one of the AIDT dancers in the cast weighed the pros and cons of altering the steps of the dance. The dancer felt Geiogamah's idea was "a little off" compared with the rest of the dance and too closely resembled a powwow step. Geiogamah, however, did not mind it. The change was "roundly contested by some Cherokee members of the audience," highlighting the continued challenges surrounding authenticity and entertainment. The head drummer, Eastern Band member John-John Grant, similarly questioned Geiogamah's vision after the director asked that drums be used in the Children's Suite of dances—Bear, Corn, and Quail—instead of the traditional rattles. See Thompson, "Staging the Drama," 243, 248.

82. Thompson, 282.

83. Hosmer, *American Indians in the Marketplace*, xi–xii.

84. Thompson, "Staging the Drama," 306.

85. Interview with John Tissue, conducted by Katrina Phillips in Cherokee, North Carolina, August 2, 2012.

86. Interview with Eddie Swimmer, conducted by Katrina Phillips in Cherokee, North Carolina, on July 31, 2012.

87. Interview with Linda Squirrel, conducted by Katrina Phillips in Cherokee, North Carolina, on August 2, 2012.

88. Thompson, "Staging the Drama," 24, 85.

89. Smithers, "Cherokee Epic," 15.

90. Nees, "'Indian' Summers," 135; Lewis, *Sovereign Entrepreneurs*.

91. John Tissue, as cited in Nees, "'Indian' Summers," 179.

92. Thompson, "Staging the Drama," 126, citing Hayes, "Study of Hero-Building and Mythmaking."

93. Sturken, *Tourists of History*, 31.

94. Peers, *Playing Ourselves*, 61.

95. Saunooke, "Cherokee Royalties," 13; Nees, "'Indian' Summers," 146.

96. "Oconaluftee Indian Village," Visit Cherokee NC. For more, see "Oconaluftee Indian Village," Cherokee Historical Association.

97. Peers, *Playing Ourselves*, 104, citing Clifford, "Looking Several Ways," 8.

98. Holland, "Oconaluftee Indian Village," 841.

99. Beard-Moose, *Public Indians, Private Cherokees*, 47.

100. See King, *Cherokee Heritage*, 6–7.

101. Beard-Moose, *Public Indians, Private Cherokees*, 104; Anderson, "Museum of the Cherokee Indian," 774.

102. Beard-Moose, *Public Indians, Private Cherokees*, 106.

103. "'People of the Clay: Contemporary Cherokee Potters' to open at Cherokee Museum," *Cherokee One Feather*, March 29, 2019.

104. Lewis, *Sovereign Entrepreneurs*, 3, 13.

105. Lewis, 5. Lewis notes that Ron Blankenship's Talking Leaves Bookstore is the only dedicated bookstore in Cherokee (32). The coffee shop, Qualla Java, was originally opened as Tribal Grounds but did not survive the separation of its co-owners (1, 157–58). The Long House Funeral Home opened in the summer of 2009, and its owners call it the "First Funeral Home of the First People" (150–53).

106. In 2012, American Indians played fourteen of the thirty-four named characters, and ten were Eastern Band. The program proudly noted, "The presence of these descendants of the Cherokee who were forced from their homes in 1838 lends tremendous authenticity and power to the play." See *Unto These Hills* souvenir program (Cherokee Historical Association, 2012). Later programs did not necessarily follow suit. The 2019 program, for instance, does not delineate Eastern Band and Native cast members unless the performer notes it in their biography. See *Unto These Hills* souvenir program (Cherokee Historical Association, 2019).

107. Interview with John Tissue, conducted by Katrina Phillips in Cherokee, North Carolina, August 2, 2012.

108. Thompson, "Staging the Drama," 22–23.

109. Lewis, *Sovereign Entrepreneurs*, 121, 123–24.

110. Interview with Eddie Swimmer, conducted by Katrina Phillips in Cherokee, North Carolina, July 31, 2012.

Chapter Five

There are a number of different spellings of the name of this Suquamish and Duwamish chief, including Seattle and Seathl. In most instances, I have chosen to follow the lead of scholar Coll Thrush, who refers to the leader as Seeathl in *Native Seattle: Histories from the Crossing-Over Place*.

1. The title for this chapter comes from "Description of the Drama 'TECUMSEH!,'" Scioto Society, 1976, IOD/IOT, box 150, folder f. The quoted information in the epigraph can be found here: 1986 souvenir program for *Blue Jacket*, First Frontiers, IOD/IOT, box 146, folder a.

2. "Sugarloaf Mountain Amphitheatre over 70% Complete," Scioto Society, undated (likely 1972–73), IOD/IOT, box 149, folder g.

3. Undated (likely early 1970s) *Tecumseh!* promotional flier, 3, IOD/IOT, box 149, folder g.

4. Interview with Al Heierman, conducted by Katrina Phillips in Chillicothe, Ohio, August 2015.

5. "The Playwright," Scioto Society, June 18, 1973, IOD/IOT, box 150, folder f.

6. Letter from Jack Zierold to Mark Sumner, August 6, 1973, IOD/IOT, box 149, folder g.

7. "Description of the Drama 'TECUMSEH!,'" Scioto Society, 1976, IOD/IOT, box 150, folder f.

8. "The Playwright," Scioto Society, June 18, 1973, IOD/IOT, box 150, folder f.

9. Hinderaker, *Elusive Empires*, xiii.

10. See Hinderaker, 134–35.

11. Hinderaker and Mancall, *At the Edge of Empire*, 99.

12. See Hinderaker, *Elusive Empires*, 154; Hinderaker and Mancall, *At the Edge of Empire*, 122; and Hurt, *Ohio Frontier*, 46–47, among others.

13. See, among others, White, *Middle Ground*, x–xiii; Middleton, "Pontiac," 1–32.

14. See Calloway, *Scratch of a Pen*, 77–78, among others.

15. Hurt, *Ohio Frontier*, 59–60.

16. See Parkinson, "From Indian Killer to Worthy Citizen," 97–122.

17. See Hinderaker, *Elusive Empires*, 189; Hinderaker and Mancall, *At the Edge of Empire*, 159.

18. Hinderaker, *Elusive Empires*, 218.

19. L. Jones, *William Clark*, 41.

20. See Harper, "State Intervention," 233–48; and Harper, "Looking the Other Way," 621–44.

21. See, for example, Bowles, *Land Too Good for Indians*.

22. Buss, *Winning the West with Words*, 69.

23. Peck, *Images of America*, 96–97.

24. See Centennial Exposition of the Ohio Valley and Central States, "Official Guide."

25. Buss, *Winning the West with Words*, 2.

26. Buss, 4.

27. See Buss.

28. Bodnar, *Remaking America*, 128–35.

29. Bodnar, 153.

30. Gordon, *Spirit of 1976*, 35.

31. Rymsza-Pawlowska, *History Comes Alive*, 44.

32. Rymsza-Pawlowska, 2.

33. Rymsza-Pawlowska, 2.

34. Rymsza-Pawlowska, 3–4.

35. Gordon, *Spirit of 1976*, 50.

36. Richard Handler and Eric Gable argue that social history came to Colonial Williamsburg in the 1970s, developing out of "the turmoil of the previous decade as a new way of telling the American story." See Handler and Gable, *New History in an Old Museum*, 4.

37. See "Sauder Village," Sauder Village; "History of Sauder Village," Sauder Village.

38. Rymsza-Pawlowska, *History Comes Alive*, 129.

39. Rymsza-Pawlowska, 134.

40. Rymsza-Pawlowska, 135.

41. Gordon, *Spirit of 1976*, 69–70.

42. For more information on the American Indian Movement, see Smith and Warrior, *Like a Hurricane*.

43. Smith and Warrior, 114–15.

44. Smith and Warrior, 128–29.

45. For more on AIM's survival schools, see J. Davis, *Survival Schools*.

46. Smith and Warrior, *Like a Hurricane*, 134 (on Plymouth Rock protest), 112–15 (death of Raymond Yellow Thunder).

47. Byrd, *Transit of Empire*, 81.

48. P. Deloria, *Playing Indian*, 156.

49. Cave, "Shawnee Prophet," 671.

50. *Indiana Centinel* [*sic*], quoted in Tucker, *Tecumseh*, 325.

51. Emmons, *Tecumseh*, 35.

52. Drake, *Life of Tecumseh*, 223–25.

53. Progress Report from the OOHDA, n.d. (likely 1969), IOD/IOT, box 149, folder a. By the summer of 1969, the OOHDA had raised $190,000, and the state legislature had voted to give $350,000 to the drama, supervised by the Ohio Arts Council. The Department of Public Works supervised construction. See Press Release from the OOHDA, August 30, 1969, IOD/IOT, box 149, folder b. The title for this epigraph comes from Ohio's Symphonic Drama Newsletter, vol. 1, no. 6 (November 1968), IOD/IOT, box 149, folder b.

54. "Ohio's Historic Drama," fund-raising brochure (Ohio Outdoor Historical Drama Association, Inc., n.d.), IOD/IOT, box 149, folder b.

55. In the OOHDA's October 1967 newsletter, Redinger noted that tourism did not require increased taxes for building schools and other facilities that permanent residents required. Ohio's Symphonic Drama Newsletter, vol. 1, no. 2 (October 1967), IOD/IOT, box 149, folder b. By September 1968, the newsletter conceded that the OOHDA had struggled to convince people in Tuscarawas County that the drama would be an economic asset. See Ohio's Symphonic Drama Newsletter, vol. 1, no. 5 (September 1968), IOD/IOT, box 149, folder b.

56. Letter from Mark Sumner to Doug McIntire, April 20, 1970, IOD/IOT, box 149, folder d.

57. Letter from Rachel Redinger to Mark Sumner, September 2, 1970, IOD/IOT, box 149, folder d.

58. Letter from Mark Sumner to Rachel Redinger, September 15, 1970, IOD/IOT, box 149, folder d.

59. Letter from Mark Sumner to the Honorable John J. Gilligan, Governor, July 21, 1971, IOD/IOT, box 149, folder d.

60. Attendance Comparison for Ohio Drama, 1970–1995, IOD/IOT, box 144, folder h.

61. *Blue Jacket* souvenir program, 2007, IOD/IOT, box 146, folder c.

62. *Blue Jacket* souvenir program, 2007, IOD/IOT, box 146, folder c.

63. Institute of Outdoor Drama informational packet, n.d. (but maybe 1999), IOD/IOT, box 145, folder a.

64. "First Frontier Gets OAC Grant," newspaper unknown, August 5, 1978, IOD/IOT, box 145, folder c.

65. "Outdoor Drama May Purchase County Land," *Xenia Daily Gazette*, August 8, 1978, IOD/IOT, box 145, folder c.

66. "Outdoor Drama Is Prospering," *Xenia Daily Gazette*, March 28, 1981, IOD/IOT, box 145, folder c. In 1983, the Ohio Office of Travel and Tourism granted $90,000 to each of the three Ohio outdoor dramas to boost their marketing for the upcoming tourist season, demonstrating the state's commitment to this sector of the state's tourism economy. See "Outdoor Dramas Receive Funds," *Dover New Philadelphia Bargain Hunter*, August 10, 1983, IOD/IOT, box 145, folder d.

67. The *Xenia Daily Gazette* cited his "life-long interest in the American Indian" as a reason for the drama's decision to focus on the Shawnee leader. See "'Blue Jacket' an Inspiring Story," *Xenia Daily Gazette*, March 28, 1981, IOD/IOT, box 145, folder c.

68. "'Blue Jacket' an Inspiring Story," *Xenia Daily Gazette*, March 28, 1981, IOD/IOT, box 145, folder c.

69. This long-disproven narrative suggested that Marmaduke Van Swearingen and his brother were captured by a band of Shawnee during the Revolutionary War, and Marmaduke gallantly agreed to peacefully accompany the Shawnee in exchange for his brother's freedom. See "'Blue Jacket' an Inspiring Story," *Xenia Daily Gazette*, March 28, 1981, IOD/IOT, box 145, folder c. The legend allegedly began in an 1877 publication called "Very Interesting Facts about a Noted Indian Chief," whose author was a Van Swearingen descendant. Despite a wide range of historically disparate information—and vehement rejection of the narrative by the Shawnee—the legend stuck for more than a century.

70. Rowland and others, "Was the Shawnee War Chief," 129.

71. Gary Gregory, "Fragmentary," paper unknown, June 25, 1983, IOD/IOT, box 145, folder d.

72. "Paid Attendance 1982–1993," in Report of Survey Results and Attendance, 1993 (First Frontier), IOD/IOT, box 145, folder b; "The Legacy of Blue Jacket," paper unknown, 1987, IOD/IOT, box 145, folder d.

73. Hal Lipper, "Preview: *Blue Jacket*," *Dayton Daily News*, June 23, 1983, IOD/IOT, box 145, folder d.

74. Richard Schwarze, "Blue Jacket: Script Improvements No Match for Major Flaws Elsewhere," *Journal-Herald* (Dayton), June 23, 1983, IOD/IOT, box 145, folder d. Schwarze also wrote that he did not feel sympathy for Blue Jacket, and he did not think the audience got to know him well enough to feel for him by the end of the drama.

75. Undated *Tecumseh!* promotional flier, 3, IOD/IOT, box 149, folder g.

76. Samuel Selden, "Outdoor Historical Play Project Trip Report," September, 1967, IOD/IOT, box 150, folder h.

77. Letter from Mark Sumner to Rusty Mundell, August 12, 1969, IOD/IOT, box 150, folder a.

78. "Response to Outdoor Drama Plan Pleases Officials," *Chillicothe Gazette*, November 3, 1970, IOD/IOT, box 150, folder g.

79. Letter from Rusty Mundell to Mark Sumner, July 16, 1970, IOD/IOT, box 150, folder a.

80. Letter from Rusty Mundell to Mark Sumner, June 15, 1970, IOD/IOT, box 150, folder a.

81. Letter from Rusty Mundell to Mark Sumner, April 1, 1971, IOD/IOT, box 149, folder l.

82. Interview with Brandon Smith, 2015. Rhodes, a Republican, was governor from 1963 to 1971, and again from 1975 to 1983. Democrat John Gilligan was governor from 1971 to 1975.

83. "Scioto Society at Heart of Drama's History," "The 25th Anniversary of *Tecumseh!*," special section of *Chillicothe Gazette*, June 11, 1997, IOD/IOT, box 150, folder g.

84. Dudley Saunders, "'Tecumseh!' Warms the Tepee," *Louisville Courier-Journal & Times*, July 22, 1973, IOD/IOT, box 150, folder g.

85. "Man Recalls Beginnings of 'Tecumseh!' Tradition," "The 25th Anniversary of *Tecumseh!*," special section of *Chillicothe Gazette*, June 11, 1997, IOD/IOT, box 150, folder g.

86. Letter from Rusty Mundell to Mark Sumner, May 10, 1972, IOD/IOT, box 151, folder d.

87. Letter from Mark Sumner to Rusty Mundell, May 23, 1972, IOD/IOT, box 149, folder l.

88. Letter from Mark Sumner to Rusty Mundell, May 23, 1972, IOD/IOT, box 149, folder l.

89. Letter from Mark Sumner to Rusty Mundell, May 23, 1972, IOD/IOT, box 149, folder l.

90. Letter from Samuel Selden to Mark Sumner, June 19, 1972, IOD/IOT, box 151, folder d.

91. "Sugarloaf Mountain Amphitheatre over 70% Complete," Scioto Society, undated (likely 1972–1973), IOD/IOT, box 149, folder g.

92. "'TECUMSEH! Ohio's Newest Outdoor Epic Drama Fact Sheet," Scioto Society, June 22, 1973, IOD/IOT, box 150, folder f.

93. "'TECUMSEH! Drama Gets Governor's Recognition," Scioto Society, June 22, 1973, IOD/IOT, box 150, folder f.

94. *Blue Jacket* and *Tecumseh!* attendance comparison, 1970–2002, IOD/IOT, box 145, folder f.

95. Dudley Saunders, "'Tecumseh!' Warms the Tepee," *Louisville Courier-Journal & Times*, July 22, 1973, IOD/IOT, box 150, folder g.

96. Jill Wiltberger, "'Tecumseh!' Review," *Chillicothe Gazette*, July 2, 1973, IOD/IOT, box 151, folder b.

97. Jim Bruney, "Involved Author Views Development of Drama," *Chillicothe Gazette*, June 28, 1973, IOD/IOT, box 151, folder b.

98. "Extract from a Letter Dated Sept. 12 from Dr. Christian Moe to Mark Sumner," September 12, 1973, IOD/IOT, box 149, folder g.

99. *Blue Jacket* and *Tecumseh!* attendance comparison, 1970–2002, IOD/IOT, box 145, folder f.

100. Gary Brock, "Xenia Drama Being Revamped," *Xenia Daily Gazette*, March 27, 1986, IOD/IOT, box 145, folder d.

101. Memo from Marion Waggoner to Mark Sumner, n.d., but late March or early April 1986, IOD/IOT, box 145, folder d.

102. Jeff Louderback, "'Blue Jacket' Drama True to Shawnee Spirit," *Cincinnati Enquirer*, July 9, 2000, IOD/IOT, box 145, folder d.

103. "2003 Marketing & PR Plan," First Frontier, January 29, 2003, IOD/IOT, box 145, folder c.

104. Performance audit for *Blue Jacket*, Institute of Outdoor Drama, 2003, IOD/IOT, box 145, folder f.

105. Patricia A. West-Volland, "Ohio History Comes Alive in Blue Jacket Drama," *Zanesville Times-Recorder*, July 8, 2007, IOD/IOT, box 145, folder d.

106. "Bankruptcy Kills Outdoor Drama 'Blue Jacket,'" *Columbus Dispatch*, June 3, 2009, http://www.dispatch.com/content/stories/local/2009/06/03/blue_jacket.html.

107. Terry Morris, "'Blue Jacket' Could Use Bit of Tightening," *Dayton Daily News*, June 27, 2007, IOD/IOT, box 145, folder d.

108. "State Awards $40,000 Grant to Blue Jacket," *Xenia Daily Gazette*, October 6, 2007, IOD/IOT, box 145, folder d.

109. The Board of Directors initially emphasized that it would be a postponement, not a closure. Elizabeth Studebaker, "'Blue Jacket' a No-Show for 2008," *Greene County Dailies*, April 4, 2008, IOD/IOT, box 145, folder d.

110. Aaron Keith Harris, "Outdoor Drama Group Vows to Return Next Year with New Show," *Greene County Dailies*, August 5, 2008; Christopher Magan, "Blue Jacket Production Group Sued over Lease, Debt," *Dayton Daily News*, April 14, 2010, IOD/IOT, box 145, folder d.

111. Terry Morris, "Loss of 'Blue Jacket' Outdoor Drama Has Wide Effects," *Dayton Daily News*, July 4, 2009, https://www.daytondailynews.com/news/local/loss-blue-jacket-outdoor-drama-has-wide-effects/QGVtMemvCirVTsP54hTcpN/; Richard Wilson, "Festival Planned to Reopen Former Outdoor Drama Blue Jacket Site," *Dayton Daily News*, June 3, 2018, https://www.daytondailynews.com/news/breaking-news/festival-planned-reopen-former-outdoor-drama-blue-jacket-site/fAiJW5ntlMjcZRr4Xj7PMJ/.

112. "New Lead in Outdoor Drama," Scioto Society, 1991, IOD/IOT, box 150, folder f.

113. Allan W. Eckert, "Why *Tecumseh?*" *Tecumseh!* souvenir program, 2003, IOD/IOT, box 153, folder d.

Chapter Six

1. The quoted information in the epigraph can be found here: Adena region tourism brochure, undated, but published during James Rhodes's tenure as governor of Ohio. That would place it between 1963–1971 or 1975–1983, IOD/IOT, box 151, folder c.

2. Interview with Albert Heierman, conducted by Katrina Phillips in Chillicothe, Ohio, in August 2015.

3. Research notes, August 2015.

4. Interview with Brandon Smith, conducted by Katrina Phillips in Chillicothe, Ohio, in August 2015.

5. Interview with Brandon Smith, August 2015.

6. Interview with Ken Factor, conducted by Katrina Phillips in Chillicothe, Ohio, in August 2015.

7. Kilpatrick, *Celluloid Indians*, 8.

8. Edmunds, *Tecumseh and the Quest*, 224.

9. Jortner, *Gods of Prophetstown*, 187.

10. "Tecumseh!" http://tecumsehdrama.com/.

11. "The Scioto Society, Incorporated Presents Allan W. Eckert's Tecumseh!, an Epic Outdoor Historical Drama," Ross County Historical Society Archives.

12. White, *Middle Ground*, 518.

13. Lynn Ducey, "History of Play's Namesake, Shawnees Examined" in "The 25th Anniversary of Tecumseh," *Chillicothe Gazette*, June 11, 1997 (courtesy of Ross County Historical Society Archives).

14. White, *Middle Ground*, 517.

15. See, for instance, Edmunds, *Shawnee Prophet* and *Tecumseh and the Quest*; Jortner, *Gods of Prophetstown*.

16. Edmunds, *Tecumseh and the Quest*, 218.

17. "New Biography Dispels Myths about Tecumseh," paper unknown, included in 1992 Public Relations Report (Chillicothe, OH: Scioto Society), IOD/IOT, box 150, folder c.

18. "Tecumseh Descendants Dance at Drama," *Chillicothe Gazette*, July 2, 1973, IOD/IOT, box 151, folder b.

19. Jill Zegeer, "News Flash: Tecumseh, Becky Were Just Friends," paper unknown, included in 1992 Public Relations Report (Chillicothe, OH: Scioto Society), IOD/IOT, box 150, folder c.

20. "Drama Need Not Change," paper unknown, included in 1992 Public Relations Report (Chillicothe, OH: Scioto Society), IOD/IOT, box 150, folder c.

21. See Edmunds, *Tecumseh and the Quest*, 225.

22. P. Deloria, *Playing Indian*, 5.

23. P. Deloria, 7.

24. Sturken, *Tourists of History*, 10.

25. Eckert, "Author's Note."

26. Kirkus Reviews, *Sorrow in Our Heart*.

27. Eckert, *Frontiersmen*, 322.

28. Letter from Rusty Mundell to Mr. George M. Montgomery, Manager of Economic and Industrial Development at the Springfield Area Chamber of Commerce, November 17, 1976, IOD/IOT, box 149, folder l.

29. Letter from Mark Sumner to Rusty Mundell, November 30, 1973, IOD/IOT, box 149, folder l.

30. Letter from Philip R. Warner, Promotion Director, to Ms. Marion Meginnis, Institute of Outdoor Drama, May 1, 1974, IOD/IOT, box 149, folder l.

31. "A Word About Last Season—And This," *Tecumseh!* souvenir program, 1974, IOD/IOT, box 152, folder b.

32. *Tecumseh!* souvenir program, 1974, IOD/IOT, box 152, folder b.

33. "A Word About Last Season—And This," *Tecumseh!* souvenir program, 1974, IOD/IOT, box 152, folder b.

34. "A Word About Last Season—And This," *Tecumseh!* souvenir program, 1974, IOD/IOT, box 152, folder b.

35. Letter from Rusty Mundell to Mr. George M. Montgomery, Manager of Economic and Industrial Development at the Springfield Area Chamber of Commerce, November 17, 1976; letter from Rusty Mundell to Mark Sumner, August 8, 1974, IOD/IOT, box 149, folder l.

36. Letter from Mark Sumner to Rusty Mundell, August 12, 1974, IOD/IOT, box 149, folder l.

37. Letter from Mark Sumner to "the Nameless Indians and Settlers of TECUMSEH!," August 28, 1974, IOD/IOT, box 149, folder l.

38. Letter from Mark Sumner to Allan W. Eckert, September 5, 1974, IOD/IOT, box 149, folder l.

39. Letter from Mrs. J. Stansbury to the Institute of Outdoor Drama, July 18, 1975; Letter from Marie Maddox at the IOD to Rusty Mundell, July 22, 1975, IOD/IOT, box 149, folder l.

40. Letter from Allen A. Witt, Promotion Director, to Mark Sumner, n.d., 1975; Letter from Rusty Mundell to Mr. George M. Montgomery, Manager of Economic and Industrial

Development at the Springfield Area Chamber of Commerce, November 17, 1976, IOD/IOT, box 149, folder l.

41. Letter from Rusty Mundell to Mr. George M. Montgomery, Manager of Economic and Industrial Development at the Springfield Area Chamber of Commerce, November 17, 1976, IOD/IOT, box 149, folder l.

42. Letter from President Gerald Ford to the Scioto Society, April 5, 1976, IOD/IOT, box 150, folder f.

43. "America's Greatest Frontiersman?," 1976 Scioto Society press release. Errors in original. IOD/IOT, box 150, folder f.

44. "Description of the Drama," 1976 Scioto Society press release, IOD/IOT, box 150, folder f.

45. "Mel Cobb to Play Tecumseh," 1976 Scioto Society press release, IOD/IOT, box 150, folder f.

46. "Teenager Wins a Place in History," 1976 Scioto Society press release, IOD/IOT, box 150, folder f.

47. "The Shawnee Prophet," 1976 Scioto Society press release, IOD/IOT, box 150, folder f.

48. There are a number of different spellings of the name of this Suquamish and Duwamish chief, including Seattle and Seathl. In this instance, I have chosen to follow the lead of scholar Coll Thrush, who refers to the leader as Seeathl in *Native Seattle*.

49. "'Tecumseh!' 1977 audition packet," Scioto Society, 1977, IOD/IOT, box 151, folder c.

50. *Blue Jacket* souvenir program, 1986, IOD/IOT, box 146, folder a.

51. Thrush, *Native Seattle*, 5–6.

52. Thrush, 187–88.

53. P. Deloria, *Playing Indian*, 167.

54. "Shake Hands with Ohio. Adena Region" tourism brochure, n.d. (likely mid-1970s to the early 1980s, given the tenure of Governor James Rhodes and that of James Duerk, the director of the Department of Economic and Community Development for the State of Ohio), IOD/IOT, box 151, folder c.

55. "Future Projects of the Scioto Society, Inc.," n.d. (likely 1977), IOD/IOT, box 150, folder d.

56. Interview with Brandon Smith, August 2015.

57. Bob Derby, "'Tecumseh' a Mighty Lesson," *Troy Daily News*, July 15, 1988, IOD/IOT, box 150, folder g.

58. Jeff Reed, "Summer Thunder atop Sugarloaf Mountain," *Country Living*, June 1994, IOD/IOT, box 150, folder g.

59. Jeff Reed, "Summer Thunder atop Sugarloaf Mountain," *Country Living*, June 1994, IOD/IOT, box 150, folder g.

60. "1991 Outdoor Drama Attendance Leads Industry," Scioto Society, 1991, IOD/IOT, box 150, folder f.

61. "Outdoor Drama Marks 25 Years of Memories and History," "The 25th Anniversary of *Tecumseh!*," a special section of *Chillicothe Gazette*, June 11, 1997, IOD/IOT, box 150, folder g.

62. "History of Play's Namesake, Shawnees Examined," "The 25th Anniversary of *Tecumseh!*," special section of *Chillicothe Gazette*, June 11, 1997, IOD/IOT, box 150, folder g.

63. "Drama Continues Strong in 18th Season," Scioto Society, 1990, IOD/IOT, box 150, folder f.

64. "New Lead Actor for *Tecumseh!* in 1996," Scioto Society, 1996; "*Tecumseh!* Is Shining during 25th Season," Scioto Society, 1997; "Kohler Returns as Drama's Lead," Scioto Society, 1999, IOD/IOT, box 150, folder f.

65. Tonya Ewing Sharp, "Tecumseh Celebrates 25th Season," *Ohio's Country Journal*, July 1997, IOD/IOT, box 150, folder g.

66. Interview with Brandon Smith, August 2015.

67. Interview with Brandon Smith, August 2015.

68. Interview with Brandon Smith, August 2015.

69. Interview with Brandon Smith, August 2015.

70. Interview with Brandon Smith, August 2015.

71. Interview with Al Heierman, August 2015.

72. P. Deloria, *Playing Indian*, 186–87.

73. Sturken, *Tourists of History*, 279.

74. The title for this epigraph comes from Eckert, *Tecumseh!*, 173.

75. White, *Middle Ground*, 518.

76. Eckert, *Tecumseh!*.

77. Eckert, *Tecumseh!*, 73–74.

78. Eckert, *Tecumseh!*, 82.

79. Eckert, *Tecumseh!*, 89.

80. Eckert, *Tecumseh!*, 95–96.

81. Eckert, *Tecumseh!*, 116.

82. Eckert, *Tecumseh!*, 150.

83. Eckert, *Tecumseh!*, 155.

84. Eckert, *Tecumseh!*, 160.

85. Research notes from *Tecumseh!*, August 2015.

86. Research notes from *Tecumseh!*, August 2015.

87. Research notes from *Tecumseh!*, August 2015.

88. Warren, "Eastern Shawnees," 3. This volume was part of a grant called "A Search for Eastern Shawnee History," administered by the Administration of Native Americans, wherein the tribe intended to repatriate its own history. The tribe's efforts included the digitization of thousands of documents, which became part of a digital collection on the *Ohio Memory* website. The Eastern Shawnee Cultural Preservation Department also hosted annual history summits between 2014 and 2016. The book, as editor Stephen Warren notes, was designed for the use and benefits of the Eastern Shawnee.

89. Nick Trougakos, "Shawnee Tribe, GGS Breaks Ground on Golden Mesa Casino," *Miami News-Record*, June 1, 2018.

90. Barnes, "Becoming Our Own Storytellers," 218.

91. Barnes, 219.

92. Peers, *Playing Ourselves*, xxiii.

Conclusion

1. Memo to Mark Sumner, July 28, 1972, IOD/IOT, box 236, folder h.

2. Letter from Mark Sumner to Bernard Atz, August 10, 1972, IOD/IOT, box 236, folder h. The title for this chapter comes from Longfellow, *Song of Hiawatha*, 1.

3. Letter from Mark Sumner to Bernard Atz, August 10, 1972, IOD/IOT, box 236, folder h.

4. Defunct Outdoor Dramas, supplement to letter from Mark Sumner to Bernard Atz, August 10, 1972, IOD/IOT, box 236, folder h.

5. Outdoor Drama Failures, August 10, 1972, IOD/IOT, box 236, folder h.

6. Outdoor Drama Failures, August 10, 1972, IOD/IOT, box 236, folder h.

7. This may have become the outdoor drama called *To Forge a Nation*, but I have yet to see conclusive evidence to support that hypothesis.

8. "Ten Points that Should Be Considered by Everyone Planning to Produce an Outdoor Play," undated, IOD/IOT, box 236, folder h.

9. Feasibility Study for Dover–New Philadelphia, Ohio, 1967, IOD/IOT, box 273, folder h.

10. Feasibility Study for Robeson Historical Drama Association, 1999, IOD/IOT, box 273, folder a.

11. Feasibility Study for Battle Ground, Indiana, 1980s, IOD/IOT, box 267, folder g.

12. Feasibility Study for Greenville, Ohio, 2002, IOD/IOT, box 273, folder j.

13. Steil, "Pipestone's Hiawatha Pageant."

14. National Park Service, "Park and Its Neighbors." As with Happy Canyon, *Unto These Hills*, and *Tecumseh!*, the *Song of Hiawatha* pageant has a complicated history. In the 1930s, children at the Pipestone Indian School acted in the pageant under the direction of one of their teachers, who also happened to be the principal's wife. The initial pageant only lived for a few years—drought claimed the creek that had served as the backdrop, and World War II soon became a more pressing issue. The pageant was resurrected shortly after the war ended, continuing the publicized connection, however slight, between Pipestone's quarries and Henry Wadsworth Longfellow's poem.

15. Gabler, "Pipestone's Hiawatha Pageant."

16. Southwick, *Building on a Borrowed Past*, 9–10.

17. Steil, "Pipestone's Hiawatha Pageant."

18. Troutman, *Indian Blues*, 154; P. Deloria, *Indians in Unexpected Places*, 191.

19. Sturken, *Tourists of History*, 4.

Bibliography

Archives

Bayfield, WI
    Bayfield Heritage Association
Cherokee, NC
    Cherokee Historical Society
    Museum of the Cherokee Indian
Chillicothe, OH
    Ross County Historical Society
Greenville, NC
    East Carolina University Joyner Library
    Institute of Outdoor Theatre
Pendleton, OR
    Pendleton Round-Up and Happy Canyon Hall of Fame
    Umatilla County Historical Society

Newspapers

Asheville Citizen (Asheville, NC)
Asheville Citizen-Times (Asheville, NC)
Athena Press (Athena, OR)
Bayfield County Journal (Bayfield, WI)
Bayfield Progress (Bayfield, WI)
Carolina Times (Durham, NC)
Charlotte Observer (Charlotte, NC)
Cherokee One Feather (Cherokee, NC)
Chillicothe Gazette (Chillicothe, OH)
Cincinnati Enquirer (Cincinnati, OH)
Columbus Dispatch (Columbus, OH)
Concord Daily Tribune (Concord, NC)
Daily East Oregonian (Pendleton, OR)
Dalles Daily Chronicle (The Dalles, OR)
Dayton Daily News (Dayton, OH)
Dover New Philadelphia Bargain Hunter (Millersburg, OH)
Duplin Times (Kenansville, NC)
Durham Morning Herald (Durham, NC)
East Oregonian (Pendleton, OR)

East Oregonian Round-Up Souvenir Edition, September 11, 1913 (Pendleton, OR)
Gate City Journal (Nyssa, OR)
Greene County Dailies (Xenia, OH)
Heppner Gazette-Times (Heppner, OR)
Jackson County Journal (Sylva, NC)
Journal-Herald (Dayton, OH)
Louisville Courier-Journal & Times (Louisville, KY)
Miami News-Record (Miami, OK)
Morning Oregonian (Portland, OR)
New York Times (New York, NY)
News & Observer (Raleigh, NC)
News-Topic (Lenoir, NC)
Northwest Opinions, East Oregonian (Pendleton, OR)
Oregon Arbus (Oregon City, OR)
Oregonian (Portland, OR)
Outer Banks Sentinel (Nags Head, NC)
Ruralite (Sylva, NC)

Spilyay tymoo (Warm Springs, OR)
Statesman Journal (Salem, OR)
Sunday Oregonian (Portland, OR)
Troy Daily News (Troy, OH)

Willamette Collegian (Salem, OR)
Waynesville Mountaineer (Waynesville, NC)
Xenia Daily Gazette (Xenia, OH)
Zanesville Times-Recorder (Zanesville, OH)

Published Books, Articles, and Essays

Abbott, Carl. *The Great Extravaganza: Portland and the Lewis and Clark Exposition.* Portland: Oregon Historical Society Press, 1981.

Allison, Mildred. "Annual Event Comes Long Way." Repr. in "East Oregonian Souvenir Edition, September 1959," Umatilla County Historical Association, *Pioneer Trails* 4, no. 1 (September 1979).

Anderson, William L. "Museum of the Cherokee Indian." In *Encyclopedia of North Carolina*, ed. William S. Powell, 774. Chapel Hill: University of North Carolina Press, 2006.

Archabal, Nina Marchetti. Introduction to *Chippewa Customs*, by Frances Densmore. St. Paul: Minnesota Historical Society Press, 1979.

Arnold, David. "Work and Culture in Southeastern Alaska: Tlingets and the Salmon Fisheries." In *Native Pathways: American Indian Culture and Economic Development in the Twentieth Century*, ed. Brian Hosmer and Colleen O'Neill, 156–83. Boulder: University Press of Colorado, 2004.

Aron, Cindy S. *Working at Play: A History of Vacations in the United States.* New York: Oxford University Press, 2001.

Avery, Laurence G. *A Paul Green Reader.* Chapel Hill: University of North Carolina Press, 1998.

Bales, Michael, and Ann Terry Hill. *Pendleton Round-Up at 100: Oregon's Legendary Rodeo.* Norman: University of Oklahoma Press, 2009.

Barnes, Benjamin J. "Becoming Our Own Storytellers: Tribal Nations Engaging with Academia." In *The Eastern Shawnee Tribe of Oklahoma: Resistance through Adversity*, ed. Stephen Warren. Norman: University of Oklahoma Press, 2017.

Bauer, William J., Jr. *We Were All Like Migrant Workers Here: Work, Community, and Memory on California's Round Valley Reservation, 1850–1941.* Chapel Hill: University of North Carolina Press, 2009.

Bayfield Civic League. *Indian Pageant Cook Book.* Bayfield: Bayfield Civic League, 1924.

Bayfield Heritage Association. "Second Annual Apostle Islands Indian Pageant." Souvenir program, 1925.

Beard-Moose, Christina Taylor. *Public Indians, Private Cherokees: Tourism and Tradition on Tribal Ground.* Tuscaloosa: University of Alabama Press, 2009.

Bederman, Gail. *Manliness and Civilization: A Cultural History of Gender and Race in the United States.* Chicago: University of Chicago Press, 1995.

Bernardin, Susan, Lisa MacFarlane, Nicole Tonkovich, and Melody Graulich. *Trading Gazes: Euro-American Women Photographers and Native North Americans, 1880–1940.* New Brunswick, NJ: Rutgers University Press, 2003.

Blee, Lisa. "Completing Lewis and Clark's Westward March: Exhibiting a History of Empire at the 1905 Portland World's Fair." *Oregon Historical Quarterly* 106, no. 2 (Summer 2005): 232–53.

Blegen, Theodore Christian, and Minnesota Historical Society. *Minnesota History Bulletin.* St. Paul: Minnesota Historical Society, 1920.

Bodnar, John. *Remaking America: Public Memory, Commemoration, and Patriotism in the Twentieth Century.* Princeton: Princeton University Press, 1992.

Borstelmann, Thomas. *The Cold War and the Color Line: American Race Relations in the Global Arena.* Cambridge, MA: Harvard University Press, 2001.

Bowles, John P. *Land Too Good for Indians: Northern Indian Removal.* Norman: University of Oklahoma Press, 2016.

Brock, Emily K. *Money Trees: The Douglas Fir and American Forestry, 1900–1944.* Corvallis: Oregon State University Press, 2015.

Brown, Dona. *Inventing New England: Regional Tourism in the Nineteenth Century.* Washington, DC: Smithsonian Institution Press, 1995.

Bruyneel, Kevin. *The Third Space of Sovereignty: The Postcolonial Politics of U.S.-Indigenous Relations.* Minneapolis: University of Minnesota Press, 2007.

Buss, James Joseph. *Winning the West with Words: Language and Conquest in the Lower Great Lakes.* Norman: University of Oklahoma Press, 2011.

Byrd, Jodi A. *The Transit of Empire: Indigenous Critiques of Colonialism.* Minneapolis: University of Minnesota Press, 2011.

Caison, Gina. "'We're Still Here': Eddie Swimmer on Cherokee History, Life, and Outdoor Drama in the Appalachian Mountains." *North Carolina Literary Review* 19 (2010): 46–59.

Calloway, Colin G. *The Scratch of a Pen: 1763 and the Transformation of North America.* New York: Oxford University Press, 2006.

Cattelino, Jessica R. "Casino Roots: The Cultural Production of Twentieth-Century Seminole Economic Development." In *Native Pathways: American Indian Culture and Economic Development in the Twentieth Century,* ed. Brian Hosmer and Colleen O'Neill, 66–90. Boulder: University Press of Colorado, 2004.

———. *High Stakes: Florida Seminole Gaming and Sovereignty.* Durham, NC: Duke University Press, 2008.

Cave, Alfred A. "The Shawnee Prophet, Tecumseh, and Tippecanoe: A Case Study of Historical Myth-Making." *Journal of the Early Republic* 22, no. 4 (Winter 2002): 637–73.

Centennial Exposition of the Ohio Valley and Central States. "Official Guide of the Centennial Exposition of the Ohio Valley and Central States, Cincinnati, O., U.S.A., 1888." Cincinnati: John F. C. Mullen, 1888.

The Cherokee Historical Association. *History of Cherokee Historical Association, 1946–1982.* Cherokee, NC, 1982.

———. *Unto These Hills* souvenir program, 2012.

———. *Unto These Hills* souvenir program, 2019.

Chiltoskey, Mary Ulmer. *Cherokee Fair and Festival: A History thru 1978.* Asheville, NC: Gilbert Printing, 1995.

Clifford, James. "Looking Several Ways: Anthropology and Native Heritage in Alaska." *Current Anthropology* 45, no. 1 (2004): 5–30.

Confederated Tribes of the Umatilla Indian Reservation. *2016 Annual Report.*

Conner, Roberta. "From Generation to Generation: Tribal Participation." In *Pendleton Round-Up at 100: Oregon's Legendary Rodeo,* ed. Michael Bales and Ann Terry Hill. Norman: University of Oklahoma Press, 2009.

———. "Round-Up Reminiscences: 'You Can't Eat Lound-Up!'" In *Pendleton Round-Up at 100: Oregon's Legendary Rodeo*, ed. Michael Bales and Ann Terry Hill. Norman: University of Oklahoma Press, 2009.

Connor, William P., Jr. *History of Cherokee Historical Association, 1946–1982*. Cherokee, NC: Cherokee Historical Association, 1982.

Corning, Howard. *Dictionary of Oregon History*. Hillsboro, OR: Binfords & Mort, 1956, 1989.

Cothran, Boyd. "Working the Indian Field Days: The Economy of Authenticity and the Question of Agency in Yosemite Valley, 1916–1929." *American Indian Quarterly* 34, no. 2 (Spring 2007): 194–223.

Cronon, William. "Foreword: Dreams of Plenty." In *Landscapes of Promise: The Oregon Story 1800–1940*, ed. William G. Robbins, xi. Seattle: University of Washington Press, 1997.

Dann, Kevin. "Pageants, Parades, and Patriotism: Celebrating Champlain in 1909." *Vermont History* 77, no. 2 (2009): 87–98.

Davis, Harry. "Theatre of the People." Official program of Kermit Hunter's *Unto These Hills*. 1957.

Davis, Julie L. *Survival Schools: The American Indian Movement and Community Education in the Twin Cities*. Minneapolis: University of Minnesota Press, 2013.

Deloria, Philip J. *Indians in Unexpected Places*. Lawrence: University Press of Kansas, 2004.

———. *Playing Indian*. New Haven, CT: Yale University Press, 1998.

Deloria, Vine, Jr. *Custer Died for Your Sins: An Indian Manifesto*. Norman: University of Oklahoma Press, 1988.

Denson, Andrew. *Monuments to Absence: Cherokee Removal and the Contest over Southern Memory*. Chapel Hill: University of North Carolina Press, 2017.

———. "Native Americans in Cold War Public Diplomacy: Indian Politics, American History, and the US Information Agency." *American Indian Culture and Research Journal* 36, no. 2 (2012): 1–22.

Desmond, Jane. *Staging Tourism: Bodies on Display from Waikiki to Sea World*. Chicago: University of Chicago Press, 1999.

Donahue, Mike. *Portland Rose Festival: For You a Rose in Portland Grows*. American & World Geographic, 1996.

Drake, Benjamin. *Life of Tecumseh and of His Brother the Prophet; with a Sketch of the Shawanoe Indians*. Cincinnati: E. Morgan, 1841.

Dudziak, Mary L. *Cold War Civil Rights: Race and the Image of American Democracy*. Princeton, NJ: Princeton University Press, 2011.

Duncan, Barbara R., and Brett H. Riggs. *Cherokee Heritage Trails Guidebook*. Chapel Hill: University of North Carolina Press, 2003.

Eckert, Allan W. "Author's Note: November 1966." In *The Frontiersmen: A Narrative*. New York: Bantam Books, 1970. Orig. pub. Little, Brown, 1967.

———. *The Frontiersmen: A Narrative*. New York: Bantam Books, 1970. Orig. pub. Little, Brown, 1967.

———. *Tecumseh!: A Play*. New York: Little, Brown, 1974.

Edmunds, R. David. *The Shawnee Prophet*. Lincoln: University of Nebraska Press, 1983.

———. *Tecumseh and the Quest for Indian Leadership*. Boston: Little, Brown, 1984.

Ellis, Clyde. "Five Dollars a Week to Be 'Regular Indians': Shows, Exhibitions, and the Economics of Indian Dancing, 1880–1930." In *Native Pathways: American Indian Culture and Economic Development in the Twentieth Century*, ed. Brian Hosmer and Colleen O'Neill, 184–208. Boulder: University of Colorado Press, 2004.

Emmons, William. *Tecumseh: Or, The Battle of the Thames, A National Drama, In Five Acts*. New York: Elton & Harrison, 1836.

Encyclopedia Americana. New York: Grolier, 1962.

Federal Writers' Project. *Kansas: A Guide to the Sunflower State, Comp. and Written by the Federal Writers' Project of the Work Projects Administration for the State of Kansas*. New York: Hastings House, 1949.

Feldman, James W. *A Storied Wilderness: Rewilding the Apostle Islands*. Seattle: University of Washington Press, 2011.

Finger, John R. *Cherokee Americans: The Eastern Band of Cherokees, 1819–1900*. Lincoln: University of Nebraska Press, 1991.

———. *The Eastern Band of Cherokees, 1819–1900*. Knoxville: University of Tennessee Press, 1984.

———. "Termination and the Eastern Band of Cherokee." *American Indian Quarterly* 15, no. 2 (Spring 1991): 153–70.

Free, William J., and Charles B. Lower. *History into Drama: A Source Book on Symphonic Drama Including the Complete Text of Paul Green's* The Lost Colony. New York: Odyssey, 1963.

French, Laurence A., and Jim Hornbuckle, eds. *The Cherokee Perspective: Written by Eastern Cherokees*. Boone, NC: Appalachian Consortium Press, 1981.

Frome, Michael. *Strangers in High Places: The Story of the Great Smoky Mountains*. Knoxville: University of Tennessee Press, 1966.

Furlong, Charles Wellington. "The Epic Drama of the West." *Harper's Monthly Magazine*, vol. 133 (June–November 1916): 368–77.

———. *Let 'Er Buck: A Story of the Passing of the Old West*. New York: Overlook, 1921. Repr. 2007.

Gabler, Jay. "Pipestone's Hiawatha Pageant Ends 60-Year Run." *Twin Cities Daily Planet*, July 24, 2008. http://www.tcdailyplanet.net/article/2008/07/22/pipestones-hiawatha -pageant-ends-60-year-run.html.

Gassan, Richard H. *The Birth of American Tourism: New York, the Hudson Valley, and American Culture, 1790–1830*. Amherst: University of Massachusetts Press, 2008.

Gassner, John. "Broadway in Review." *Educational Theatre Journal* 5, no. 4 (December 1953): 349–54.

Geiogamah, Hanay. "American Indian Theater 2013: Not Running on Empty Yet." In *The World of Indigenous North America*, ed. Robert Warrior, 330–46. New York: Routledge, 2015.

Glassberg, David. *American Historical Pageantry: The Uses of Tradition in the Early Twentieth Century*. Chapel Hill: University of North Carolina Press, 1990.

Gordon, Tammy S. *The Spirit of 1976: Commerce, Community, and the Politics of Commemoration*. Amherst: University of Massachusetts Press, 2013.

Grafe, Steven L. "Lee Moorhouse: Photographer of the Inland Empire." *Oregon Historical Quarterly* 98, no. 4 (Winter 1997–1998): 426–77.

Green, Paul. "Author's Note." *The Common Glory*. Chapel Hill, NC, 1948.

———. *The Lost Colony: A Symphonic Drama of American History*. Chapel Hill: University of North Carolina Press, 1954.

———. *The Lost Colony: A Symphonic Drama of American History*. Edited by Laurence G. Avery. Chapel Hill: University of North Carolina Press, 2001.

———. "Playmaker's Progress." *Theatre Arts*. August 1957, 86. In *History into Drama: A Source Book on Symphonic Drama, Including the Complete Text of Paul Green's* The Lost Colony, ed. William J. Free and Charles B. Lower, 125. New York: Odyssey, 1963.

———. "Preface." *The Lost Colony*. Chapel Hill, NC: University of North Carolina Press, 1946.

Gross, Ariela. *What Blood Won't Tell: A History of Race on Trial in America*. Cambridge, MA: Harvard University Press, 2008.

Gruber, Jacob W. "Ethnographic Salvage and the Shaping of Anthropology." *American Anthropologist, New Series* 72, no. 6 (December 1970): 1289–99.

Handler, Richard, and Eric Gable. *The New History in an Old Museum: Creating the Past at Colonial Williamsburg*. Durham, NC: Duke University Press, 1997.

Harper, Rob. "Looking the Other Way: The Gnadenhutten Massacre and the Contextual Interpretation of Violence." *William and Mary Quarterly* 64, no. 3 (July 2007): 621–44.

———. "State Intervention and Extreme Violence in the Revolutionary Ohio Valley." *Journal of Genocide Research* 10, no. 2 (2008): 233–48.

Heape, Rich. *Trail of Tears*. Rich Heape Films, 2006.

Hill, Ann Terry. "Happy Canyon—Going Strong Since 1913." In *Pendleton Round-Up at 100: Oregon's Legendary Rodeo*, ed. Michael Bales and Ann Terry Hill. Norman: University of Oklahoma Press, 2009.

Hinderaker, Eric. *Elusive Empires: Constructing Colonialism in the Ohio Valley, 1673–1800*. Cambridge: Cambridge University Press, 1997.

Hinderaker, Eric, and Peter C. Mancall. *At the Edge of Empire: The Backcountry in British North America*. Baltimore: Johns Hopkins University Press, 2003.

Hochman, Barbara. *"Uncle Tom's Cabin" and the Reading Revolution: Race, Literacy, Childhood, and Fiction, 1851–1911*. Amherst: University of Massachusetts Press, 2011.

Holland, Ron. "Oconaluftee Indian Village." In *Encyclopedia of North Carolina*, ed. William S. Powell. Chapel Hill: University of North Carolina Press, 2006.

Hosmer, Brian. *American Indians in the Marketplace: Persistence and Innovation among the Menominees and Metlakatlans, 1870–1920*. Lawrence: University Press of Kansas, 1999.

Hoxie, Frederick. *A Final Promise: The Campaign to Assimilate the Indians, 1880–1920*. Lincoln: University of Nebraska Press, 2001.

Hunter, Kermit. "History or Drama?" *South Atlantic Bulletin*, May 1953, as cited in Raymond Carroll Hayes, "A Study of Hero-Building and Mythmaking in Three of Kermit Hunter's Outdoor Historical Epic-Dramas." PhD diss., Indiana University of Pennsylvania, 1982, 61.

———. "The Story of the Cherokee." In *Unto These Hills: A Drama of the Cherokee, 1540–1950* souvenir program. Cherokee: Cherokee Historical Association (1950): 20–21.

———. "The Theatre Meets the People." *Educational Theatre Journal* 7, no. 2 (1955): 128–35.

———. *Unto These Hills*. Cherokee: Cherokee Historical Association, 1950.

Hurt, Douglas R. *The Ohio Frontier: Crucible of the Old Northwest, 1720–1830*. Bloomington: Indiana University Press, 1996.

Imada, Adria. *Aloha America: Hula Circuits through the U.S. Empire*. Durham, NC: Duke University Press, 2012.

Jones, Edward Gardner. *The Oregonians Handbook of the Pacific Northwest*. Portland: Oregonian, 1894.

Jones, Landon Y. *William Clark and the Shaping of the American West*. New York: Hill and Wang, 2005.

Jortner, Adam. *The Gods of Prophetstown: The Battle of Tippecanoe and the Holy War for the American Frontier*. New York: Oxford University Press, 2012.

Kelly, Lawrence. "The Indian Reorganization Act: The Dream and the Reality." *Pacific Historical Review* 44, no. 3 (August 1975): 291–312.

Kenny, Vincent. *Paul Green*. New York: Twayne, 1971.

Kilpatrick, Jacquelyn. *Celluloid Indians: Native Americans and Film*. Lincoln: University of Nebraska Press, 1999.

King, Duane H., comp. *Cherokee Heritage: Official Guidebook to the Museum of the Cherokee Indian*. Cherokee: Museum of the Cherokee Indian, 1982.

———. "The Origin of the Eastern Cherokees as a Social and Political Entity." In *The Cherokee Indian Nation: A Troubled History*, ed. Duane H. King. Knoxville: University of Tennessee Press, 1979.

Kirkus Reviews. *A Sorrow in Our Heart*. February 14, 1992.

Koch, Frederick H. "The Drama of Roanoke Island." *The Lost Colony Official Program*. Manteo, NC, 1938.

———. *Raleigh: The Shepherd of the Ocean; A Pageant Drama*. Raleigh, NC: Edwards & Broughton, 1920.

Kramer, Paul A. *The Blood of Government: Race, Empire, the United States, & the Philippines*. Chapel Hill: University of North Carolina Press, 2006.

Kutsche, Paul. "The Tsali Legend: Culture Heroes and Historiography." *Ethnohistory* 10, no. 4 (Autumn 1963): 329–57.

Laegreid, Renee M. "Rodeo Queens at the Pendleton Round-Up: The First Go-Round, 1910–1917." *Oregon Historical Quarterly* 104, no. 1 (Spring 2003): 6–23.

Larsen, Dennis M. *The Missing Chapters: The Untold Story of Ezra Meeker's Old Oregon Trail Monument Expedition, January 1906 to July 1908*. Puyallup, WA: Ezra Meeker Historical Society, 2006.

Lewis, Courtney. *Sovereign Entrepreneurs: Cherokee Small-Business Owners and the Making of Economic Sovereignty*. Chapel Hill: University of North Carolina Press, 2019.

Limerick, Patricia Nelson. *The Legacy of Conquest: The Unbroken Past of the American West*. New York: W. W. Norton, 1987.

Löfgren, Orvar. *On Holiday: A History of Vacationing*. Berkeley: University of California Press, 1999.

Lomax, Alfred L. "Thomas Kay Woolen Mill Co.: A Family Enterprise." *Oregon Historical Quarterly* 54, no. 2 (June 1953), 102–39.

Longfellow, Henry Wadsworth. *The Song of Hiawatha*. 1855, repr. Chicago: J. G. Ferguson, 1968, 1.

Lowery, Malinda Maynor. *Lumbee Indians in the Jim Crow South: Race, Identity, and the Making of a Nation*. Chapel Hill: University of North Carolina Press, 2010.

Marsh, Tom. *To the Promised Land: A History of Government and Politics in Oregon*. Corvallis: Oregon State University Press, 2012.

May, Keith F. *Pendleton: A Short History of a Real Western Town*. Pendleton, OR: Drigh Sighed Publications, 2005.

McCann, Dennis. *This Superior Place: Stories of Bayfield and the Apostle Islands*. Madison: Wisconsin Historical Society Press, 2013.

McDougall, Allan K., Lisa Philips, and Daniel L. Boxberger. *Before and After the State: Politics, Poetics, and People(s) in the Pacific Northwest*. Vancouver: UBC Press, 2018.

McNally, Michael. "The Indian Passion Play: Contesting the Real Indian in Song of Hiawatha Pageants, 1901–1965." *American Quarterly* 58, no. 1 (March 2006): 105–36.

Middleton, Richard. "Pontiac: Local Warrior or Pan-Indian Leader?" *Michigan Historical Review* 32, no. 2 (Fall 2006): 1–32.

Miles, Tiya. *Ties That Bind: The Story of an Afro-Cherokee Family in Slavery and Freedom*. Berkeley: University of California Press, 2006.

Miller, George R., and the Portland Rose Festival Foundation. *Portland Rose Festival*. Charleston, SC: Arcadia, 2013.

Miller, Stuart Creighton. *The Unwelcome Immigrant: The American Image of the Chinese*. 1969; Berkeley: University of California Press, 1974.

Minto, John. "Sheep Husbandry in Oregon: The Pioneer Era of Domestic Sheep Husbandry." *Quarterly of the Oregon Historical Society* 3, no. 3 (September 1902): 219–47.

Mooney, James. *Myths of the Cherokee*. 1891. Repr. *James Mooney's History, Myths, and Sacred Formulas of the Cherokees*. Fairview, NC: Bright Mountain Books, 1992.

Moylan, Michele. "Materiality as Performance: The Framing of Helen Hunt Jackson's *Ramona*." In *Reading Books: Essays on the Material Text and Literature in America*, ed. Michele Moylan and Lane Stiles. Amherst: University of Massachusetts Press, 1996.

Murphy, Jacquelyn Shea. *The People Have Never Stopped Dancing: Native American Modern Dance Histories*. Minneapolis: University of Minnesota Press, 2007.

Nash, Roderick Frazier. *Wilderness and the American Mind*. New Haven, CT: Yale University Press, 2001.

Norrgard, Chantal. *Seasons of Change: Labor, Treaty Rights, and Ojibwe Nationhood*. Chapel Hill: University of North Carolina Press, 2014.

Olmanson, Eric. *The Future City on the Inland Sea: A History of Imaginative Geographies of Lake Superior*. Athens: Ohio University Press, 2007.

O'Neill, Colleen. "Rethinking Modernity and the Discourse of Development." In *Native Pathways: American Indian Culture and Economic Development in the Twentieth Century*, ed. Brian Hosmer and Colleen O'Neill, 1–24. Boulder: University Press of Colorado, 2004.

Oregon Trail: A Plan to Honor the Pioneers. New York: Oregon Trail Memorial Association, 1929.

Parkinson, Robert G. "From Indian Killer to Worthy Citizen: The Revolutionary Transformation of Michael Cresap." *William and Mary Quarterly* 63, no. 1 (January 2006): 97–122.

Peck, G. Richard. *Images of America: Chillicothe, Ohio*. Charleston, SC: Arcadia, 1999.

Peers, Laura. *Playing Ourselves: Interpreting Native Histories at Historic Reconstructions*. New York: AltaMira, 2007.

"Pendleton's Roots Began Nearly 140 Years Ago." *Textile World*, September 1, 2001.

Perdue, Theda. *Cherokee Women: Gender and Culture Change, 1700–1835*. Lincoln: University of Nebraska Press, 1998.

Perdue, Theda, and Michael D. Green, eds. *The Cherokee Removal: A Brief History with Documents*. Boston: Bedford–St. Martin's, 2005.

Peterson del Mar, David. *Oregon's Promise: An Interpretive History*. Corvallis: Oregon State University Press, 2003.

Phillips, Katrina. "Performance over Policy: Promoting Indianness in Twentieth-Century Wisconsin Tourism." *Radical History Review* 129, "Unpacking Tourism" (Fall 2017): 34–50.

Philp, Kenneth R. *Termination Revisited: American Indians on the Trail to Self-Determination, 1933–1953*. Lincoln: University of Nebraska Press, 1999.

Pierce, Jason. *Making the White Man's West: Whiteness and the Creation of the American West*. Boulder: University Press of Colorado, 2016.

Prucha, Francis Paul. *The Great Father: The United States Government and the American Indians*. Lincoln: University of Nebraska Press, 1986.

Raibmon, Paige. *Authentic Indians: Episodes of Encounter from the Late-Nineteenth-Century Northwest Coast*. Durham, NC: Duke University Press, 2005.

"Real Indians in Pageant of the Dalles, Oregon." *The Playground* 15, no. 1 (April 1921): 378. Cooperstown, NY: Playground and Recreation Association of America.

Reid, Robert A. *The Lewis and Clark Centennial Exposition Illustrated*. Portland, OR: Robert Allan Reid, 1905.

Robbins, William G. *Landscapes of Promise: The Oregon Story 1800–1940*. Seattle: University of Washington Press, 1997.

Roland, Charles P. *The Improbable Era: The South Since World War II*. Lexington: University Press of Kentucky, 1975.

Rosenthal, Nicholas G. "The Dawn of a New Day? Notes on Indian Gaming in Southern California." In *Native Pathways: American Indian Culture and Economic Development in the Twentieth Century*, ed. Brian Hosmer and Colleen O'Neill. Boulder: University Press of Colorado, 2004.

Rothman, Hal. *Devil's Bargain: Tourism in the Twentieth-Century American West*. Lawrence: University Press of Kansas, 1998.

Rowland, C. D., R. V. Van Trees, Marc S. Taylor, Michael L. Raymer, and Dan E. Krane. "Was the Shawnee War Chief Blue Jacket a Caucasian?" *Ohio Journal of Science* 106, no. 4 (2006): 126–29.

Rydell, Robert W. *All The World's a Fair: Visions of Empire at American International Expositions, 1876–1916*. Chicago: University of Chicago Press, 1984.

Rymsza-Pawlowska, M. J. *History Comes Alive: Public History and Popular Culture in the 1970s*. Chapel Hill: University of North Carolina Press, 2017.

Santee, J. F. "Pio-Pio-Mox-Mox." *Oregon Historical Quarterly* 34, no. 2 (June 1933): 164–76.

Schneider, Wolf. "Pendleton: No Oregon Town Has More Western Cachet." *Cowboys and Indians: The Premier Magazine of the West*, September 2009.

Sears, John F. *Sacred Places: American Tourist Attractions in the Nineteenth Century*. Amherst: University of Massachusetts Press, 1998.

Selden, Sam. "American Drama in the Open Air." Official program of Kermit Hunter's *Horn in the West*, 1952.

Shakespeare, William. *As You Like It*. New York: Simon & Schuster; Reissue edition, 2004.

Shaffer, Marguerite S. *See America First: Tourism and National Identity, 1880–1940*. Washington, DC: Smithsonian Institution Press, 2001.

Sinks, James. "A Drive Down Eastern Oregon: Plan a Trip for Pendleton." *1859: Oregon's Magazine*, August 25, 2015.

Smith, Gordon. "Foreword." In Michael Bales and Ann Terry Hill, *Pendleton Round-Up at 100: Oregon's Legendary Rodeo*. Norman: University of Oklahoma Press, 2009.

Smith, Paul Chaat, and Robert Warrior. *Like a Hurricane: The American Indian Movement from Alcatraz to Wounded Knee*. New York: New Press, 1996.

Smithers, Gregory D. "A Cherokee Epic: Kermit Hunter's *Unto These Hills* and the Mythologizing of Cherokee History." *Native South* 8 (2005): 1–30.

Southwick, Sally J. *Building on a Borrowed Past: Place and Identity in Pipestone, Minnesota*. Athens: Ohio University Press, 2005.

Stephens, George Myers. "The Beginnings of the Historical Drama, 'Unto These Hills.'" *North Carolina Historical Review* 28, no. 2 (April 1951): 212–18.

Sturken, Marita. *Tourists of History: Memory, Kitsch, and Consumerism from Oklahoma City to Ground Zero*. Durham, NC: Duke University Press, 2007.

Thrush, Coll. *Native Seattle: Histories from the Crossing-Over Place*. Seattle: University of Washington Press, 2007.

Trachtenberg, Alan. *Shades of Hiawatha: Staging Indians, Making Americans, 1880–1930*. New York: Hill and Wang, 2004.

Trafzer, Clifford E. "The Legacy of the Walla Walla Council, 1855." *Oregon Historical Quarterly* 106, no. 3, The Isaac I. Stevens and Joel Palmer Treaties, 1855–2005. (Fall 2005): 398–411.

Trotman, William. "Does *The Lost Colony* 'Work'?" In *History into Drama: A Source Book on Symphonic Drama, Including the Complete Text of Paul Green's* The Lost Colony, ed. William J. Free and Charles B. Lower. New York: Odyssey, 1963.

Troutman, John. *Indian Blues: American Indians and the Politics of Music, 1879–1934*. Norman: University of Oklahoma Press, 2009.

Tucker, Glenn. *Tecumseh: Vision of Glory*. Indianapolis: Bobbs-Merrill, 1956; repr. New York: Cosimo, 2005.

Varley, Molly. *Americans Recaptured: Progressive Era Memory of Frontier Captivity*. Norman: University of Oklahoma Press, 2014.

Warren, Stephen. "The Eastern Shawnees and the Repatriation of Their History." In *The Eastern Shawnee Tribe of Oklahoma: Resistance through Adversity*, ed. Stephen Warren. Norman: University of Oklahoma Press, 2017.

Werry, Margaret. *The Tourist State: Performing Leisure, Liberalism, and Race in New Zealand*. Minneapolis: University of Minnesota Press, 2011.

Whelan, Robert, and Jared Rollier. "The Contributions of Indian Gaming to Oregon's Economy in 2014 and 2015: A Market and Economic Impact Analysis for the Oregon Tribal Gaming Alliance." Portland: ECONorthwest, 2017.

White, Richard. *"It's Your Misfortune and None of My Own": A New History of the American West*. Norman: University of Oklahoma Press, 1991.

———. *The Middle Ground: Indians, Empires, and Republics in the Great Lakes Region, 1650–1815*. New York: Cambridge University Press, 1991.

Wilkins, David E., and K. Tsianina Lomawaima. *Uneven Ground: American Indian Sovereignty and Federal Law*. Norman: University of Oklahoma Press, 2002.

Willingham, William F. "The First 100 Years of the Pendleton Round-Up." In *Pendleton Round-Up at 100: Oregon's Legendary Rodeo,* ed. Michael Bales and Ann Terry Hill. Norman: University of Oklahoma Press, 2009.

Wilson, Norma. "New Native American Drama: Three Plays." Review. *Studies in American Indian Literatures, New Series* 7, no. 4, Review Issue (Winter 1983): 84–87.

Wright, Muriel H. "The American Indian Exposition in Oklahoma." *Chronicles of Oklahoma* 24 (Summer 1946): 158–65.

Dissertations, Theses, and Unpublished Papers

Davis, Suzanne. "Indian Costumes for *Unto These Hills.*" Master's thesis, University of North Carolina at Chapel Hill, 1954.

Hayes, Raymond Carroll. "A Study of Hero-Building and Mythmaking in Three of Kermit Hunter's Outdoor Historical Epic-Dramas." PhD diss., Indiana University of Pennsylvania, 1982.

Lindsey, Edwin S. "Outdoor Historical Dramas of Paul Green and Kermit Hunter." Unpublished paper read at the Tennessee Philological Association, February 20, 1959.

Nees, Heidi L. "'Indian' Summers: Querying Representations of Native American Cultures in Outdoor Historical Dramas." PhD diss., Bowling Green State University, 2012.

Saunooke, Annette Bird. "Cherokee Royalties: The Impact of Indian Tourism on the Eastern Band of Cherokee Identity." Master's thesis, College of William and Mary, 2004.

Taylor, Wanda. "A Brief History of the Outdoor Drama *Unto These Hills* and Transcript of an Interview with a Former Cast Member." N.p., Cherokee Historical Association, 1992.

Thompson, Matthew D. "Staging 'the Drama': The Continuing Importance of Cultural Tourism in the Gaming Era." PhD diss., University of North Carolina–Chapel Hill, 2009.

Umberger, Wallace R. "A History of *Unto These Hills,* 1941 to 1968." PhD diss., Tulane University, 1970.

Websites and Online Resources

Bayfield Apple Festival Poster. Bayfield: Bayfield Chamber of Commerce and Visitor Bureau. http://bayfield.org/bayfield-activities/bayfield-apple-festival/.

Cherokee Indian Fair and Folk Festival souvenir program, 1935. Cherokee Indian Fair Association. "Motoring through the Mountains—1930s: Cherokee." Travel Western North Carolina, Hunter Library Digital Programs and Special Collections at Western Carolina University. http://www.wcu.edu/library/digitalcollections/travelwnc/1930s /1930cherokee.html.

"Company History." Pendleton Woolen Mills. http://www.pendleton-usa.com/custserv /custserv.jsp?pageName=CompanyHistory&parentName=Heritage.

"Department of Anthropology: A History of the Department, 1897–1997." Smithsonian Institution. http://anthropology.si.edu/outreach/depthist.html.

"Fair History." Umatilla County Fair. http://www.co.umatilla.or.us/fair/fair_history.html.

"Foundation History." Wildhorse Foundation. http://www.thewildhorsefoundation.com /foundation-history/.

"Heroic at 80." Tamástslikt Cultural Institute. December 16, 2011. https://tamastslikt
.wordpress.com/2011/12/16/heroic-at-80/.

"History: City of Pendleton." City of Pendleton. http://www.pendleton.or.us/history.

"History and Culture." Confederated Tribes of the Umatilla Indian Reservation. http://
ctuir.org/history-culture.

"History of Sauder Village." Sauder Village. https://saudervillage.org/about/history-of
-sauder-village.

National Park Service. "The Park and Its Neighbors: The Hiawatha Club." 2004. http://
www.nps.gov/parkhistory/online_books/pipe/adhi8.htm.

"Oconaluftee Indian Village." Cherokee Historical Association. https://www.cherokee
historical.org/oconaluftee-indian-village/.

"Oconaluftee Indian Village." Visit Cherokee NC. http://visitcherokeenc.com/play
/attractions/oconaluftee-indian-village/.

The Oregon History Project. https://oregonhistoryproject.org/articles/historical-records
/act-to-prohibit-the-intermarriage-of-races-1866/#.XRpMXOhKjMX.

"Park Statistics." National Park Service, Great Smoky Mountains National Park. https://
www.nps.gov/grsm/learn/management/statistics.htm.

"Pendleton Fabric Expertise—A Story of Generations." *Pendleton Woolen Mills.* https://
blog.pendleton-usa.com/tag/thomas-kay/. January 30, 2019.

"Pendleton Round-Up & Happy Canyon Hall of Fame." Pendleton Round-Up and Happy
Canyon Hall of Fame. http://pendletonhalloffame.com/?page_id=40.

"Ramona" Outdoor Play. Ramona Bowl Amphitheatre. http://ramonabowl.com/.

"Sauder Village." Sauder Village. https://saudervillage.org/.

"The Show." *Tecumseh!* http://tecumsehdrama.com/the-show/.

Steil, Mark. "Pipestone's Hiawatha Pageant to Close after 60 Years." *Minnesota Public Radio
News*, December 30, 2007. http://www.mprnews.org/story/2007/12/21/hiawathawraps.

"Tecumseh!" http://tecumsehdrama.com/.

UNC News Release. "'Unto These Hills' Rewritten, Staged by Cherokee from Tribe's
Viewpoint." April 28, 2006. http://www.unc.edu/news/archives/apr06/seas042806.htm.

"*Unto These Hills,*" Cherokee Smokies. http://www.cherokeesmokies.com/unto_these
_hills.html.

"Video Presentation: Foreigners in Native Homelands: Lewis and Clark and the
Pioneers." Tamástslikt Cultural Institute. https://www.tamastslikt.org/video
-presentation-foreigners-in-native-homelands-lewis-and-clark-and-the-pioneers/.

"Visit Cherokee." Visit Cherokee NC. http://visitcherokeenc.com/play/attractions/unto
-these-hills-outdoor-drama/.

"Welcome to 'Unto These Hills.' Where Cherokee History Dramatically Comes to Life."
Cherokee, North Carolina. http://visitcherokeenc.com/play/attractions/unto-these
-hills-outdoor-drama/.

Willingham, William. "Pendleton Woolen Mills." *Oregon Encyclopedia.* https://
oregonencyclopedia.org/articles/pendleton_woolen_mills/#.XxywrfjKi3I. 2018.

Index

CPSIA information can be obtained
at www.ICGtesting.com
Printed in the USA
LVHW090741071221
705491LV00005B/815

9 781469 662312